HANDBOOK
ON
SIKHS

HANDBOOK
ON
SIKHS

Revised at the request of the Government of India in 1928

By

Major A. E. BARSTOW, 2/11th Sikh Regiment
(late 15th Ludhiana Sikhs)

Uppal Publishing House
NEW DELHI-110002

UPPAL PUBLISHING HOUSE
3, Ansari Road, Daryaganj, New Delhi-110002

Reprinted 1989
ISBN 81-85024-54-5

PRINTED IN INDIA
Published by B.S. Uppal, UPPAL PUBLISHING HOUSE
3, Ansari Road, Daryaganj, New Delhi-110002, and Printed
at Mehra Offset Press, Daryaganj, New Delhi-2

LIST OF THE PRINCIPAL AUTHORITIES CONSULTED IN THE PREPARATION OF THIS WORK.

Akbar—*Malleson.*
Census Reports—Punjab—1881, 1891 and 1911—1931—*Official.*
Districts' Customary Law.
Districts' Gazetteers, Parts 1 and 2.
Ethnography of the Punjab—*Denzil Ibbetson.*
Ethnographical Handbook—*Crooke.*
Ethnology of India—*Campbell.*
Encyclopædia Britannica.
Encyclopædia of India—*Balfour.*
Gazetteers of the Punjab—*Official.*
Ghadr Conspiracy—*Isemonger and Slattery.*
History and Philosophy of the Sikh Religion—*Khazan Singh.*
History of India—*Wheeler.*
History of the Sikhs—*Cunningham.*
Historical Records of the Bengal Army—*Cardew.*
Handbook on Sikhs—*Bingley.*
History of the Sikhs—*McGregor.*
India—*Strachey.*
Jats of Hindustan—*Ryall.*
Notes on Sikhs—*Crowther.*
Notes on Sikhs—*Rie.*
Notes on Jats—*Ostrehan.*
Ranjit Singh—*Lepel Griffin.*
Translation of the Adi Granth—*Trumpp.*
The Punjab and the War—*Leigh.*
The Truth about Jaito—*District Sikh Publicity Committee.*
Punjab Secretariat Memoranda.
War Speeches—*Sir Michael O'Dwyer.*
Sikh Martyrs—*Bhagat Lakshman Singh.*
Sikh Gurdwaras Act, 1925.

COMPILER'S PREFACE.

The Handbook on Sikhs was first published in 1899. It has been re-written in the present instance at the request of Army Headquarters, in order to embody in brief outline the salient features of Sikh History in the first quarter of the present century, and in other ways to bring it up to date.

It thus consists of 10 chapters, with the addition of appendices and map.

The first chapter relates briefly to the Punjab,—the home of the Sikh,—and gives certain data of general interest, which is perhaps frequently not fully realised.

Chapter II contains a short survey of the origin of Sikhism and its history; it is divided into two parts, the latter of which deals more particularly with the Sikh religious and political outlook in the present century. The materials for this chapter have been collected largely from official sources, and the personal knowledge of civil, and other authorities, intimately connected with events in the Punjab in the period under review.

Chapter III describes the distribution of the Sikhs, and their ethnology, and includes a glossary of castes.

The fourth chapter deals very briefly with the salient features of the lives of the Gurus, the details of which were omitted from the second chapter in order to keep the main outline of the history of the Sikhs as clear as possible.

The fifth chapter relates to the Sikh religion.

Chapter VI deals in considerable detail with the different Sikh sects and their clans, or sub-divisions. These have been dealt with by Districts, in order that information may be readily accessible for any particular District. The material has been largely obtained from the Census Reports and District Gazetteers. It should be noted that although figures are bound to vary with every subsequent census, yet they have been included mainly as a guide for recruiting purposes.

Chapters VII and VIII deal with Sikh customs and their characteristics. The data from which these chapters have been compiled, has been mainly obtained from Punjab and District Census Reports, District Gazetteers, and the personal knowledge of certain authorities and leading Sikh gentlemen. It must, however, be remembered that the

Punjab covers a large area, that customs not only vary considerably in each individual district, but even in different villages in each district, and, therefore, variations in the conduct of ceremonies and in characteristics must be held to be the rule, and not the exception. In the main an endeavour has been made to describe the usual formalities.

Chapter IX contains a short account of agriculture. It has been included for the chief reason that the Jat Sikh is primarily an agriculturist, and that an understanding of what this implies is essential to those who have any dealings with him. It is also hoped that its inclusion will lend a greater interest to the visits of British Officers who may tour the Districts.

Chapter X has been devoted to recruiting, and deals firstly with war measures in the Great War, and secondly to peace conditions. The data has been largely obtained from the "Punjab and the War", to the author of which the writer is greatly indebted, and also to those who have had practical experience.

The writer would finally wish to express his special acknowledgments and thanks to the following, without whose assistance, especially in regard to unravelling the tangled thread of events from 1914 onwards, his task would have been exceedingly difficult of achievement:—

to Mr. C. M. G. Ogilvie, I.C.S., Deputy Commissioner, Lahore, who throughout has rendered the most willing co-operation, and kindly consented to criticise the M. S. before publication; to Mr. V. W. Smith, Indian Police of the Punjab, who assisted with publications and other data; to the Deputy Commissioners of Districts in kindly placing at my disposal the Gazetteers and books on Customary Law of their Districts; and to Colonel Lachman Singh of the Patiala Imperial State Forces

A. E. BARSTOW, *Major*,
2/11th Sikhs.

NORTHERN COMMAND,
MURREE,
15th May 1927.

CONTENTS.

APPENDICES.

CHAPTER I.

INTRODUCTORY.

The Sikhs, for many reasons, are of especial interests, to any body engaged in maintaining British rule in India. Their modern developments are especially difficult to understand and appraise aright. On the one hand overweening confidence must be avoided, and on the other, undue suspicion. The exact point at which the Sikhs require guidance, stimulation or restraint from Government in their efforts to improve themselves, calls not only for statesmanship, but for accurate knowledge of their history, characteristics, and aspirations generally.

The time when military and civil departments regarded each other as water tight departments has long since passed. They can mutually derive great benefit and assistance from each other, and it is essential that close liaison between the two Services should at all times be preserved. It is therefore incumbent on all military officers to have a good working knowledge of the civil administration, and this cannot be attained unless every opportunity is taken of touring in the areas from which the men belonging to their units are enlisted. It may be confidently asserted that they will derive great benefit therefrom; they will receive a warm welcome in the villages, and will retain that personal touch between their units and their pensioners, which in the interests of recruiting and the service generally, it is so essential to maintain.

This book therefore represents an earnest endeavour to interpret in a readable form, the masses of information on record in connection with the Sikh, his origin, history, customs, characteristics and modern developments, which those, under whose charge or command he may be, may require to know.

Before proceeding however with the subject matter of this volume, it is proposed to devote this chapter to an outline of the Punjab and certain factors connected therewith, in order that the pages that follow may be more readily understood.

The Punjab.—The Punjab, or "Five Waters" is the name of the home of the Sikh. It includes all the tract of country lying between the Himalayas and the Rajputana Desert, and between the rivers Jumna and Indus; it also extends up into the Himalayas to the borders of Tibet, and across the Indus to the borders of Baluchistan. It measures in all 135,773 square miles, that is to say, it is roughly one-eighth as large again as the British Isles, and in area and population is one-thirteenth of the whole of India.

Not quite one-third of the province is hilly, the remainder being level plain. Of the latter less than half lies in the fertile basins of the "Five Rivers". and the rest consists of the dry uplands of the west.

Less than three-fourths of the total area, and five-sixths of the population are in British territory; the rest are in the Indian States—43 in number.

The British area is divided into 29 Districts, grouped into 5 divisions, each in charge of a Commissioner.

These are as follows ;—

1. *Ambala.*	2. *Jullundur.*	3. *Lahore.*	4. *Rawalpindi*	5. *Multan.*
Hissar.	Kangra.	Lahore.	Gujrat.	Montgomery.
Rohtak.	Hoshiarpur.	Amritsar.	Shahpur.	Lyallpur.
Gurgaon.	Jullundur.	Gurdaspur.	Jhelum.	Jhang.
Ambala.	Ludhiana.	Sialkot.	Rawalpindi.	Multan.
Karnal.	Ferozepore.	Gujranwala.	Attock.	Muzaffargarh.
Simla.			Mianwali.	Dera Ghazi Khan

The Sikhs are concentrated mainly in the second and third divisions and their distribution therein is referred to again in a subsequent chapter.

Of the States, the three which are known collectively as the "Phulkian States" (Patiala, Nabha, Jind) form a single political agency, as do also Faridkot, Malerkotla, and Bahawalpur. For the others the Commissioner of the adjacent division acts as Political Agent.

Each division is sub-divided for revenue into Tehsils (usually about four). A Tehsil consists of a few hundred villages. The village is the unit of land revenue assessment, all landowners of a single village being in theory jointly responsible for the sum assessed on the village. Each village, according to size, has one or more 'Headmen' called "Lumbardars", and in most districts the headmen of several villages are represented by one of their number, called a "Zaildar" in their dealings with the official administration.

The Tehsildar, the Deputy Commissioner of the district, the Commissioner of the division, and the two Financial Commissioners (each of whom deals with certain subjects for the province as a whole) and the Governor are, in ascending scale, the officials with whom the villagers are concerned in matters affecting their land, and with whom recruiting and regimental officers frequently come into contact.

The people.—The province has a population of 28,490,857, or nearly three-fourths that of the British Isles. Of these the Sikhs number 4,071,624. There are more than 13 men to every 11 women—a fact which is of importance to the army. It is estimated that very nearly one third of the men of all religions, that is to say about four million, are of military age. The towns-people only amount to one-tenth of the total, and, for the most part, differ considerably in race, habits and interests from the villagers. This is one of the reasons why they are rarely, if ever, recruited.

Out of every ten Punjabis, nine live in villages and six make their living by agriculture; it is from these in the plains, from the great tribe of Jats, that our recruits are obtained. A large proportion of these own the land they cultivate; thus we can think of the Punjab in general as a land of peasant proprietors.

Not learned men! only 6 out of every 100 could read and write an ordinary letter. But at least the men are ten times as learned as the women.

Of the prevailing religions, Islam is most important, and commands the allegiance of just one-half of the population; next comes Hinduism, 36 per cent.; the Sikhs, 12 per cent.—have earned by their military record and loyalty to their traditions, a prominence out of all proportion to their numbers.

Local politics.—The differences of geography, race and religion, are reflected in a marked variety of political organisation. In the Indian States are divers degrees of autocracy; the Baluchis of the border have a patriarchal system well suited to their primitive way of life; at the opposite end of the province the Jats are markedly democratic, and their ideals of local government are not unlike those of ancient Greece. In between are many gradations between feudalism and democracy.

In general it can safely be said that there is a well-developed sense of clanishness, and that the rank and file look for leadership to certain individuals who are allowed by common consent to have some superiority, whether of family or of sanctity.

On the whole it may be fairly claimed that the political sense of the Punjab was, up to the end of the War, satisfied by the officially recognised system of village headmen and zaildars described above. These were the men to whom officials had to turn when the Great War called for the Punjab's best efforts, and it was due to the excellent manner in which most of them responded that the results obtained were so good.

The Punjab History.—Thanks to its situation, the Punjab has always been the first Province in India to feel the force of invasion by land. It divides the hungry Highlanders of Central Asia from the tempting plains of Hindustan. Time and again the fate of Delhi and the lands beyond has been decided upon the plains.

The invaders have been, for the past thousand years, Mohamedans. The most effective re-action against the encroachment of Islam, the Sikh Khalsa, was a purely Punjabi product. Both these religions are essentially militant in contrast to the "quietism" of the orthodox Hindu.

The Asiatic rulers of the province, whether they held sway from Hindustan or Afghanistan, were generally content to allow considerable independence to the local chieftains. Occasionally the Central Government was powerful enough to exercise a real control; the great Akbar and his successors could certainly make their influence felt. After the break up of the Moghal Empire, the greater part of the Punjab was once more welded into a real kingdom by the genius of Ranjit Singh.

Of him it has been said that :—"He succeeded to the leadership of a single tribe in the Punjab when it was distracted by the contests of a dozen chieftains, and to the command of a body of matchlock horsemen. He bequeathed to his successor a great kingdom enriched with the spoils of its neighbours, together with an army of 80,000 lances strong with 300 pieces of cannon, superior in discipline, in equipment, and in valour, to any force ever before assembled under a native chief".

It will be necessary to relegate to the next chapter how this great force originated, and to trace the principles and development of Sikhism to the present day.

Meanwhile it may be stated that even "The Lion of the Punjab" never succeeded in mastering thoroughly the lands west of the Jhelum, nor was he able to include in his kingdom the country east of the Sutlej. In the absence of strong Central Government, security of life and property is always far to seek. As Lord Minto was constrained to write to the Board of Directors in 1812 :—"With the native princes, was rapine and conquest constitute an avowed principle of action, a just and legitimate pursuit, and the chief source of public glory". This fairly describes the state of things which ensued upon the death of Ranjit Singh in 1839. The power passed into the hands of Army Committees, and finally, the Rani, who, a long series of murders having left in power, felt obliged to send them against the British, as the only means of keeping them from ruining the country.

The same position that had exposed the Punjab to invasion by land, had kept it aloof from the great powers which came to India by sea. So the British left the Punjab alone. In 1809 they had, at the request of the Cis-Sutlej Chiefs, made a treaty with Ranjit Singh which put an end to his designs of conquest towards east and south, but it took no less than two direct challenges by the Khalsa Army to drive them into annexing the territories of the Sikh Maharajah.

The King of Delhi was maintained upon his throne until he made himself impossible by his treachery during the Mutiny. In each case annexation was the result of fierce and protracted fighting; victors and vanquished could not but form a high opinion of each other's soldierly qualities. It is a notable fact that in the Mutiny the victors' staunchest comrades-in-arms were those who had fought so hard against them in the Sikh Wars.

The immediate effect of the establishment of British rule was the substitution of law and order for insecurity and anarchy. The revenue assessment was materially reduced, titles in land were accurately tested and recorded, and cash payments took the place of the collections in kind which had been such a fruitful source of extortion and annoyance. More than 2,000 miles of good roads were built in five years. The year after the suppression of the Mutiny, a railway was built from Amritsar to Multan and the Bari Doab Canal began to work.

This was the beginning of a system of irrigation which has grown to be the greatest in the world. Thanks to the canals, most of the uplands between the Jumna and the Jhelum have been brought under cultivation; these tracts were once barely able to provide grazing for sheep and camels; they are now amongst the great wheat markets of the world.

Widespread famine has become practically unknown. Railways and roads now cover the Province in a regular network; hospitals and schools have been built and are everywhere increasing in astonishingly large numbers. Post and Telegraph Offices have been opened up in even the most outlaying districts, and the advent of the motor car, universally popular in the remotest villages, has made communication and travel a matter of easy attainment. Again the system of co-operative credit societies introduced and fostered by the Government has taken firm root and has done much to solve problem of agricultural indebtedness, whilst the securing of the landowners by law in their ownership of the land from the usurpers, who, at one time, threatened to oust them by trading on their lack of business instinct, has all tended to a contented peasantry.

In all these developments the relation of the Government to the people has been, to use a common expression, that of "father and mother". But side by side with this there has grown up another bond between Britishers and the Punjab—that of comradeship-in-arms. In than 10 years from the second Sikh War, the Bitrish and Punjabis saved India from the Mutineers. Since then, more than ever, has India looked to the Punjab for a very large part of its fighting force. At the outbreak of the Great War the Punjab supplied half of the Indian soldiers in the Army, of whom 33,000 were Sikhs, and the proportion gradually increased in the successive vears of the War. During the period 1st August 1914 to 30th November 1918 no less than 88,925 Sikh combatants were enlisted, exclusive of non-combatants.

A no mean figure! and if this fine record has been somewhat overclouded by the events which followed in the years immediately after the War and which are but imperfectly understood by the majority, it must be remembered that this was a phase of religious reform, of which the mass of the population but improperly understood the real points at issue; their religious feelings were worked up and played upon by those who had not so much religious as political motives as their objective, and who utilized the uneducated masses in the rural districts to help achieve their purpose—as will appear in the following chapter.

Between religion and politics there is no wide gulf fixed, especially in the East; frequently it is difficult to detect the division between the two; a knowledge of one will assist to an understanding of the other and a comprehension of both should be within the radius of vision of every officer.

CHAPTER II.

THE ORIGIN OF SIKHISM AND ITS HISTORY.

PART I.

Sikhism as founded by Nanak.—The Sikh religion was founded by Baba Nanak, the first of the ten Sikh Gurus, who was born in the Lahore District, and flourished about 1500 A. D.

It is by no means easy to define "Sikh"; the word is derived from "SHISHYA," meaning "disciple".

The followers of Nanak were called Sikhs, and, as the creed spread, this appellation became the descriptive title of the whole people. It is necessary, however, to emphasize that the term Sikh is a religious and not a racial designation, and that if belongs only to those who have accepted the faith of the Khalsa.

Sikhism, like Buddhism, was inspired by a spirit of revolt against the ceremonial and social restrictions of the Hindu religion, as well as against the bigotry and arrogance of its hereditary priesthood, the Brahmans.

The religion of Nanak was essentially quiescent and non-aggressive. His teaching was to the effect that there was but one God, who was neither the God of the Hindu nor of the Mohamedan, but that He was the God of the universe, and that all men were equal in His sight. He rejected the authority of the Brahmans, their incantations and sacrifices, holding that salvation was to be obtained by uprightness and purity of life, rather than by a rigid observance of unintelligible and superstitious rites.

It is to be noted that the doctrine of Nanak was thus, in many respects, essentially unlike that of the tenth and last Guru, Govind Singh, which will presently be made clear.

In this connection it should be noticed that the very surprising—in fact amazing—transformation of the Sikhs from being a quiet quaker-like sect of peaceful reformers to a fanatical and ferocious race of warriors is perhaps unique in history. For all practical purposes the teachings of Nanak might never have been. The reasons why the innovations of Govind Singh and the foundation of the Khalsa have completely obscured the teachings of the great master is that the Granth Sahib is written in archaic Punjabi with a strong admixture of Sanskrit and other languages, even Persian, and that it is unintelligible to the ordinary villager. Probably not more than a dozen living Sikhs can interpret the whole book. Guru Amar Das, when asked why he did not preach and teach in Sanskrit as being the only language in which great truths could be expressed, replied: "Sanskrit is like well-water with which a garden plot can be beautifully cultivated, but Punjabi is like the rain which falls over all the country." This advice the Sikhs have neglected and the Granth has never been translated into the village Punjabi of to-day.

Govind Singh's struggles and vicissitudes impressed the imagination of the people, and the persecutions which followed deepened that impression—his teachings also appealed to the natural instincts of the Jat, with the result that the faith which Govind Singh was out to defend has been more completely extinguished than the most ardent and successful persecutors could have hoped.

The opportunity will also be taken at this point of emphasizing the fact that the Khalsa has no priesthood. Until recently the Sikhs of Govind Singh has been quite content to leave their shrines in the keeping of Mahants, who, in the majority of cases, had never even taken the "Pahul". This refers especially to the Gurdwaras of other Gurus Govind. The Udasis who held most of the important shrines were the spiritual descendants of Siri Chand, the son of Nanak. In brief the priesthood represented the old pre-Govind Singh and as such had very little in common with the Khalsa.

Introduction of the political element.—Nanak died in 1539, and was succeeded by Angad, the second Guru.

The new religion ran an uneventful course until the succession of the fifth Guru, Arjun, in 1581. This Guru first gave the Sikhs their scriptures in the shape of the "Adi Granth," (*vide* Appendices) and also a common rallying point in Amritsar, which he made his religious centre. Though a man of eminent piety, Arjun was also a dabbler in politics, and having embroiled himself with the Emperor Jehangir, he was summoned to Lahore, where a rigorous imprisonment in the custody of a powerful Hindu minister, Chandu Lal, accelerated, if it did not actually cause, his death.

The arrest of Arjun inaugurated that Mohamedan persecution which was the turning point in Sikh history, and from that time onward, Sikhism was perpetually in conflict with the Islamic power and religion.

Har Govind, his successor, was a warrior and a political leader. Though essentially a mercenary, and prepared to fight for or against the Moghal as convenience or profit dictated, yet from the fact that most of his forays were against the Mohamedans, the Guru came to be regarded as a champion of the down-trodden Hindus, while his camp grew to be the rallying point of free lances and adventurers.

The policy of Har Govind was continued by his two successors, and under Tegh Bahadur, the ninth Guru, the Sikhs, while constantly growing in power, so far degenerated into mere marauders and disturbers of the peace as to constitute a menace to the prosperity of the country. The Imperial troops were sent against them, and they were at least defeated and Tegh Bahadur taken prisoner. Tegh Bahadur himself was executed by the Moghal authorities as an infidel, a robber and a rebel, and his followers who resisted conversion to Islam were cruelly persecuted.

Tegh Bahadur appointed his son Govind Rai as his successor, and enjoined on him the necessity and merit of revenge.

The Khalsa nation as founded by Govind Singh.—Govind Rai was only fifteen years of age at the time of his father's death, and for some years subsequently he appears to have remained inactive, brooding over his wrongs, and devising measures for the accomplishment of his mission against the Mohamedans. Emerging from his retirement he preached the doctrine of the "Khalsa," the faith of the 'pure,' the 'elect'. His teachings were calculated to convert the followers of Guru Nanak into a militant body without affecting their relationship with the Hindus whom it was intended to protect. It is for this reason that, until the development of the recent movement of Sikh separatism, the Hindus did not look upon Sikhism as an alien religion or social group.

Admission to the 'Khalsa' was gained by the baptismal ceremony of the "pahul," and its military nature was marked by the bestowal of the title of "Singh," or "lion," on all who entered it.

[The essence of the above ceremony is the drinking, in the presence of five believers, of a mixture of sugar and water which has been stirred by a steel dagger, the baptismal fluid being known as "Amrit". It also demanded by the recipient as the outward and visible symbols of Sikhism, the wearing of the five K's; *i.e.*, (*i*) the 'Kes', or uncut hair; (*ii*) the 'Kachh', or short drawers; (*iii*) the Kara, or iron bangle; (*iv*) the 'Kirpan', or steel dagger; and (*v*) the 'Kanga', or comb.]

The Guru taught his followers that they must practise arms, and never show their backs to the foe in battle. He preached the democratic doctrine of equality with even less reservation than Nanak himself, and enjoined on his Sikhs that they were to consider themselves members of one family, and that previous caste distinctions were erased.

Religious fervour, however, was entirely eclipsed by military zeal, and thus "a religion became a political power, and for the first time in India a nation arose, embracing all races, all classes, and all grades of society and banded them together in face of a foreign foe.". (*Ibbetson.*)

Rise of the Sikh power.—Govind Singh's next step was to adapt the Sikh scriptures to his own views. With this object, he endeavoured to induce the custodians of the "Adi Granth" to permit him to make additions to the work but the "Sodhis," the Sikh priests, who had the guardianship of the sacred volume, and who were the descendants of Guru Ram Das, refused to accept the authority of the new leader. When they understood that the object of Govind Singh was to preach the democratic doctrine of equality in a far more liberal fashion than it had been promulgated by even Nanak himself, and that the lowest classes, and even outcastes, were to be admitted equally with themselves to the higher privileges of the "Khalsa," they rose in revolt to a man.

They with their great establishments, had already become the Brahmans of the Sikh creed, with all the unbounded spiritual pride of their prototypes. They, therefore, denounced him as an imposter, and told him if he were a true Guru he should compile scriptures for himself, which he at once proceeded to do, the work being completed in 1696.

The Granth of Guru Govind Singh is known as the "Daswan Badshah ki Granth." (*Vide* appendices). In this compilation it was not his object to overturn, or indeed modify any important particulars of the doctrine bequeathed by Nanak, but to produce a work which should have on his excitable and fanatical followers the effect which he desired of launching them as a militant power against Islam, and recovering the Punjab for the new congregation of the faithful.

In this he was fairly successful, and, at the head of a continually increasing band of devoted followers, he commenced his life work of propagating the Sikh faith.

Govind Singh's struggles with the Moghal authorities.—The life of Govind Singh, was spent in a series of petty wars, sometimes with the Hindu Rajputs of the Hills, but more often with the Mohamedan governors of the Emperor. In one of these battles his two eldest sons were killed, and his followers reduced to forty. His mother, his wives, and two youngest children escaped with difficulty to Sirhind where the latter were cruelly buried alive by the Moghals. After this, Govind Singh was hard pressed by his enemies, who closely besieged him in his fort at Chamkaur. The last of his sons having fallen, and further resistance being hopeless, the Guru determined to take advantage of a dark night to make his escape with a handful of devoted followers. After many adventures, he escaped into the desert country round Bhattinda, where the Imperial troops gave up the pursuit. From thence the dispirited fugitive repaired to Talwandi in Patiala, which he declared should be as sacred to the Sikhs as Benares was, and is, to Hindus. This Sikh shrine is now known as the Dam Damma, or 'breathing place of the Guru,' a distinction which is also claimed by Bhattinda.

Govind Singh enters the service of the Moghals.—In 1707 Aurangzeb died, and his eldest son, Bahadur Shah, hastened from Kabul to secure the succession. He vanquished and overcame one of his brothers near Agra, and marching to the Dekhan, there defeated another, who soon after died of his wounds. While engaged in the last campaign, Bahadur Shah summoned Govind to his camp. The Guru obeyed, and was rewarded with a military command in the valley of the Godavery. "The Emperor probably thought that the leader of the insurrectionary Jats might be usefully employed in opposing rebellious Mahrattas, and Govind perhaps saw in the imperial service a ready way of disarming suspicion and of reorganising his scattered followers."

Death of Govind Singh.—At any rate, whatever may have been Govind Singh's reasons for adopting a line of conduct which was certainly opposed to the tenor of his life and teaching, there is no doubt that he travelled at the head of his followers to the Dekhan, where he was assassinated by the sons of an Afghan horse-dealer whom he had slain in a fit of anger. He died in 1708 at Naderh, on the Godavery which is still known to the Sikhs as Abchalnagar, *i.e.*, the town of the Guru's departure'. Naderh is also known as *Gurdwara*, or the 'house of the Guru,' and numerous religious establishments, and a Sikh colony, testify to its importance as one of the holiest shrines of the religion of the "Khalsa".

Govind Singh did not live to see his ends accomplished, but he had roused the dormant spirit of the people.

His successor Banda Bairagi.—He was succeeded by his chosen disciple, a Bairagi ascetic named Banda, who is said to have been a native of the Dekhan. After his master's death, Banda returned to the Punjab, where he carried on a guerilla warfare against the Moghals with varying success for some years. He was at length driven to earth at his fort near Gurdaspur, where, in 1716, after a heroic resistance, he was forced to surrender to his enemies.

Mohamedan persecutions.—A period of persecutions followed, so sanguniary and so terrible, that for a whole generation nothing was heard of the Sikhs. A hundred Sikhs were put to death, daily, contending among themselves for priority of martyrdom. Banda himself was torn in pieces by red hot pincers after having been compelled to take the life of his only son. These and other cruelties are generally ascribed to Mohamedan fanaticism, but it must be remembered that the Sikhs were mostly bandits and outlaws, and that they brought punishment upon themselves by their excesses and defiance of the law. So long as they were merely a religious body, they were left unmolested; but when they began to band themselves together for political purposes, the Moghal authorities naturaly took alarm, and commenced a series of repressive measures which increased in severity and eventually took the form of bitter religious persecutions.

From the death of Aurangzeb in 1707, began the gradual break up of the Moghal Empire. Provincial governors asserted their independence, and in the general anarchy that followed, the Delhi sovereigns became mere puppets in the hands of a Mahratta confederacy.

The invasion of Nadir Shah.—In 1738 India was invaded by the Persians under Nadir Shah. Nadir's march through the Punjab in 1739, met with no opposition to speak of; but the Sikhs, who were fast reviving from the brutal treatment their fathers had undergone under Bahadur Shah, kept up a system of desultory plunder, robbing both the invaders and the people fleeing before them. Some years later, after the assassination of Nadir Shah, Ahmed Shah Abdali, who had succeeded him as the ruler of Afghanistan, invaded the Punjab, and advanced as far as Sirhind where he was defeated by the Moghals and forced to retire across the Indus. During his retreat the Sikhs plundered his baggage, cut off his stragglers, and took advantage of the prevailing anarchy to throw up a small fort near Amritsar. Their leader at this time was one Jassa Singh, a distiller by caste, who boldly proclaimed the birth of a new power in the state—the Khalsa, or army of the Sikh theocracy.

The invasions of Ahmed Shah.—Between 1748 and 1761 the Punjab was three times invaded by Ahmed Shah. In 1758 the Mahrattas, assisted by the Sikhs, drove out the Afghans from Lahore; but returning in 1761, Ahmed Shah totally defeated them at Panipat, after which he again retired to Kabul.

For a time the Sikhs seemed to have some prospect of holding the Punjab for themselves. The Moghals and their allies the Mahrattas had been defeated by the Afghans, while the latter had retired once more across the Indus. The number and power of the Sikhs had also greatly increased.

The Sikhs confederacies or Misls.—They had grouped themselves into associations, called Misls, in which a number of robber chiefs agreed, after a somewhat democratic and equal fashion, to follow the flag and fight under the orders of one powerful leader. This organization made them formidable. The several chiefs built their forts in convenient places, and gradually over-ran the whole plain country of the Punjab, shutting up the Mohamedan governors in their strongholds at Sirhind and Lahore, which last city they twice seized and occupied for a short time.

The Sikh insurrection of 1761.—The years 1761-62 are memorable in the history of the Sikhs. Hardly had Ahmad Shah turned his face homeward, than the Sikhs, collecting in great numbers, attacked the troops he had left in garrison at Sirhind. The Afghans were hard pressed, and the capture of the place seemed certain, when Ahmed Shah, by a series of rapid marches, returned to their assistance, and totally defeated his enemies. Some 20,000 Sikhs were killed and captured, among the latter being Ala Singh, the chief of Patiala. Ahmed Shah, who was a man of great sagacity, thinking it would be wise to conciliate his opponents after having given them so signal a proof of his power, embraced his prisoner and bestowed on him a dress of honour and title of Raja. This unwonted dignity aroused against Ala Singh the jealousy and anger of all the other chiefs, who declared that he had betrayed them, and that it was disgraceful for a Sikh to accept an honour conferred by a Mohamedan, a foreigner and an enemy. Matters, however, were at length smoothed over, but Ala Singh was called upon to prove by his deeds that he was a true Sikh, and no servant of the Afghan.

Capture of Sirhind by the Sikhs in 1763.—The Sikhs were not cast down by their defeat, and no sooner had Ahmed Shah returned to Kabul than the confederacies, both north and south of the Sutlej, for once laid aside their feuds and jealousies, and united for another great effort against Sirhind, a city which to them was peculiarly obnoxious, being the place where Govind Singh's children had been so cruelly martyred. Zin Khan, the Afghan Governor, came out of the town to meet them, but was defeated and killed, and his troops utterly routed. The Sikhs immediately took possession of the city, which they plundered and destroyed in revenge for the sufferings inflicted on the family of their Guru.

Thus the Sikhs, both by their defeat and their victory, acquired a status which they did not before possess, and had they known how to put aside private jealousies and unite habitually as they had done for the conquest of Sirhind, they would have become as formidable in Northern India as the Mahrattas in the south and west. But the democratic nature of the Sikh faith, responding to the natural sentiments of the people, resisted all attempts at dictation by a central authority, until Maharaja Ranjit Singh broke down all opposition, and reduced rivals and enemies to a common obedience.

The tribal quarrels of the Sikh Sirdars.—The history of the Sikhs from the middle of the 18th to the beginning of the 19th century is a record of struggles for pre-eminence among the chiefs of the different Misls or confederacies, who fought against each other more often than against their common enemies the Mohamedans. Even within the borders of each Misl itself, the Sirdars were always quarrelling, and first one chief and then another took the lead. This was due, no doubt, to the constitution of Sikhism, under which no such thing as vassalage or feudal superiority was acknowledged. The principle of the creed was fraternity, and it was the boast of the Sikhs that they were communities of independent soldiers.

Causes which led to the rise of the great Sikh chieftains.—While the Khalsa was still in its infancy, this idea of independence represented a state of things not far removed from the truth; but as the more important chiefships gradually increased in power, their smaller neighbours were compelled, either for security against others, or to avoid absorption altogether, to place themselves under the protection of some leader able to defend them, rendering service in the field in return. "All that a Sikh chief asked from a follower in those days was a horse, a sword, and a matchlock. All that a follower sought was protection and permission to plunder in the name of God and the Guru, and under the banner of his chief or Sirdar." All the great Sikh families owe their origin to the power of the sword. To attract followers by his power and success was the main desire of every Sikh chieftain. Who they were and what were their antecedents, were matters of no consequence, if only they could fight and ride. In those days every village became a fort. A neighbour, as with the Jews and Pathans, was synonymous with an enemy, and cultivators ploughed their fields with matchlocks by their sides. No man could consider his land, his horse, or his wife, secure, unless he was strong enough to defend them; for although the Sikh leaders were best pleased with the spoil of Mohamedans, or the capture of an Imperial convoy, they were really more robbers than patriots, and plundered all with the frankest impartiality. "Yet, while the Sikhs were undoubted robbers, and though cattle lifting was as honourable a profession amongst them, as it was on the Scottish border a few hundred years ago, their enthusiasm for their faith, coupled with their hatred for Musalmans who had so long trampled them under foot, gave them a certain dignity, and to their objects and expeditions an almost national interest."

Invasion of Zaman Shah, 1797.—Lahore was held by three Sikh chiefs, when, in 1797 and the following years, Zaman Shah, grandson of Ahmed, brought an army from Kabul, with a view to recovering the Punjab, only to be recalled on each occasion by troubles nearer home. He secured Lahore without opposition, and on leaving in 1798, made over the city to a young noble who had attracted his attention and rendered him valuable service. This was Ranjit Singh the son of a Sikh Sirdar who had risen to considerable power towards the end of the 18th century.

Rise of Maharaja Ranjit Singh.—Ranjit was a man of strong will and immense energy; of no education but of great acuteness in acquiring knowledge that would be of practical use to him. He soon united all the separate confederacies of Sikhs under his own control, and thus acquired a general authority over all the Sikhs of the Punjab. In 1808 his endeavours to include within his jurisdiction the Sikh principalities south of the Sutlej, forced the chiefs of these states to place themselves under British protection. Foiled in this direction, Ranjit Singh strengthened his authority in the Punjab proper, and steadily extended his dominions in the west. In 1809 he obtained possession of Kangra which the Nepalese were then besieging. In 1813 he acquired the fort at Attock on the Indus; and in the same year obtained from Shah Shuja, the fugitive Amir of Kabul, what he coveted as much as territory—the celebrated Koh-i-Nur diamond, which Nadir Shah had carried off as loot from Delhi. In 1818, after some failure in previous years, he captured the fortress of Mooltan. Kashmir, which had successfully opposed him on several occasions, was annexed soon afterwards, also the southern portion of the country that lay between the Indus and the hills. The Peshawar valley was not added until some years later. The Trans-Indus districts, however, were left very much to themselves, and only received a visit when revenue had to be collected.

The Sikh Army.—The Sikh army was generally known as the Dal Khalsa, or 'Army of God'. It consisted for the most part of cavalry, who found their own horses, and received a double share of prize money. Each chief, in proportion to his means, furnished horses and arms to his retainers, who were called Bargirs; and as the first tribute exacted from a conquered district was invariably horses, the infantry soldier was, after a successful campaign, generally transformed into a trooper. The infantry, previous to the formation of a regular army, by Ranjit Singh, was considered an inferior service, and the only portion which enjoyed any consideration was that composed of Akalis, or 'immortals,' a band of religious enthusiasts and warriors, who were dressed in blue, and wore knife-edged quoits round their turbans, partly for show, and partly for use as missiles. These military devotees, excited by opium and "ganja," were generally the first to enter a breach; but though they often rendered excellent service, their temper was lawless and uncertain and in times of peace they enjoyed almost boundless license.

Formation of a regular army by Ranjit Singh.—The series of brilliant victories won by Lord Lake over the Mahrattas, impressed the Sikhs with the value of disciplined troops. In 1805 Ranjit Singh is said to have paid a secret visit to the British Camp, and in 1809 he witnessed in the streets of Lahore the repulse of a fanatical band of Akalis by the native infantry escort of the British envoy. This incident is said to have decided him to raise regular troops. By 1812 he had formed several battalions, drilled chiefly by men who had resigned or deserted from the East India Company's service. The majority of his troops were Sikhs, but there were several corps of Hindustanis and Gurkhas, and the artillery was chiefly composed of Mohamedans. The transformation of the feudal levies of the Khalsa into regular disciplined troops was not effected without difficulty. The Sikhs disliked the rigidity and precision of the infantry drill, and it was only by offers of liberal pay, and by himself taking part in their manœuvres, that Ranjit Singh induced his subjects to submit to the European system of discipline. In spite of much opposition from the older Sirdars, the infantry gradually became the corps d'elite, and before the Maharaja's death had come to be regarded as the true array of the Khalsa.

Conditions of service in the Khalsa Army.—During the Maharaja's reign, enlistment in the Regular Army, or "Khas Fauj," was entirely voluntary; but there was never any difficulty in obtaining recruits, the infantry, especially, being composed of the handsomest and strongest young men. Under their trained instructors the Khalsa battalions became a formidable body of troops, well disciplined and steady, though perhaps rather slow in manœuvring. Their endurance, however, was remarkable, and it was not unusual for whole regiments to make 30 mile marches often for days at a time. The cavalry was constituted in much the same manner as in the early days of the Khalsa "when clouds of irregular horsemen hung on the skirts of the Afghan armies, afraid to venture an attack, but cutting off convoys and endangering the communications of the enemy."

Employment of French and Italian officers.—Following the example of Scindia and Holkar, Ranjit Singh, while gradually raising his army, received into his service several French and Italian officers, who organised his troops and greatly improved his artillery. They were not, however, entrusted with commands in the field, as these were generally deserved for the Sikh Sirdars. Of all the generals of the Maharaja, Diwan Mokhan Chand, a Khatri, was perhaps the ablest.

Another leader of the same class, named Diwan Chand, earned considerable distinction as the conquerer of Kashmir and Mooltan. The Murat of the Khalsa was Hari Singh, a leader of infinite dash and gallantry, who died at Jamrud in 1836. His son, Jowahir Singh, who inherited all his father's valour, led the splendid charge of irregular cavalry against the British at Chillianwala, which so nearly turned that doubtful battle into a defeat.

The successors of Ranjit Singh.—Ranjit Singh died in 1839, and was succeeded by Kharrak Singh, his eldest son, a weak and incapable prince, under whose rule the history of the Punjab became a record of intrigues and deeds of violence. The reigns of Kharrak Singh and his son, Nao Nihal Singh, were short and uneventful. The former died by the hand of an assassin, the latter by the fall of a beam from a gateway. They were succeeded by two reputed sons of Ranjit—Sher Singh, who was murdered, and Dalip Singh, an infant, who was placed on the "masnad" through a palace intrigue.

Usurpation of power by the Sikh Army.—Ranjit Singh had left an army of 92,000 infantry, 32,000 cavalry, and nearly 400 guns. It was a force which his feeble successors were totally unable to control. When one after another of those nominally in power had been assassinated, and the treasury plundered, the army, unpaid and unmanageable, demanded to be led into British territory. "It was, in fact, no longer the willing instrument of an arbitrary government, but looked upon itself and was regarded by others as the representative body of the Sikh people. The soldiers were sensible of the advantages of systematic union, and were proud of their armed array as the visible body of Govind Singh's commonwealth.".

The regimental panchayats.—As a general rule the troops were obedient to their appointed officers, but the concerted action of each regiment and brigade was invariably regulated by a 'panchayat' of five representatives, chosen from each battalion in consideration of their character as Sikhs, or from their particular influence in their villages. In the crude form of representation thus achieved, the Sikh people were enabled to interfere with effect, and some degree of consistency, in the nomination and removal of their rulers. But these large assemblies sometimes added military license to the barbarous ignorance of uneducated cultivators. Their resolutions were often unstable or unwise, and the representatives of different brigades were not unfrequently bribed and cajoled by unscrupulous and ambitious ministers striving to acquire a preponderance of political power.

The treachery of the Sikh Sirdars.—The authority of the army gradually increased. In 1845, the Prime Minister Jowahir Singh was executed by order of the regimental panchayats, and the territorial chiefs, thoroughly alarmed, decided that the only way in which they could preserve their own authority was to remove the army by inducing it to engage in a war with the English, which would probably result in its defeat and dispersion.

The Sutlej campaign.—The history of the war is too well known to need recapitulation. The battles of Mudki, Firozshahr, and Aliwal, were followed by the rout of the Sikh army at Sobraon, when they were driven back into the Sutlej with great loss, and the British army advanced to Lahore. On the 9th March 1846, a treaty was concluded with the Sikh Darbar, acting on behalf of the young Maharaja Dalip Singh. By this treaty, the Julludur and Kangra districts were ceded to the British. The latter further demanded a money payment of £1,500,000; but the hill country between the Beas and the Indus, including Kashmir and Hazara, was eventually accepted in lieu. The services of Gulab Singh, Raja of Jummoo, in procuring the restoration of friendly relations between the Sikhs and the British, were rewarded by the sale to him of Kashmir for 75 lakhs of rupees. At the urgent request of the Darbar, a British force was left at Lahore for the protection of the Maharaja, and the maintenance of his authority. To restore order, and introduce a settled administration a British Resident was also appointed, who was to guide and control the Council of Regency.

The second Sikh War.—Peace was not long preserved. Early in 1848 the Governor of Mooltan, Diwan Mulraj, applied for permission to resign. Two British officers were sent by the Resident to relieve him, but they were treacherously murdered, their escort going over to the enemy. Meanwhile Herbert Edwardes, then in charge of the Derajat, hearing of the attack on his comrades, hastily collected some levies, and rapidly advanced to their assistance. He arrived too late, but at once attacked Mooltan, which proved, however, to be far too strong to be captured by a force of irregulars. Inaction caused the movement to spread, the field of operations widened, and before the end of the year the greater portion of the Punjab was in a state of insurrection, and the Khalsa Army engaged in hostilities with the British. Mooltan was taken after a lengthy siege. The hard fought battle of Chillianwala on the 13th January 1849, left the Sikhs as undaunted as they had been in the previous campaign after the two days' fighting at Firozshahr; and it needed the crushing defeat of Gujrat in 1849, like that of Sobraon in 1846, to bring the war to a conclusion.

Raising of Sikh corps for the British service.—On the termination of the Sutlej campaign, the Government of India, impressed by the stubborn valour displayed by the Sikhs, determined to utilize for the native army the splendid fighting material which the conquest of the Punjab had placed at their disposal. In 1846 orders were issued for the formation of two Sikh Battalions at Ferozepore and Ludhiana, respectively, and ten years later another regiment was raised, for service among the Sonthals, which soon became famous as 'Rattray's Sikhs'.* Besides these special corps, the commandants of regular regiments were directed to enlist 200 Sikhs per battalion; but the Hindustanis, of

* These three battalions were known as the 14th, 15th Sikhs and 45th Sikhs, and under their present designation are the 1/11th, 2/11th and 3/11th Sikhs.

which they were then composed, disliked the introduction of strangers, and through the lax state of discipline which then prevailed, the order was only partially carried out. In 1849 the policy of giving military employment to the Sikhs was extended yet further by the formation of the Corps of Guides and a brigade of all arms, for police and general purposes on the border, both of which were largely composed of the former soldiers of the Khalsa, and formed the nucleus of the Punjab Frontier Force.

The loyalty of the Punjab secured by an able system of administration.—The annexation of the Punjab was followed by a settlement of the land-tax at an assessment very much lower than that which had been levied by the Sikhs. Roads and canals were laid out, and a simple but equitable code of civil and criminal procedure established, thoroughly suited to the temper of the people. The security to life and property enjoyed under the new Government, and the enormous personal influence of such able officials as the two Lawrences, Nicholson, and Herbert Edwardes, was felt in the furthest corner of the province, and caused the Punjab to remain quiet and loyal after only eight years' experience of English rule, while the people of the old North-West Provinces, who had been British subjects for upwards of half a century, revolted almost to a man.

The Mutiny.—The story of the Mutiny is too well known to need more than a passing notice. After the escape of the Meerut mutineers to Delhi, where they placed themselves under the nominal authority of the titular Moghal Emperor, the rebellion was given a rallying point, and identified with the restoration of the Mohamedan power. In the old North-West Provinces and Oudh, the revolt spread like wild-fire. The people sympathised with, and in most instances supported the insurgents, while the British troops serving in this district were too few to do much more than hold their own, and protect the women and children entrusted to their care.

The disarmament of the sepoys.—In the Punjab our position was equally precarious, but certain circumstances rendered it rather more hopeful. In the first place the administration of the province was in the hands of conspicuously able men, who, knowing the dangerous condition of the native army, forestalled the revolt of the sepoys by a timely and general disarmament. Owing to the recent annexation of the Punjab, the British garrison was larger there than it was elsewhere, and, from their being scattered over a large area, the native troops were unable to act in concert; the latter, moreover, where in the midst of a hostile population which regarded them with indifference and suspicion——an indifference which was converted into absolute hatred when it became known that the avowed object of the Hindustani sepoys was to restore the dominion of the hated Moghals.

The Sikh revival, and services of the Sikhs in the Mutiny.—The spirit of the Khalsa, which had been humbled by the defeats on the Sutlej, was aroused at the thought of a combat between Sikhism and

Islam. Delhi, the centre of the Sepoy Mutiny, was associated in their minds with the memory of bitter persecutions and the torture and martyrdom of their Gurus; thus when urgent demands for troops caused Lawrence to raise local levies, the Sikhs flocked in numbers to our standards, and identified themselves with the British cause with a loyalty which never wavered. While the newly raised regiments and the corps of the Frontier Force were earning fame and distinction before Delhi, their comrades of the 14th and 45th Sikhs were rendering splendid service in Oudh and the North-West Provinces. The former, besides saving the fort at Allahabad from falling into the hands of the rebels, took a distinguished part in Havelock's advance on Lucknow, and in the subsequent defence of the Residency. The latter, rejecting the numerous efforts made to seduce them from their allegiance, took a prominent share in the suppression of the Mutiny in Behar, and gained special distinction by the gallantry of a small detachment in defending a house at Arrah against the Dinapore mutineers.

Reorganization of the Bengal Army.—The reorganization of the Bengal Army which followed the Mutiny, led to a complete change in its class constitution. The Hindustanis of the regiments which had either revolted or been disbanded, were replaced by the Sikhs, Dogras, Punjabis, and Pathans, of the levies raised by Lord Lawrence, and the history of India since that time bears ample testimony to the military qualities of these races. It would be difficult indeed to select a more striking example of military constancy and devotion than that given by the heroic band of the (36th) 4/11th Sikhs who defended Saraghari. True to the martial instincts of their faith, they died to a man at their posts, covering themselves with glory, and giving imperishable renown to the grand regiment to which it was their privilege to belong.

PART II.

Decay of Sikhism after the British Conquest.—On the conclusion of the Mutiny, and with the disappearance of the wars and tumults which had fostered the growth of Sikhism, re-action again became visible. The younger generations began to find the restrictions imposed by their religion irksome; further, there were no longer raids, looting or reprisals to compensate for the austerities entailed by the observance of religious formalities. As a natural consequence there was in the last half of the 19th century a considerable relapse of Sikhism into the Hinduism from which it sprung. It must be remembered that by the performance of a few expiatory rites, and the payment of a certain sum of money to Brahmans, the Sikh reverts as a Jat peasant into the ordinary Hindu community.

SIKHISM IN THE LATTER HALF OF THE NINETEENTH AND COMMENCEMENT TWENTIETH CENTURIES.

Influence of Hinduism on Sikhism.—This era of the history of the Sikhs requires close study in view of the developments which occurred during the first quarter of the 20th century. It must not be imagined, however, that the decay of Sikhism above referred to was purely fortuitous or dependent on mere circumstances. Hinduism has always been hostile to Sikhism, whose Gurus successfully attacked the principle of caste, which is the foundation on which the whole fabric of the Brahminical religion has been reared. The activities of Hinduism have, therefore, been constantly directed to the undermining of Sikhism, both by preventing the children of Sikh fathers from taking the "pahul", and by seducing professed Sikhs from their allegiance to their faith. Hinduism has strangled Buddhism, once a formidable rival to it, and it made serious inroads on the domains of Sikhism.

The movement to declare the Sikhs Hindus, though widespread and of long duration, is, according to Macauliffe, "in direct opposition to the teaching of the Gurus". Nevertheless, it incidentally receives support from certain of those who profess themselves Sikhs.

Besides the "Singhs", or followers of the 10th Guru, there is the important class of "Nanak panthi", or "Sajdhari" Sikhs, who while following the faith of Nanak, have not thought it incumbent on them to adopt the ceremonial and social observances of Govind Singh, who do not observe the five K's, and do not even in theory reject the authority of the Brahmans.

Again many "Sodhi" (sub-sections of Khatris; Nanak was a "Bedi", and the Gurus from the fourth onwards were "Sodhis") and "Bedi" Sikhs, have never been able to bring themselves to resign the quasi-sacredotal position and privileges which attach to them as members of the class (Khatris) which gave the Sikhs most of their Gurus, and has given them a priesthood also, in so far as the Sikhs can be said to have one. Such spiritual leaders number among their followers not only "Sajdharis" and "Singhs" indiscriminately, but also many pure Hindus, some of whom, apparently out of deference to the religious tenets of their leaders, wear their hair long, and outwardly appear to be Sikhs, though they cannot be classed with any precision either as Sikhs, or as Hindus.

There is thus a considerable body of Sikhs between whom and Hindus the dividing line is far from clearly demarcated, and who, if they have not actually accepted, have never been at any pains to repudiate the contention that the Sikhs are part and parcel of the Hindu nation.

Hinduism, owing to its wonderfully assimilative character, had thus reabsorbed a good part of Sikhism, as it had absorbed Buddhism before it, notwithstanding that much of these religions is opposed to caste and the supremacy of the Brahmans.

More recently the militant Hindu sect known as the "Arya Samaj" has not been content, like orthodox Hinduism, to trust to the slow process of time, but has carried war into the Sikh domains, by "reclaiming" certain low castes who are socially inferior to the rank and file of the Khalsa, but who are unquestionably Sikh by tradition and religion.

The pro-Hindu and the orthodox Sikh parties.—Briefly, therefore, there are thus in the Sikh community two sections which are pulling in totally different directions. The first which favours, or at any rate views with indifference the re-absorption of the Sikhs into Hinduism, and which is powerfully supported by the Hindu community. The second which maintains that there is a distinct line of cleavage between Hinduism and Sikhism, and devotes itself to maintaining the Sikh faith in its original purity. This latter party has the support of the best authorities in claiming that it is the champion of orthodoxy, and it has set itself to watch and oppose Hindu, and more particularly Arya, aggression.

Present day Sikhism and Hinduism.—In spite of the efforts of the orthodox Sikh party to prevent abuses from creeping into their religion, it is doubtful whether many of the orthodox Sikhs of the present day are entitled to call themselves, such, if judged strictly by the articles of faith of the tenth Guru. It must be remembered that the Gurus attacked caste distinctions, and the authority of the priesthood. Orthodox Sikhs, however, still refuse to mingle with "Mazbhis", "Ramdasias", and other low classes, who are theoretically their social equals; moreover instances frequently occur where they are brought into the world, married and buried by Brahmans whose authority and influence their Gurus were at one in repudiating. Again, numbers flock annually to Hardwar, and other Hindu places of pilgrimage, though this is repugnant to the teaching of their Scriptures.

Sikhism in the Indian Army.---It has already been seen how the teachings of Govind Singh sufficed to weld the members of a quiescent religious order into a warlike and politically ambitious nation. The peculiar value of the Sikh faith in imbuing its followers with a military spirit is generally admitted; the history of the Sikh Mazbhi regiments conclusively proves the value of the teachings of the Guru in transforming this class, through an interminable line of heredity, into brave and staunch soldiers. The soldierly qualities of the Sikhs have been fittingly recognised in the extent to which they have been employed in the Indian Army, in which on the outbreak of the war they numbered 33,000 out of 174,000, or somewhat less than 1/5th of the total strength.

Throughout the era under review, as is the case at the present time, one of the principal agencies for the preservation of the Sikh religion has been the practice of military officers commanding Sikh Regiments, to send Sikh recruits to receive the "pahul" or baptism, according to the rites prescribed by Guru Govind Singh. Sikh soldiers, too, are required to adhere rigidly to Sikh customs and ceremonial and every effort has been made to preserve them from the contagion of Hinduism. Sikhs in the Indian Army have been studiously "notionalised", or encouraged to regard themselves as a totally distinct and separate nation; their national pride has been fostered by every available means, and the "Granth Sahib", or Sikh Scriptures, are saluted by British Officers of Indian Regiments. The reason of this policy is not far to seek. With his relapse into Hinduism, and re-adoption of its superstitions and vicious social customs, it is notorious that the Sikh loses much of his martial instincts, and greatly deteriorates as a fighting machine. Macauliffe, in alluding to the fact that loyalty to the British is enjoined by various prophecies in Sikh holy writ, considers that—"it is prophecies such as these, combined with the monotheism, the absence of superstitions and restraint in the matter of food, which have made the Sikhs among the bravest, the most loyal and devoted subjects of the British Crown". Later, in describing the pernicious effects of the upbringing of Sikh youths in a Hindu atmosphere, Macauliffe writes "Such youths are ignorant of the Sikh religion and of its prophecies in favour of the English, and contract exclusive social customs and prejudices to the extent of calling us "Malechhas", or persons of impure desires, and inspiring disgust for the customs and habits of Christians.

It will thus be clear that the policy pursued in the Indian Army has been directed, and rightly directed, to the maintenance of the Sikh faith in its pristine purity, for the reason that any falling off from orthodoxy not only detracts from the fighting value of the Sinkh soldier, but inevitably tends at the same time to affect adversely his whole attitude to the British power.

The good services of the Army in buttressing the crumbling edifice of the Sikh religion have been freely acknowledged by orthodox Sikhs.

The institutions the Sikhs themselves have established in their endeavours to maintain their separate national individuality, will now be described.

The Singh Sabhas and the Lahore and Amritsar Khalsa Diwans.—The first Singh Sabha, or Society, was established at Amritsar in 1873. Owing, however, to the fact that the President and Secretary endeavoured to secure absolute control, the more disinterested members broke away and established another Singh Sabha at Lahore. The objects of the Lahore Branch were to interpret more truly the teachings of the 'Adi Granth", and other sacred books, and to demolish false doctrines and improper customs. In 1883 the Amritsar Sabha, which had suffered considerably from the secession of the founders of the Lahore branch, was re-established, and, several new Sabhas having sprung up, it was deemed advisable to have a central controlling body.

Foundation of the Khalsa Diwan in 1883.—In pursuance of this policy the Khalsa Diwan was founded in 1883, at Amritsar. This newly constituted body was far from making an auspicious start, and it was torn from the very beginning of its existence by internal dissensions. These finally resulted in the splitting up of the Diwan into two sections, known as the Lahore and Amritsar parties. From the year 1887 onwards, the Lahore and Amritsar Diwans existed as separate and distinct societies, neither of them being able to claim to represent the Sikhs as a body. The Lahore Diwan, however, was larger in point of members, and stronger as regards educational attainments and general ability, and may thus be regarded as the real Sikh representative body of the time. It was owing to the exertions of this Diwan that the long discussed scheme for a Sikh national educational institution at length took practical shape, in the founding at Amritsar, in 1892, of the "Khalsa College". Dissension and disunion between the parties, however, still continued. The Sikhs themselves were generally coming to recognise that their communal interests were only hindered thereby, and in November, 1901, at a special meeting of the Amritsar Singh Sabha, attended by influential Sikhs from all over the Punjab, it was decided that the Amritsar Branch was in future to be considered the ruling one in the Society.

The Chief Khalsa Diwan, founded in 1902.—The result of this meeting was the Chief Khalsa Diwan, which was founded at Amritsar in 1902. The ostensible objects of this Diwan were religious and secular instruction, the reformation and improvement of the Sikh community, and the representation of its needs to Government. It was thus a sort of central controlling agency for the management of the numerous Sabhas which exist all over the country.

It was not only the self-constituted leader and spokesman of the Sikhs in all social and political matters, but it was also able through its preachers, to wield in spiritual matters a degree of influence. The supporters of the Chief Khalsa Diwan formed essentially what was referred to by Hindus, as the "Separatist" party among the Sikhs;

that is they dissociated Sikhs from Hindus, discouraged the employment of Brahmans at Sikh social and religious ceremonies, and generally endeavoured to keep their religion pure from the thraldom of Hinduism and its priesthood.

In so far as they strove to arrest the decay of orthodox Sikhism, the objects of the Chief Khalsa Diwan were in every way commendable. "This body undertook for the first time to separate Sikhs entirely from Hindus, as their interpretation of the 10th Guru's orders was that "Sikhs were not Hindus". This provided on the one hand the Hindu Sanatists who were alarmed on religious as well as social grounds, and on the other, the Arya Samajists, who did not like the average Sikh owing to his military importance and pro-British views", but towards the end of the first decade of the 20th century, the zeal of the Diwan for the cause of Sikh nationality caused it to out-run its discretion and led it to embark on a programme of social and religious reform which was neither acceptable to the Sikh laymen of the Orthodox School, nor to the religious authorities at the Amritsar Golden Temple.

The Khalsa College.—The same instinct of communal self-preservation which led orthodox Sikhs to establish Singh Sabhas and Khalsa Diwans, was responsible also for the foundation of the Sikh national educational institution, known as the Khalsa College. The Sikhs were long alive to the fact that they were backward in education as a community, and also that their youths, if left to be reared by teachers of other denominations were exposed to many influences which were hostile to their traditionary habits and character. The Khalsa College was thus founded, not only with the idea of making good educational deficiencies, but of ensuring that Sikh youths should be reared in a genuinely Sikh atmosphere, and receive such moral and religious instruction as would mould them into true Sikhs and loyal citizens. The foundation stone was laid on 1892, and was managed in the first instance by an Executive Committee selected by the Council. Owing to certain defects in its internal administration and financial status, the old regime was abolished in 1908, and some element of Government control was introduced into the management. This was the more desirable, as the tone of the College left much to be desired.

The political activity discernible among the Sikhs about this period was the resultant of forces some of which were purely political, or purely religious, whilst others did not fall wholly within the domain either of politics or religion but which were, as it were, an admxiture of both. Politics and religion are closely allied, and this is no more in evidence than with the Sikhs. If a clear understanding of Sikh history is to be arrived at, with special reference to the Gurdwara Reform Movement, this aspect must be duly considered as a fraction of the whole, and it will now be necessary to allude to some of the political, or politico-religious movements which have influenced the Sikhs in common with the other sections of the Indian population, in recent years.

Politico-Religious Movements in the 20th Century.—The loyalty of the Sikh is traditional, and the tradition rests on the substantial basis of a long and honourable record of loyal and devoted service rendered to the Crown in peace, as well as in war. There is in fact among British officers a very general disposition to suppose that loyalty is inherent in the Sikh, and that it is an attribute of him which can always be safely assumed to be above suspicion. In the majority of cases it is so, yet, there are among their ranks a leavening of disaffected persons, as in all communities there always must be. The fanatical "Kuka" set among the Sikhs were always overtly hostile to the British supremacy, and had to be put down with a strong hand. In the early eighties the rumoured advent of Dalip Singh had a decidedly unsettling effect on a large section of the Sikhs. Bearing these, and other facts in mind, as also the remarkable advance of Indian political life and thought towards the end of the 19th Century, it is in no way surprising that the Sikhs did not remain unaffected by the wave of disloyal unrest which swept over the Punjab in 1907.

An agitator will always obtain a hearing amongst a certain section of the community, this is no less true in England than it is in India, and the psychology of the masses must in no way be lost sight of. The inflammatory speeches, therefore, of the notorious agitator Ajit Singh, and the advent of Mr. Gokhale to the Punjab in 1907 left an unsettling influence, which, even in the quieter years which succeeded it, was never entirely eliminated.

Two objectionable Gurmukhi papers appeared in 1909, which were largely echoes of the violently nationalistic writings which were then appearing in the Punjab press, and which culminated in a series of press prosecutions during 1909-1910. From America it was reported that several ex-sepoys had publicly burnt their medals and discharge certificates, whilst a spirit of anti-British disaffection was commonly prevalent amongst Sikhs in Canada.

These incidents have been quoted in order to show clearly that the Sikhs have not been, and are not, immune from the disloyal influences which have been at work among other sections of the populace. The contention that some of them are disloyal is in no wise meant to impugn the loyalty of the Sikhs, but it is necessary to realise that an anti-British spirit has existed for some years in certain quarters, and is a factor which must be taken into account in deciding from what standpoint certain recent Sikh movements should be viewed.

The Depressed Classes Movement among Sikhs.—An influence which powerfully affected the character and trend of Sikh political activities, early in the present century, was what, for want of a better name, may be termed the 'depressed classes movement'. According to the teachings of the tenth Guru, all Sikhs, are, strictly speaking, socially equal after baptism, and there are none of the caste distinctions which are so characteristic a feature of Hindu society. Sikhism, however, is only one of the many religions in which practice has over ridden precept, and the Jat Sikh has never been able entirely to divest himself of the caste prejudices which pertained to him as a Hindu, or to regard as his social equals his co-religionists recruited from classes of lower social standing than his own. This attitude accounts for the existence of the Mazbhis, Ramdasias, Rehtias, Rangretas, and other classes of Sikhs, with whom the general body of the Khalsa neither inter-dine, nor inter-marry; and whom they regard in much the same light as Hindus view the lower strata of their society.. These low-class Sikhs have never had any attractions held out to them by orthodox Hinduism by which they would be assigned, if anything, a still lower social position; on the other hand proselytising religions like Christianity and Islam have secured some converts from among them, though such small defections as have occurred never seem to have caused much anxiety to the Sikhs.

Effect of Arya Samaj influence.—With the advent of "Arya Samaj" this attitude of indifference had to be abandoned. The Samaj, theoretically at all events, admits all religions and all classes on terms of social equality, and its attractions for low-caste Hindus and Sikhs are, therefore, peculiarly strong. Moreover, the most rigid observance of the religion and rites of the tenth Guru have never given the low caste Sikh the social equality which the Arya religion confers on him immediately on conversion.

The success which attended the proselytising activities of the militant Arya sect greatly disquietened the Sikhs, among whom the more advanced and liberal minded recognised that a rigid observance of caste barriers must result in the gradual atrophy of the outlying portions of their social system. In 1907, therefore, a society was formed in Amritsar which had as its object the levelling up of class distinctions, and which advocated the reception into the Sikh brotherhood of all persons of whatever class who were previously included in Sikhism. The actual promoters were persons of no great position or influence. and the Society as such seemingly never wielded much influence, but the impetus given by it to the proselytising movement has remained, and the reclamation and admission on terms of equality of low class Sikhs was the avowed policy of the Chief Khalsa Diwan.

Though probably originally aiming at nothing more than social and religious improvement, the depressed classes movement came to have at least as great a political as either a social or religious significance. The "Arya Samaj" frankly devoted itself to producing a homogeneous national body, and as Christianity and Islam, in theory at least, subscribe to the doctrine of social equality, orthodox Hinduism and sikhism have been compelled, to some extent, to keep pace with the more progressive religions, or, to witness a constant shrinkage of their members. Recent events in India, also, if they have brought into existence the idea of a united Indian nation, have also done much to accentuate the lines of cleavage between the different communities. There has been a great awakening of inter-communal jealousy, and there is no community that is not fired with the idea consolidating and improving itself to the utmost of its power. Losses in numerical strength are no longer regarded with indifference.

The problem of raising their depressed classes has thus, in spite of themselves, been obtruded on the Sikhs, and they have been driven to choose between closing up their ranks, or seeing the outlying portions of their social system gradually falling away. The choice of the former alternative was almost inevitable, and it was adopted.

It should be noted that in theory there should be no 'untouchability' amongst followers of the Sikh religion, but in practice it has never ceased to exist, and is not likely to die out as long as it is observed amongst Hindus with whom Sikhs will always have so much in common.

The uplifting of the 'depressed classes' and 'untouchables' has recently been taken up in right earnest by the leading lights amongst Akalis, but they do not find it easy to pursuade the Jat Sikhs to give up their traditional prejudices and to bring them down to the level of an 'untouchable', even though he be a Sikh.

In so far as the movement tends to consolidate the Sikh nation, and to enable it to present a solid front to external aggression, it must command the most unqualified approval; among the Sikhs, however, as among the Hindus. religion is indissolubly bound up with the social system, and a relaxation of social rules is bound to have a disturbing effect on religious beliefs; such a disturbance has been clearly visible in the case of those Sikhs who have subscribed to the reform movement, and this falling away from orthodoxy, which in Sikhism is synonymous with loyalty, has again altered the political outlook of those who have been affected by it. These various changes are all accurately reflected in the "Tat Khalsa" Sect which has grown up, and which requires description.

The new Tat Khalsa Sect or Neo-Sikh party.—The tenth Guru, Govind Singh, appointed no spiritual successor except the Granth Sahib, or Sikh Scriptures, though in various temporal matters he commisisoned one of his disciples named Banda, to fill his place. This person was led to put forward claims to the Guru-ship as well, with the result that the Sikhs of that time split into two parties, one of them obeying the behests of their late Guru, and the other supporting the pretensions of Banda. The former were known as the "Tat", (the real or true) Khalsa, and the others as the "Bandai" Khalsa. In later times the term Tat Khalsa has been applied by Hindus to what they are pleased to call the "Separatist" party among the Sikhs, and every orthodox Sikh, if questioned, would claim with pride that he belongs to the Tat. or true Khalsa. But just as the term "Swaraj", which originally meant colon, self-government for India within the Empire, has come to denote complete national autonomy, so the expression "Tat Khalsa", from meaning the orthodox Sikhs generally, has come to be applied to the "advanced Sikh reforming party", which is not merely not orthodox in its religion, but would seem to have been in some danger of falling away from Sikhism altogether.

Though Guru Govind Singh advocated the admission of all castes on a footing of perfect social equality, after they had received the "pahul", it seems quite clear that even in his time the Hindu Jat who embraced Sikhism, never actually did accept as his social equals his co-religionists who had been received into the Khalsa, from a lower social level than his own. The mere existence of Sikhs such as Mazbhis, and others, affords practical proof of this, and between them and the Jat Sikhs, as well as Brahman and Khatri Sikhs, there have always existed clearly defined social distinctions. Inter-marrying and inter-dining among the higher and lower classes, though theoretically permitted and even inculcated, have been as little practised as within the orthodox Hindu community itself. Consequently, when in pursuance of the policy of the Chief Khalsa Diwan, its leaders began to receive as co-equals, and to eat with low caste Sikhs, they at once found themselves in collision with the religious authorities of the Amritsar Golden Temple, and the Sikh hierarchy controlling the different "dharamsalas" and "gurdwaras" (Sikh temples) all over the country. The rupture between the Tat Khalsa and the Golden Temple was complete.

The Tat Khalsa party contended that their reforming activities were justified by their scriptures, and that they, and not the adherents of the religion of the Golden Temple, were entitled to claim to be Tat or true Sikhs, and it seems fairly free from doubt that the Tat Khalsa party had the weight of the teachings of the tenth Guru behind them in this contention; still, their indiscriminate and somewhat reckless proselytising was a thing so far unknown in Sikh History, and they were prepared to receive direct into the fold of Sikhism individuals with far less scruple than was shown even by the tenth Guru himself. The Sikh body politic was thus bound to receive accretions which were neither Sikh by tradition nor sentiment.

Another aspect of the Tat Khalsa movement gave rise to a more serious matter. With their anxiety to swell the members of the Sikh community, it would be imagined that a corresponding quickening of religious zeal would also have manifested itself. This, however, was not the case. The Tat Khalsa Party turned their backs on their priesthood because of their difference of opinion on the depressed classes movement, and ceased to attend at places of worship, or to participate in the religious observances enjoined by their religion. The freedom of thought and laxity of observance displayed by this party were looked upon with something like dismay by orthodox Sikhs.

On the face of it there appeared but little to urge against the Tat Khalsa creed. There were no doubt amongst its followers a number of zealous Sikhs who desired nothing more than the homogeneity of the Sikh body politic, and the protection of it from any risk of further disintegration. Still, the Sikh is an exceedingly important miltary asset, and any lukewarmness which he may develop in his attachment to his hereditary faith, which in itself inculcates a spirit of loyalty to the British throne, would be regrettable. This was in no way allayed when it is remembered that the new Sikhism appeared to be modelling itself more and more closely on the Arya Samaj, which is admittedly not only a religion, but a policy, and aims at creating not only a vedic Church, but an Aryan nation. Therefore, if the whole of the adherents of the Tat Khalsa were not politically minded, there were many members who were imbued with nationalistic ideals. These aimed not merely at forming a homogeneous Sikh community which would be able to defend itself against other rival bodies, but hoped for the revival of a Sikh nation. This party may be described as the Neo-Sikh party, which were very greatly in evidence in the Gurdwara Reforms.

The Sikh Educational Conferences.—A factor in Sikhism which figured largely in the present century was the Sikh Educational Conference. This, as its name implies, is a body of Sikhs which is devoted to the promotion and encouragement of education among its co-religionists. The Conference was founded in 1908, and met annually subsequently. It has already been remarked that the happenings of recent years have served greatly to intensify inter-communal rivalry in India. There has been a corresponding quickening of interest in educational matters, education having come to be regarded as the most essential condition of communal and political advancement. These influences have been at work amongst the Sikhs as among others, and a realisation of the indispensability of education has been accompanied in this case by a growing consciousness of the educational backwardness which hitherto characterised them as a community. The movement commanded the hearty support of all classes among the Sikhs, because the need of education was universal, and generally recognised.

The Conference, though it had as one of its objects to ameliorate and propagate Sikhism, was declared in the statement of aims and objects to be a non-political body. It was attended by delegates from different provinces, who were elected by the different Khalsa Diwans and Singh Sabhas, or by general meetings or local Sikhs; also by delegates from Sikh Schools and Colleges.

Though the Sikh educational conference was th[illegible] movement which in its ostensible aims and objects was above reproa[illegible], and which received the most hearty support of all classes of Sikhs, yet, the fact that it was originated and controlled by the Chief Khalsa Diwan gave rise at the time to some anxiety as to the direction its activities might eventually take. That the Sikhs were backward in education, and that advancement was urgently needed, was accepted as axiomatic truths by Sikhs of all classes and shades of opinion, who, therefore, regarded the conference as a cause in respect of which all sectarian differences might be sunk in furtherance of the common weal; they gave freely, therefore, not only moral support, but financial assistance. The actual nature of the objects, however, to which the moneys subscribed in the name of education were to be devoted, rested within the decision of the Chief Khalsa Diwan.

There was a considerable section among the adherents of the Chief Khalsa Diwan which viewed its management with dislike, not only because of the advanced character of its religious and political outlook, but because also of the ascendancy which the Aroras had gained in its councils. The Arora Sikhs are recruited from a socially inferior class of Khatris of the same name, and who have always been notorious for the sharpness of their business instincts.

Another cause which lessened the prestige and influence of the Chief Khalsa Diwan was the starting in 1909 of a new body called the Central Khalsa Diwan, with its headquarters at Bhagrian in the Ludhiana District. The movement is chiefly of interest as showing how Malwa-Manjha jealousy can still interfere with concerted action on the part of Sikhs as a community; as there are not known to be any fundamental political differences between the two bodies.

The Chief Khalsa Diwan was totally eclipsed by the Akali movement in which it refused to participate and consequently it has since been labelled as a moderate institution.

It is simply lingering on and at present is almost lifeless.

THE GHADR CONSPIRACY.

Growth of discontent among emigrants.—It will be convenient at this point to consider certain events which had led to the growth of discontent among Indian emigrants in America, and which led in the early years of the war to what is known as the Ghadr conspiracy. This had an unsettling effect on the Punjab, not only during the period of the Great War, but for several years after, and which only terminated with the passing of the Second Gurdwara Reform Bill in 1925.

The conspiracy derived its origin from the Pacific Coast of America, its centre being at San Francisco, and its chief promoter was one Lala Hardayal.

Canadian Government ordinance of 1910.—In 1910, the Canadian Government passed an ordinance enabling the immigration authorities to prohibit the entrance of any Asiatic into Canada, unless he came from his country of origin by direct voyage, and was in possession of a sum of 200 dollars. This prohibition caused considerable disappointment, particularly amongst the Sikh community, which furnishes annually the greater number of emigrants, as it has debarred them from obtaining labour in a country where high rates of wages prevail, and very large profits are to be made.

Sikh emigrant deputation of 1911.—In 1911 a deputation of Sikhs went to Ottawa to represent their grievances before the Canadian authorities, but without result.

In 1912 the general discontent was given a strong fillip in a refusal for admission to two wives of two prominent provincial members of the Sikh community at Vancouver.

Sikh emigrant deputation of 1913.—In 1913 a deputation of three Sikhs visited London and India in order to represent both to Government and the public the disabilities under which Indian emigrants were suffering. In India they utilised their opportunities to stir up mischief, and with this object in view addressed public meetings, and visited cantonments with a view to bringing their propaganda to the notice of the troops, in which they were disappointed. Nevertheless, their actions formed a distinct step in the development of the revolutionary movement, and was intended to establish a link of sympathy between Indians at home and emigrants abroad.

In America meanwhile, in 1913, Hardayal commenced an intensive campaign, touring and lecturing. His lectures were enthusiastically received, and his popularity grew rapidly. The restrictions imposed on Indian immigration formed a real grievance, and there was a general feeling of discontent against the British Government. The Sikh Khalsa Diwan in California was in sympathy with Hardayal, and supported his actions.

Full details of the events which subsequently took place fill a volume in themselves, and are detailed in great length in the account of the Ghadr conspiracy 1913-1915, published in 1919. The leading features can alone be described.

Salient feature of Conspiracy.—By the end of the summer of 1913 Hardayal had collected sufficient funds to establish a press for the publication of the newspaper "Ghadr" and the first Gurmukhi edition was brought out in December of that year. The paper amply fulfilled the worst anticipations that could have been formed from such an introduction. Its circulation was very rapidly extended, and very large numbers were posted weekly to India, and in fact to every place where Indians were known to be residing. Within a few weeks it was found that copies were being received in India from all ports on the Chinese coast, and even from Africa. Precautions were taken to deal with the menace, but in spite of these, copies found their way to the villages, and were a potential source of unrest in the Punjab.

Minnesota and Komagata Maru incidents.—In 1913 the refusal of the Canadian authorities to allow 200 Indian labourers to land from the Minnesota, accentuated the feeling of irritation against the immigration laws, and supplied fresh material for those engaged in fomenting discontent. By April 1914 feeling was running very high, and in May the venture of the Komagata Maru added greatly to the general discontent. Proceedings under the immigration laws were instituted against the 300 passengers which this ship contained, and no one was allowed to land. Orders of deportation were then served on all the passengers who, however, assumed a very truculent attitude, locked up the captain and his officers, and refused to all the ship to leave. An attempt on the 19th July to place police on board to regain possession of the ship was beaten off with sticks and other missiles. The ship eventually left at the end of July with orders to proceed to Hong Kong, and after causing considerable trouble at various ports of call, arrived at the mouth of the Hugli on the 26th September. Meetings meanwhile had been held all over America, at which the audiences were addressed in violent language, and urged to hasten back to India in order to create a general feeling of hatred against the Government, and to take the opportunity of the War in Europe to raise a revolution.

It is not possible to quote the events that followed during 1914, and the succeeding years 1915-17, which were the result of this revolutionary campaign. Suffice it to say that six vessels containing returned emigrants arrived in India in 1914-1915, and endeavoured to carry out the teachings that had been instilled into them in America.

Ingress into India Ordinance of 1914.—In order to meet the situation, the Government of India took powers on the 5th September 1914, under an Ordinance known as the "Ingress into India Ordinance", to provide for the control of persons entering British India, whether by sea or land, in order to protect the State from anything prejudicial to its safety, interests or tranquility. On the 22nd March 1915, the Act was brought into force in sixteen specified districts of the Punjab.

Budge-Budge Riot.—The arrival of the Komagata Maru caused a riot at Budge-Budge. This riot showed the necessity for strong action in dealing with revolutionary suspects from America. Their avowed policy was to procure arms, and that every means should be adopted to cause injury and harassment to Government. Post-offices, railway lines and bridges, telegraphic communications and tehsil treasuries were to be pillaged and destroyed. Jails were to be broken open, and their inmates to be released and induced to join in the work. In addition, efforts were to be made to tamper with the loyalty of the Indian Army, and to inculcate ideas of mutiny.

On the 27th February 1915, the leading Sikh gentry of the districts to which the emigrants mainly belonged, met at Government House, Lahore. As a result of this Conference, Sikh Advisory Committees were established in the Central Districts to assist the District Magistrates in the supervision of the returned emigrants. These gave most valuable advice in regard to restrictions, internments, relaxations and releases, and the influence exerted by the members on the side of the law and order was of the utmost value.

Plans of the Revolutionaries in India.

Earlier activities.

The plan of action which the revolutionaries set before themselves was, briefly, that they would preach Ghadr to the villagers of the Punjab, and win new adherents to its doctrines; procure arms by plundering police stations, and funds by looting treasuries and committing dacoities; tamper with troops, and generally raise the country against the Government. The details for carrying out the plans, except as regards the dacoities, were vague, and understood only by a very few. Until February 1915 the Punjab revolutionaries left to their own devices accomplished practically nothing to forward their plot. The various gangs wandered about from village to village to meet other returned emigrants, organise gatherings, and look for likely places in which to commit dacoities.

Acts of violence.—The first act of violence in the Punjab was at the Chauki Man railway station, in the Ludhiana District, with the object of securing an expected consignment of arms.

The next outrage planned was an attack on the Tehsil Treasury at Moga. Owing to the activities of the police, this was frustrated, but in the subsequent skirmish against a gang of fifteen the Sub-Inspector of Police, and a zaildar were killed.

During this period also there had been important activities in the Amritsar, Lahore and Jullundur Districts, meetings taking place at the annual Sikh Fair at Nankana Sahib, Gujranwala, and at Khasa, Tarn Taran, and at a small Sikh Temple called the Jhar Sahib, which stands alone near the village of Bhure in the Amritsar District. The assembly determined finally on the 26th of November as the date for general concerted action. Some of the conspirators had got into communication with Sikh sowars of a cavalry regiment quartered in Lahore Cantonments, and were confident that on the date fixed that the sowars, having mutinied, would ride out and join them with arms. The sowars, however, did not appear, much to the disappointment of the revolutionaries. These decided to gather again on the night of the 27th at a site known as the Khairon mound, from where they would proceed to attack the Sirhali Police Station to secure arms. The attack, however, failed.

With the failure of the Jhar Sahib meetings, and the breakdown of the projected attacks on Lahore and Ferozepore Cantonments, the conspiracy in the province entered on a period of quiesence. The rank and file of the movement in their own way had diagnosed the reason for the failure so far to accomplish anything. There was no cohesion among the men scattered through the various districts, nor was there any definite plan pursued by all Worst of all, there were no arrangements for the supply of arms, the consignments promised them by the American originators of the movement being found to be a myth. Such weapons as they had consisted of a type known as a "Chavie". This consists of a large blade like that of the old battle axe, with an attachment by means of which it can be readily put on, or taken off, an ordinary bamboo stave. When not mounted for use, the blade is carried concealed about the person. The "Chavie" is the traditional weapon of the Central Punjab dacoit.

The general situation in the Punjab.

Effect of the outbreak of the war.

When the emigrants began to arrive back in September 1914, they expected to find the Punjab, if not ready for a revolution, at least in a state of uneasiness, and it is certain that in this respect, as in the matter of arms, they suffered a disappointment. The vast majority of the people were thoroughly loyal and contented, though, of course, somewhat perturbed over the European war. The peasantry were—and still are—largely illiterate, and wild rumours were everywhere in circulation, which tended to unsettle men's minds, even where they were not believed. In the Sikh Districts one such rumour was that the Sikh troops sent to Europe, had been obliged to cut their long hair, the retention of which is part of their religious observances. Most persistent of all was the legend of German invincibility; fantastic tales were told of her Zeppelins, her cannon and her various war appliances. Such wild rumours however, were to be expected among ignorant people, and they did not affect the underlying loyalty of the peasantry to their rulers.

Agitation causes weakening of loyalty.—Agitation in the two or three years immediately preceding, however, had caused a weakening of the loyalty of some persons here and there in the Mohamedan and Sikh communities. Agitation among the Sikhs had appeared in 1913 at first, over a proposal to limit the size of the "kirpan". In 1914 certain improvements at Delhi rendered it necessary to straighten out the boundary wall of an old Sikh temple called the Rikabganj Gurdwara, which no one regarded locally as being of particular sanctity or importance; this gave excuse for further agitation. These incidents, coupled with the emigrants question, involved considerable commotion, causing some of the Sikh peasantry, who had hitherto shown unquestioning loyalty, to ask themselves whether Government was not hostile to them. As the tracts which supplied the greatest number of the Sikh Regiments of the Indian Army were also those which furnished the greatest number of emigrants to the Far East, the effect of the Budge-Budge Riot was great, and the shaking which Sikh loyalty had received was the most serious matter of the moment. The returned emigrants set themselves to inform their kins-men of the unequal treatment that was meted out to them in Canada and the United States; gave exaggerated versions of what had happened to the Komagata Maru, and to preach their doctrines of revolution that they had learned from the Ghadr, and the crude socialism that they had picked up in America. They met nowhere with wide success in their efforts to corrupt, and on the better classes they had no influence whatever. Among the lower classes, however, they met with a certain amount of success. Some were won over by the hope of plundering the rich, others were attracted by the spirit of adventure; a few were seduced through their religious or patriotic feelings—being led to feel that it was the policy of Government to interfere with their religion, of which the Rikabganj Gurdwara was cited as an instance, or that Government was an oppressor of their brethren, both abroad and at home. As most of the returned emigrants had relatives in the Army, their capacity for mischief was greatly increased. The assistance rendered to Government by the better classes of the Sikh community was most praiseworthy. When reports were received that any particular individuals were striving to cause mischief, orders of internment in jail, or of restrictions to villages were issued immediately. The loyal members of society rallied stoutly on the side of law and order.

Effects of acts of Violence.—Despite the precautions taken and the drastic measures employed, the sympathisers with the movement grew in some areas. Soon, however, this rapid increase of partisans stopped for several reasons. The Ferozeshahr murders and the dacoities in Jullundur, and the other central districts, brought home effectively to all men with a stake to lose where the movement led, and what it might cost them and theirs. The allies in Europe were holding their own; Germany was not winning; the Government of India was as before. The inherent loyalty of the peasantry came to the top. Finally, the entry of Turkey into the war had caused a number of uneducated Musalmans to dream of an invasion by Afghanistan on the side of the Central Powers. The Sikhs realised as a whole that the Government was their defence against aggression, and the possibility of the emigrants seducing them from their allegiance was at an end.

This, however, did not make the returned emigrants incapable of mischief, and they continued as before to seduce villagers, students and soldiers, and committed a large number of dacoities all over the Punjab.

The influence that these dacoities exerted on the countryside was of great importance. Murder, senseless cruelty and robbery of the unoffending, cost the revolutionaries whatever sympathy their objects might otherwise have received. The peasantry saw nothing justifiable in these acts, from whatever ulterior motive they might have been committed. To them the revolutionaries became murderers and plunderers of honest men, the more dangerous for their organisation and arms, but to be resisted by all means possible and captured. These dacoities had been recommended by the "Ghadr" for the collection of funds; but the authors of the scheme failed to consider the mentality of the Punjab peasant. The outrages committed, far from terrorising, only made him more keen to stamp out the perpetrators of them.

CONCLUDING STAGES OF THE CONSPIRACY.

Advent of Rash Behari Bose.

Attempts on Lahore and Ferozepore.

February—September 1915.

During early February the headquarters of the revolutionists were moved to Lahore, as a better centre from which to spread revolutionary doctrines among Indian Troops. The chief instigator, one Rash Behari, at once set himself to make plans for a rising on the 21st February, and a press was set up for the production of revolutionary leaflets. Agents were despatched to all the various Cantonments with information that the outbreak was fixed for the 21st, and that it was to begin at Lahore and Ferozepore, other troops to join in on hearing that it had started. The audacity with which some of the agents went about this work of seduction is astounding. They went to the cantonments allotted to them, and, without preliminaries, preached revolution, murder and plunder, to whatever sepoys they met. There was no leisure, of course, for insidious sapping of the men's loyalty, as the revolt was being organised for a date only a week or two ahead.

The rising was to commence in the Lahore Cantonment on the date above mentioned, but, owing to a suspicion by the revolutionists that their plans had leaked out, the original date was changed to the 19th. Information, however, of the plot had fortunately been received, the authorities were on the alert, and the plan was forestalled, whilst at the same time the headquarters in Lahore were successfully raided by the police, and various ringleaders were arrested.

Next to the events at Lahore, the attempted raid on Ferozepore Cantonment was the most serious, but here also warning had been received, and the plans fell through.

Collapse of the Movement.—Rash Behari Bose had fled after the collapse of the plans for the rising on the 19th. Others of the leaders were arrested; others again went into hiding. The menace of the Ghadr conspiracy was at an end. The disclosure by approvers of all the plans, and the names of those concerned, and the arrest of the latter, in rapid succession, soon destroyed any hope that there may have been of the power to set the plot in movement once more. The majority of those concerned strove to conceal their connection with it; and, as time went on, the emigrants were absorbed into village life once more, and their enthusiasm for the doctrines imbibed abroad evaporated.

The Lahore Conspiracy case was heard by a Special Tribunal under the Defence of India Act, and the trial lasted from the 18th of April to the 13th of September 1915. An idea of its magnitude may be gained from the fact that the record covered 704 pages of printed matter.

The results of the Great War disillusioned the Indian Revolutionaries, most of whom were Sikhs, and gave them and the ignorant masses an idea of the magnitude of the power and resources of the British Government, but at the time left some unfortunate impression upon the minds of certain of the Indian troops which were taken to the various theatres of the war in Europe, where they came in contact with the soldiers of other allied nations.

One of the ideas borrowed by them during the war has to-day resulted in the shape of a general demand for the Indianisation of the Indian Army. It is perhaps not too much to say that there exists a certain element amongst Sikh officers who are inclined to support the demand.

They do not, however, agree with the political agitator who wants the King's Commissions to be thrown open to Indians by competitive examinations as they expect the Government to reserve the privilege mostly, if not entirely, for the candidates belonging to military classes of Indians only.

THE DISORDERS OF 1919.

Factors conducing to the disorders.—There was a marked lull in agitation after the trial of the Ghadr Conspiracy cases; there was little to complain of; the emigrants were, in due course, released, and the Province on the other hand responded, in a manner unequalled elsewhere in India, to the call for recruits, and its contributions to the War Loan. It has been suggested that the efforts made to secure these results were in themselves a pre-disposing cause of disorder, but the majority of the Hunter Commission definitely rejected this imputation. Moreover, the disorders themselves were practically confined to towns, and the town population was the least affected by the recruiting campaign.

A cause of dissatisfaction has been sought in the alleged hostility of the local Government of the day to the aspirations of the educated classes. It is possible to refute this charge by proof of the support given by the Punjab Government, then as now, to the cause of education, and the immense progress in the development of educational institutions under the control or patronage of Government. It is, however, a fact that the educated classes, or at least an element of them, inclined to political activity, with held their co-operation to a large extent in the measures deemed desirable by Government for the prosecution of the war. Either such co-operation was not fully sought, or it was deliberately withheld; but the educated classes did not retaliate by open agitation to any appreciable extent, nor were the rank and file of the town populations obviously under their influence prior to the period of disorder.

This section of the body politic had, nevertheless, other definite grievances in the severe economic depression prevailing at the time, in the incidence of the new Income Tax, and in their ancient rivalry with the landed classes. The latter had long been steadily improving the privileged position conferred upon them by the Land Alienation Act, which the trading and professional classes regarded as an invidious distinction. Their strong response to War appeals had earned a generous recognition from Government, and at the same time stimulated the jealousy of those outside the favoured circle. High prices, reacting favourably on the agricultural population were attributed by designing persons to the deliberate policy of the Government. They were in fact due to the bad monsoon of 1918, and dislocation of trade consequent upon the war, but the suffering poor of the towns had no thought for economic causes. With all this, it is improbable, although the atmosphere was fatally disposed towards uneasiness and suspicion, that disorder would have been precipitated, but for the passage of the Rowlatt

Act on the 18th March 1919; or the agitation against it have developed so dangerously, but for Mr. Gandhi, and his passive resistance movement.

Origin of Sikh Non-Co-operation and causes of.—The beginnings of Sikh non-co-operation may be said to date, like most other manifestations of the same movement, from the disturbances of 1919. The violent speeches of the Amritsar Congress at Christmas 1919-20 had a marked effect on Sikh sentiment, who were easily persuaded that they had grievances which should be remedied. There was first an outstanding grievance that Government had, some 14 years ago, taken over control of the Khalsa College. There was also the grievance that the Golden Temple was under an old arrangement, dating shortly after the Mutiny, managed by a "Sarbarah," approved by Government, who was not liked by the educated Sikh community. There was also a general feeling that war services had not been sufficiently rewarded, and this again was aggravated later on by the argument that Council representation was not commensurate with the importance of the Sikh community, or their loyal record in the past.

The Sikh League.—In 1919 a Sikh League was formed, with the intention of securing full communal representation in the new reforms, and to guide Sikh political opinion without estranging them from Government. In 1920, as a result of the various causes of discontent, an agitation began to oust the original office holders from their position in the Sikh League. The membership increased, and an attitude of hostility to Government, emulating the extreme wing of the Congress party, was presently apparent.

Non-Co-operation Resolutions.—Towards the end of October, an important meeting was held at Lahore, when Mr. Gandhi, and the Ali Brothers, appealed to the league to support the policy of council boycott, swadeshi goods and educational campaign. A resolution flavouring non-co-operation was accordingly passed. At Jullundur on the 6th December a large Sikh Diwan expressed itself to the same effect. The district leagues, like that of Jullundur, which were founded as branches of the parent body, assumed from the beginning a complexion different from that which characterised the main body. This was probably due to the admixture of Ghadr convicts, and returned emigrants in the rural committees, but the lapse of the league from constitutional methods dated from the advent of Mr. Gandhi.

Effects of Mr. Gandhi's visit to the Punjab.—His visit to Amritsar had other significant results. The students of the Khalsa College responding enthusiastically to the magnetism of his personally, went on strike, and several professors submitted their resignations, with the result that the Government voluntarily relinquished its control over that institution, Impatience of official supervision presently manifested itself in a desire to place the management of the Golden Temple also on a footing equally satisfactory to Sikh sentiment, with the result that the extreme reformers suddenly seized the Akal Takht Bunga, an appanage of the Golden Temple; Government admitted the claim without hesitation, and, after the case had been gone into, a Committee of management emerged with 179 members under the name of the Shiromani Gurdwara Parbandhak Committee (Committee for the management of sacred shrines).

The Gurdwara Movement.—It is necessary at this stage to examine the Gurdwara movement. The zeal for reforms which now inspired Sikh religious opinion brought into strong relief the antagonism of long standing between two sections of the Sikh community, *viz.*, the Sanatanist, or old Sikh party, and the new—or reforming party. The former had been for years past in possession of practically all the Sikh Gurdwaras, where the "Mahants" or Sikh priests usually administered the shrines and the attached revenues, on a general understanding that they should provide the necessary facilities for worship, and discharge the educational and charitable obligations entailed by their position as managers. The mahants were not necessarily Sikhs, or followers of the 10th Guru; some of them were Hindus pure and simple; most of them had been so long in secure and unchallenged possession that they had come to regard themselves as owners, or at least hereditary tenants, with considerable personal power over the endowments attached to their shrines.

The new, or reforming, party, who were composed entirely of Singhs, complained that the Sikh ritual at these temples was much tainted with Hinduism, and in short charged the mahants with embezzlement, irreligion and profligacy. They maintained finally that the temples and attached endowments were the rightful property of the whole Sikh nation, and that they should be administered by them on lines acceptable to the Sikh community. These accusations were probably justified in many cases, but there can be no doubt that material, as well as moral, considerations weighed with the reformers in their desire to obtain control of the lands and endowments attending to these shrines. The reforming party included among its adherents not only genuine reformers, but some few also, who were known revolutionaries, and bad characters, and who were exploited by outsiders who were bitterly antagonistic to Government. The more violent members of the party, and the instrument in every case used for the seizure of shrines, were the "Akali Jathas," or parties of volunteers, who went about in bands armed with chavies, lathis and kirpans, and who moved in a quasi-military formation. This subject will be referred to at greater length later, in order that a thorough grasp of the Akali movement may be obtained.

Policy of Shrine Seizures.—The seizure of the Akal Takht Bunga has already been referred to; this was made the occasion for a series of similar demonstrations. At the end of September 1920 local Sikhs took possession of the Baba-de-Ber shrine at Sialkot. On the 21st November a party of Akalis occupied the Panja Sahib shrine at Hasan Abdal, and a week afterwards the Mahant of the Sacha Sanda Gurdwara in the Sheikhupura district was evicted. At Tarn Taran a serious collision occurred on the 26th of January, between the "Pujaris" (priests) and the reforming party, with fatal results, and two other Amritsar shrines were occupied in quick succession.

The Nankana Tragedy.—The story of these assaults, is, however, trivial beside that of the great attack on the Janam Asthan, at Nankana, which occurred on the 20th February 1921. This noted shrine is the reputed birth-place of Guru Nanak, and enjoys an estimated revenue of some five lakhs of rupees. The Mahant, Narain Das, was a member of the sect known as Udasi Sadhus. For some months previous to the actual attack rumour had been busy, and the Mahant had expressed his fears, more than once, that forcible appropriation of the shrine by the reforming party was intended.

The number of Akalis was very much swelled by young Sikh soldiers demobilised after the termination of the War. These men were out of work, were trained in military discipline and genuinely believed that they had grievances against the Government.

The "wire-pullers" at the Akali headquarters all along attached much importance to their propaganda amongst Sikh troops. Their latest move is to sympathise with those Sikh officers and men who have in any way suffered owing to their share in the Gurdwara Reform movement, *i.e.*, the Akali trouble. The Akali of Amritsar in one of its issues in December 1921, asked all Sikh soldiers to send in their names and particulars.

It should be remarked here that the position of Government was one of the greatest delicacy; the principle of non-interference with religious matters on the part of all classes in India which it had always assumed, required to be maintained. It, therefore, did not accept responsibility for maintaining the "status quo," and maintained that the question was one between the person "claiming" possession and the person "having" possession; that police would be supplied 'on payment' to the latter for the purpose of preventing a breach of the peace; and that the courts were open either for an application for acting under section 107, or any other action which a private person might be authorised by law to take. This attitude was adopted with a view to avoiding any semblance of partiality towards one or another of two religious parties.

To continue, the Mahant unfortunately adopted a provocative attitude and took no steps to defend his interests by applications to the courts, but would have appeared to have surrounded himself with certain persons of unenviable character for his protection. The Government still hoped that a peaceful solution, by consultation with the newly formed Parbandhak Committee was possible, the more so as the Mahant did not accept the Government offer of police protection on payment. How little a conflict was anticipated was further attested by the fact that the Mahant left Nankana on the 19th of February for a Sanatanist meeting at Lahore. He was recalled, however, before his train left by receipt of information that a number of reforming Sikhs were concentrated at a village in the neighbourhood. On the following day at daybreak, a band of 100 entered the shrine enclosure. The Mahant's party were apparently taken by surprise, but speedily established themselves in positions of advantage overlooking the courtyard. Only a few had fire-arms and with these, supplemented by bricks and axes, they assailed the intruders. The Sikhs were hunted from the hiding places where they sought refuge, and exterminated without quarter or remorse. Thereafter the dead were heaped together and burnt with the aid of kerosine. The Mahant and his accomplices were brought to trial in due course, Government having from the first declared its determination to exact retribution for this act of calculated and barbarous ferocity. Space does not admit of further reference to this tragic event, which soon became widely known and discussed. In Sikh circles it aroused intense feeling, and brought the history of Sikh agitation to an acute and calamitous phase.

The Parbandhak Committee now took up the Sikh cause in real earnest. On the 20th of March 1921 they delivered an ultimatum to the effect, that, if Government did not pass suitable legislation to secure the recovery of the Gurdwaras, and at the same time release all prisoners arrested in connection with the Gurdwara movement, the Sikh community would resort to non-co-operation. The violence of this threat had the effect of alienating moderate Sikh opinion, while the narrow outlook and fanatical methods of the Akali bands, engaged in asserting the rights of the community, were disquieting to respectable persons of all sects and persuasions. The truth, however, must be admitted that the bulk of Sikh opinion was with the Shiromani Gurdwara Parbandhak Committee, whose obduracy for the time being defied all attempts at Gurdwara legislation.

The Shiromani Gurdwara Parbandhak Committee and the Akali Dal.—This committee and the Akali Dal figured so largely in affairs at this period, and in the years that followed, that it is proposed to explain their origin, activities, constitution and organisation in greater detail.

The S. G. P. C., which at this period claimed to be the sole interpreter of Sikh religious opinion, had been in existence for little over a year. Its birth can be traced in the excitement which prevailed on the occasion of Mr. Gandhi's visit to Amritsar in October 1920, which, with its consequences, has already been referred to. Its professed objects were to obtain control over all Sikh Gurdwaras and religious institutions, and to provide for their management on lines acceptable to the Sikh nation. Its moderate members exercised little influence or authority, and the Committee was in practice controlled by a section of extremists, to whom the cause of religious reform differed little from extreme nationalism. The threat of resort to non-co-operation referred to above, was re-affirmed by the Committee at a Sikh Diwan held at Nankana on the 4th and 5th April 1921.

It is important to note that just about this time the Punjab Government issued a communique explaining its attitude to the Gurdwara reform movement and Sikh aspirations generally. This pointed out that Government had not been slow in the past to tender practical sympathy and material assistance to the Sikh community in matters affecting its religious observances, and that that policy remained unaltered, as was clearly indicated by numerous recent concessions. As regards the Gurdwara movement the official attitude was one of entire sympathy for a good cause, but where violence or intimidation was employed to oust the existing incumbents of Gurdwaras, Government had no alternative but to apply the law of the land. It further pointed out that a Gurdwara Bill, then under discussion in the legislative council, had been devised with the sole object of meeting the immediate needs of the Sikh community, and providing the reform party with a system of procedure, for which no provision was made in the existing law.

In spite of the obvious desire of Government, as evinced by this communiqué, to solve the problem in favour of the reforming Sikh party, it was soon clear that matters were reaching a deadlock. In the meantime, the extreme wing of the S. G. P. C. was becoming restless and chafed at the continued inaction. The official announcement on the 30th April that negotiations had broken down, and that the postponement of remedial legislation to a future sitting of the Punjab Council was, therefore, inevitable, was followed by a meeting of the S. G. P. C. on the 10th and 11th of May, to discuss future plans of action. Less than 25 per cent of the full committee were present, the majority being non-co-operators; the result of the meeting was a further resolution in favour of general non-co-operation with the Government, and passive resistance to any executive opposition which might be encountered by the reforming party. These resolutions were passed in the face of considerable opposition on the part of the moderate members. The extremists were thus committed to a course of action which was extremely vague and difficult of execution, and found themselves faced with the secession of some of their most influential supporters, amongst whom was the President.

The working element of the committee were thus left almost entirely extremist, and being unable to arrive at any definite line of action, temporarily drifted in a state of indecision.

On the 28th August a private meeting of the newly elected committee was held, and a resolution was passed by an overwhelming majority confirming the principles of non-co-operation, whilst it was also resolved that the Sikh members of the Punjab Legislative Council should resign their seats in the cause of Gurdwara reform; finally that the Sikh Panth should furnish an army of 5,000 potentia martyrs ready to sacrifice their all.

A short description of the constitution and organisation of the S. G. P. C. is of interest. It consisted of 175 elected members with a President, Vice-President and Secretary. It was divided into an executive committee of 35 members, and a working committee of 7 members. In addition there were local committees dealing with the management of the important Sikh shrines of the Golden Temple, the Nankana Sahib and the Tarn Taran Gurdwara. The condition of membership of the general committee was that every member was to conform strictly to the teachings of the "Granth Sahib", and wear the five K's. A subscription of Rs. 1-4-0 was levied from each member.

The stage was now ready for that final struggle which the committee hoped would definitely settle in favour of the Sikhs the question of Gurdwara reform.

In the meantime, enlistment for the "Akali Dal" had been proceeding briskly, by aid of which the S. G. P. C. planned to make forcible seizures of Sikh Gurdwaras. These plans were rapidly translated into action. A number were seized in October and November 1921, some of them in sensational circumstances. Further seizures would probably have followed, had not Sikh attention been diverted temporarily by two events, the annual fair at Nankana, and the seizure of the keys of the Golden Temple by Government.

The affair of the Keys of the Golden Temple.—This latter affair marks an epoch in the history of the Gurdwara movement, and necessitates more than passing reference.

On the 29th of October the S. G. P. C. passed a resolution requiring the manager of the Golden Temple to hand over the keys of the Treasury of the Temple to the President. It pointed out that he had been appointed by Government, and, although tribute was paid to the efficiency with which he had carried out his duties, it stated that he had only been allowed by the committee to retain his position as an act of grace, that Government was no longer in control of the Golden Temple, and that it was proposed to put an end to a situation which Sikh sentiment could no longer tolerate.

The Punjab Government thereupon instructed the Deputy Commissioner to call on the manager to surrender the keys of the treasury, together with all valuable securities held by him. A bunch of 53 keys was handed over to an Indian magistrate by whom these orders were communicated, and they were then deposited for safe custody in the Government Treasury. A period of intense activity both in the press, and on the platform followed the surrender of the keys. It is not necessary to enter here upon a lengthy exposition of the merits, or demerits of the arguments brought forward, but a widespread agitation was organised in the rural areas of the Central Punjab, and the action of Government was subjected to an unprecedented volume of ill-considered criticism, in spite of the fact that on the 9th November the Punjab Government issued a communiqué explaining why such action had been taken.

These reasons may be briefly summarised :—

(1) The manager was, according to long standing custom, an official nominee.

(2) The transfer of the keys, under compulsion, from him to the Vice-President of the S. G. P. C. appeared imminent.

(3) The S. G. P. C. had not been appointed by Government, and had never received lawful authority to control the Golden Temple.

(4) The keys had merely been placed in safe custody, pending the institution and decision of a friendly civil suit, which should finally divest Government of all responsibility for the management of the Temple.

The surrender of the keys, it must be understood, in no way debarred access to the Golden Temple, and public worship could be carried on as freely as ever before.

In the institution of the civil suit there were unfortunately serious delays. The S. G. P. C. declined to be a party to it, and Government was compelled to initiate proceedings "suo motu". As the case proceeded it became clear that no body of Sikhs was prepared to contest the claims of the S. G. P. C. to represent the religious views of the community, and, in the circumstances, there was no other course open to Government than to acquiesce in the management of the Temple by that body, and to hand over the keys in the treasury to them.

This was acclaimed as a moral victory by the extremists. The stimultaneous release of Sikh political prisoners had an opposite effect from that which was intended; lawlessness became more pronounced, and a great surplus of energy was diverted into political channels.

The Akali Dal.—In the summer of 1920 certain Sikhs made their appearance wearing dark blue turbans, and large kirpans. They were none other than the spiritual descendants of the "Nihangs", or "Akalis", who were originally a band of devotees founded by Guru Govind Singh after the siege of Chamkaur. Dark blue garments and a peculiar head-dress emblematic of the martial characteristics of Sikhs were ordained for them. They were regarded as the custodians of the "Akal Takht" at Amritsar, and the directors of religious ceremonies. Turbulent and fanatical, and addicted to intoxicating drugs, they later on, became a constant source of terror to the more peaceful classes of the community. Maharaja Ranjit Singh endeavoured with some success to reduce them to a state of subjection, but for many years they were the most troublesome element in the "Khalsa".

All Sikh traditions, whether national or religious, are martial; in times of political excitement—and to the Sikhs politics and religion are closely allied—the militant spirit re-asserts itself. It was, therefore, natural that the newly awakened national spirit of the Khalsa should manifest itself in a cult essentially reminiscent of the Khalsa's militant past. Hence the appearance of the political Akali on the stage of the Sikh national drama. The word "Akali" has completely lost its original significance; to the general public it conveys little meaning beyond membership of the Akali Dal. At the same time it is important to realise that though the outward manifestations of the Akali movement were more political than religious, its inward inspiration was religious zeal.

When they first made their appearance in 1920, though militant enough in appearance, they were comparatively harmless, and were at first regarded with amused tolerance. Subsequently their numbers, and with their numbers, the size of their "kirpans", began to increase.

The Gurdwara reform movement which took shape in the summer and autumn of 1920 developed, as has already been shown, into an important political issue, and side by side the number of the Akalis increased, and well defined local associations of Akalis began to appear. No instructions were received from any central organisation, and each "jatha", as the associations began to be called, developed individually.

The Amritsar District was the first Akali recruiting ground to be essayed, and enlistment was subsequently carried on with unabated enthusiasm.

Support was soon after forthcoming from the S. G. P. C. The Akali cult soon found favour in other Sikh Districts, and "jathas" began to appear all over the central Punjab. The excuse advanced for their formation was the necessity for a radical change, by force, if moral persuasion proved unavailing, in the system of Gurdwara tenure.

The central organising agency of the Akali Dal was the "Central Akali Dal", the headquarters of which were situated at the Guru-ka-Bagh, Amritsar. It was instituted by the S. G. P. C., to relieve it of the detailed work of supervising and organising the numerous Akali jathas which had sprung into existence throughout the province. It had a working committee of 11 elected members. Its chief functions were to maintain the registers of membership of the "Jathas", which were subordinate to it, to convey to them the instructions of the S. G. P. C., and to arrange for the deputation of jathas on national work.

Subordinate to the Central Akali Dal were the jathas themselves, the numerical strength and internal organisation of which varied considerably. In districts in which the organisation of the Akalis was well advanced, it was customary to allocate a definite area to a jatha, individual villages, or groups of villages, forming distinct sub-jathas, each in charge of a "jathedar", who worked under the instructions of the head "jathedar". The more progressive jathas had a regular office staff, who performed scriptorial work, and dealt with financial matters, while the jathedar was assisted in the work of the formal admission and scrutiny of would-be Akalis, by a committee of 5 selected men, known as the "Panj Piaras", or "five beloved ones"; the term was specially chosen because of its sacred associations. Their duties were to baptise Akalis, to administer the vows of Sikhism, to convey messages and instructions from the jathedar to the sub-jathas, and generally to render assistance to the jathedar.

In theory there was no restriction of sex or caste; Mazbhis, Khatri Sikhs, Labanas, Carpenters, were all eligible for the Akali Dal, provided they subscribed to the essential principles of Sikhism, and received baptism.

Each jatha possessed its own Granthis, Ragis and Updeshaks, whose duty was to tour the villages, hold diwans, encourage the enlistment of Akalis, and dessiminate Akali propaganda. Generally they were paid servants of the Akali Dal, and received a monthly remuneration from the jatha fund, to which all members were supposed to contribute, contributions being fixed in most jathas at four annas per mensem.

The distinctive marks of the modern Akali were the "kirpan", which could be worn of any length at the discretion of the wearer, and the black, or dark blue pagri. Some also affected black shirts and trousers. In addition to the "kirpan", a "lathi", or a "safa jang" was usually carried.

The admission form to a jatha ran as follows :—"In the presence of Sri Guru Granth Sahibji I promise that I will present my body and soul for the reformation of the Gurdwaras. In this work I will always obey the command of my jathedar, and even in great distress I will not offend anyone by word or action." This formula is the nearest approach to a pledge of non-violence assumed by the Akali Dal.

It is interesting to note in passing that though the S. G. P. C. and the Akali Dal defended themselves by arguing that they were merely religious bodies yet all along amongst themselves the former institution was looked upon as the "civil Sikh" and the latter to be the "military Sikh" of the Akali administration. In some districts the Akali office bearers of the jathas assumed designations similar to those of the officers under the Government, such as "Zaildars", "Thanadars", "Tahsildars", etc.

Events subsequent to Nankana.—It will now be necessary to resume the account of affairs subsequent to the Nankana tragedy. As soon as this had become public property, large numbers of Sikhs commenced to flock to the shrine to do a pilgrimage, and to pay homage to the memory of those killed. Many thousands visited the town, where numbers of them especially "Jatha" men took up more or less permanent quarters. Many of them were armed with axes and "kirpans", and their presence gave rise to great anxiety in the countryside. To prevent the collection of armed Sikhs in the neighbourhood, a meeting was held on the 8th of March at Lahore, between certain leading Sikhs and the members of the Executive Council; one of the conclusions arrived at was, that on Government giving an assurance that the shrine would be safe-guarded from attack, the jathas then in Nankana and its neighbourhood were to be removed within five days.

In order to remove the possibility of a recurrence of bloodshed owing to opposition between the two Sikh parties, the Punjab Government on the 22nd of February 1921, had instructed District Magistrates as to the action to be taken when a dispute likely to cause a breach of the peace existed regarding any shrine or religious institution. They were in effect, as soon as it appeared advisable to do so, to attach the subject of dispute under Section 145, Criminal Procedure Code, pending an ultimate decision under that Section. Action had been taken under these orders in some cases with salutary effects, but when shrines were seized by intimidation or violence it was, of course, necessary for the ordinary law to be put in motion, and the offenders arrested.

In addition to these measures,, orders were issued in regard to the action to be taken against bands of men found marching about the country, and carrying such weapons as "chavies", "takwas" and the like. Under a Chief Court ruling persons displaying such weapons were liable to prosecution under the Arms Act, and Deputy Commissioners were instructed that the leaders or prominent men of such bands were to be disarmed, or prosecuted under Section 19 of the Act. These measures were received with relief and satisfaction by communities other than the Sikh, and even by Sikhs of more moderate views.

The black Akali safas were adopted after the Nankana tragedy.

The Akalis wanted uniformity of dress for their jathas and found this opportunity to introduce the black safa as a symbol of the mourning dress in memory of "Nankana martyrs". The idea was to show that the majority of Sikhs had become Akalis. There were several instances of black safas in the Indian Army as the Akali agitators advocated its use amongst the Sikh troops.

The Gurdwara Bill.—In the meanwhile the introduction of remedial legislation, in order to settle equitably and permanently the question of the ownership and control of Gurdwaras, had been under consideration. The Government, though unable to recognise the claim of the more extreme party to deal with this question outside the law, recognised that there were good grounds for reform, and that a quicker method of dealing will these shrines would be of value. To enable the Government to enter upon legislation a resolution was moved on the 14th of March in the Punjab Legislative Council to introduce a Bill overhauling the law relating to charitable and religious endowments in the Punjab. This Bill was drafted in a form which embodied the suggestions made by the Sikh members of Council, and attempted to deal with the problem on lines acceptable to enlightened Sikhs. Though only intended as a temporary improvisation, pending the provision of final and considered legislation, its provisions were drastic, and went far beyond the limits contemplated by the Akalis themselves when the Gurdwara reform movement was first initiated.

Amongst other matters the bill provided for the appointment of a board which was to have plenary, though only temporary, powers, of arbitration and management in the event of any dispute arising over any Sikh shrine. It also officially recognised the representative character of the S. G. P. C. The latter, however, would not consider the bill for a moment and set on foot an agitation opposing the measure and declaring that the first preliminary or any solution of the Gurdwara reform question must be the release of all Akali prisoners. Thereby it did violence to the convictions of many of its members, who were fully satisfied with the latitude contemplated by the Bill, and privately acknowledged that it was a liberally conceived measure.

Attempts to negotiate with the Parbandhak Committee proved unavailing; the Chief Khalsa Divan on being approached and requested to draft an alternative Bill was also unable to arrive at a solution likely to prove acceptable to both Government and the Committee. [The Punjab Government, therefore, eventually decided to proceed with its own legislative proposals, which were undoubtedly very liberally conceived, and the new bill was finally passed in 1925. (*Vide* Appendices.)]

The Gurdwara Bill thus met with a cold reception. It was generally accepted as an honest attempt on the part of the local Government to meet the situation but failed to satisfy the extremists on either side. Conservative and orthodox Hindus regarded the Bill as an instrument for driving the Sikhs out of the Hindu fold, and sacrificing places of worship hitherto frequented by both Hindus and Sikhs to the clamour of the separatist Akalis. Extreme Sikh opinion was equally insistent on the right of the Sikh Panth to act unfettered. It condemned the main principle of the Bill, and denied the right of Government to appoint Boards of Commissioners to arbitrate on disputed shrines. It held that the Panth should alone exercise the right to dispose of Gurdwaras in which any form of Sikh ritual was observed, and that it had vested its supreme authority in the S. G. P. C., which, therefore, should be considered as the final arbiter independent of official control.

In view of the fact, therefore, that the Punjab Government was unable to discover a "via media" which would prove acceptable to all parties, the Gurdwara Bill was postponed, and the problem was left for future solution. At the same time the Punjab Government issued a communiqué expressing its general sympathy with the Gurdwara Reform movement, and indicated how such reform could be effected, both by amicable discussion and recourse to the existing law.

That this Bill had to be postponed was most regrettable. The massacre of Nankana had shown to what lengths the Khalsa were prepared to go to gain possession of the shrines and to what lengths the Mahants would go to retain them. Otherwise the only remedy which worshippers had against a corrupt or dissolute Mahant was under the ordinary civil law—and civil litigation is at best a lengthy business. Where any ancient vested rights and property of any great value was at stake, 8 or 10 years might easily elapse before a final decision was made. Special legislation therefore was the only remedy.

The Akali leaders however, absolutely refused to accept the Gurdwara Bill and were out to secure their ends by direct action and by no other way. The reasons for this were purely political, hence the first Gurdwara Bill came to nothing.

All along there were two main agencies working behind the scenes to raise obstacles in the way of the proposed Gurdwara legislation. One was that of the Sikh revolutionaries which had an advanced base at Kabul, and the other was the Ex-Maharaja of Nabha who, being conveniently near, remained in close touch with Akali headquarters. Both of them wanted in their own interests to avoid the settlement of the

Gurdwara Reforms. They tried to prejudice the Sikh masses against the present Gurdwara Act before it was passed and were still continuing to work in order to break it.

Preparation for measures of resistance by S. G. P. C.—The weeks succeeding the postponement of the Gurdwara Bill were spent by the Gurdwara Committee preparing for the future struggle, and a peaceful atmosphere prevailed in spite of an apprehension that a general seizure of shrines was imminent.

It was not till September 1921 that the Sikh situation again began to give cause for anxiety. During this month the S. G. P. C. again affirmed its acceptance of the policy of non-co-operation, and called for 5,000 "Sahidi" (martyr) Akalis, who on behalf of the Sikh community, should take possession of all Sikh Gurdwaras and shrines not yet emancipated by the Panth. It also began to agitate for the release of all prisoners convicted in connection with the Gurdwara movement.

Seizures of Shrines.—The seizure of certain shrines during September and October took place, culminating with the affair of the "Keys of the Golden Temple" in November 1921. Towards the end of this month the Punjab Government were compelled by the grave political situation to apply the "Seditious Meetings Act" to the Lahore, Amritsar and Sheikhupura districts, exempting from the operation of the Act meetings of a purely religious nature. Thereupon the Gurdwara Committee at once signified its intention of proceeding with its defiance of the restrictions. Daily meetings were held in the "Guru-ka-Bagh" with the ostensible object of discussing the "Keys" affair; and every advance made by the local authorities with the object of arriving at an understanding, and effecting a solution of this affair, was spurned.

For the first time in the history of this agitation recruiting officers reported difficulty in obtaining Jat Sikhs for the Army.

The ominous situation which presented itself at the beginning of the year 1922 drew forth a grave warning from Government.

In January three Gurdwaras were seized at Anandpur in Hoshiarpur; in February Akali Jathas were everywhere openly hostile, and this unruly militia was rapidly passing beyond the control of the S. G. P. C.

The state of affairs was such, that on the 9th of January a press communiqué was published pointing out the serious consequences of civil disobedience, as distinct from purely negative co-operation, and preventive measures were taken by Government. On the 3rd of March the High Court delivered judgment on the Nankana case, acquitting 27 accused, and reducing the capital sentences to three.

Measures by Government.—The special measures of March 1922 were directed primarily against leaders and organizers of dangerous bands, persons guilty primarily of intimidation or violence in any form. and persons who had taken a prominent part in seditious meetings. Akalis were carefully warned that their aggressive activities, which now amounted to virtual rebellion, against constituted authority, were the only objective in the Sikh community and Government still hoped, as the defender of religious liberties, to promote a settlement of the Gurdwara movement. Meanwhile, the arrest of Mr. Gandhi on the 18th of March administered a timely reminder that Government, however long suffering, was not inert, and many waverers were moved by the atmosphere of impending reaction to confirm their doubtful loyalty. The simultaneous check thus offered to the opposing forces was momentous in its effect, and during the summer months shrine seizures were suspended.

Guru-ka-Bagh.—This period of comparative calm was, however, rudely broken by a series of events which showed that the S. G. P. C. was at least as irreconcilable as ever.

"Guru-ka-Bagh", which should be distinguished from the garden of the same name in Amritsar City, was situated some 14 miles from Amritsar in the Ajanala Tehsil. There were two Gurdwaras, the larger that of Guru Arjan Dev, and the smaller that of Guru Teg Bahadur. There were also some residential houses, a garden and 500 acres of irrigable agricultural land. The S. G. P. C. had previously turned their attention to the shrine, and according to their own account had obtained a verbal agreement from the Mahant, that he would manage the shrine in accordance with the reformed ideas of conduct. However this may be early in August 1921 the larger Gurdwara was seized forcibly by a party of Akalis, five of whom were, after certain negotiations, permitted to continue to live in the shrine. The Mahant went on living in his house, and remained in possession of the land.

On the 8th of August 1922 a party of five Akalis entered the "Guru's" land at "Guru-ka-Bagh", and cut down some branches from a grove of small kikar (acacia) trees, with the ostensible object of providing fuel for the "Guru's" free kitchen, but in reality to establish the right of the Parbandhak Committee to the land and to the trees growing thereon; for the action of these men was clearly carried out in obedience to instructions from higher authority. The Mahant made a complaint of theft to the police, who investigated the matter, and sent up the five Akalis for trial. On the 10th of August they were convicted.

This incident, apparently trivial in itself, was the origin of the protracted struggle during the following three months of September, October and November. An intensive agitation directly fomented by the Parbandhak Committee followed the conviction of the five Akalis. The whole Sikh community was urged to hold meetings, and protest against the unmerited punishment of five men who had merely been exercising an ancient right and a time-honoured custom, and the Akalis in particular were summoned to muster in strength at "Guru-ka-Bagh" and overawe the authorities. On the 22nd of August, in consequence of the deliberate repetition of the offence by others, it was found necessary to make further arrests for theft and criminal trespass. The Akali leaders were not slow to realise the advantages which would be offered by "Guru-ka-Bagh" in a trial of strength with the authorities, for they might reasonably rely on the general support of the Sikh community in their estimate of the undue privileges enjoyed by the Mahant. The ablest lawyers were briefed in order to demolish the official contention that the Mahant was entitled to the protection of the law, and to challenge the justification of the action taken by the officers of Government in preventing the Akalis from entering the disputed land. It was only on the 14th of March 1923 that judgment was finally delivered on the case of 8 prominent Akali leaders, who had been arrested on the 26th of August 1922, as instigators of the offences at "Guru-ka-Bagh".

It is impossible to follow in any detail the course of events at "Guru-ka-Bagh". Briefly, parties of Akalis began to enter the Mahant's land to cut wood, or be arrested in the attempt, day after day. For the first day or two the local authorities arrested the offenders, but subsequently as the gathering at "Guru-ka-Bagh" constituted an unlawful assembly, it was decided to have recourse to dispersal by force, not only at "Guru-ka-Bagh", but on the Ajnala road, where "Jathas" proceeding from Amritsar were met and dealt with. The Akalis were in almost all cases non-violent, but were determined not to disperse; the actions of the police piquets aroused much popular dissatisfaction, while the strain on the police was very severe. When it was found that mere dispersals were not effective, recourse was had, in the words of the official communiqué announcing the change, "to the alternative policy of making arrests".

When this was announced the Parbandhak Committee authorised an increase in the numbers of arrests, hitherto amounting to an average of 20 per diem. By the 28th of September the daily total had risen from 20 to 80 and remained at this figure until the 10th of October, when a full Jatha of 100 Akalis offered itself for arrest, while during the last three or four weeks of the struggle the number varied from 100 to 130.

The composition of the daily jathas was determined upon some time before their presence was required, at Amritsar. Each district jathedar was in receipt of definite instructions, and knew that he was required to despatch a certain number of men on a certain date to Amritsar. Each Akali before going to "Guru-ka-Bagh" was given an armlet, and his name was registered. His private property was taken charge of until he should return from jail. He was instructed to conceal his parentage and residence, and to state he was the son of Govind Singh of Anandpur. After a few days' rest and preparation at Amritsar, the Akali in command of the day's jatha paraded his men before the Akal Takht during the morning Diwan. They were then formally harangued and instructed to be non-violent, and to obey their jathedar. They then marched off to "Guru-ka-Bagh" where they were accommodated in the Gurdwara of Guru Arjan Dev until their turn for arrest arrived. Every day, at times which were more or less fixed, they emerged from the Gurdwara in parties of five each and advanced to meet the police, uttering their religious cries. On expressing an intention to cut wood for the "Guru's langer," they were formally arrested and conducted to the police camp.

Of the rights and wrongs of the "Guru-ka-Bagh" question the ordinary Akali knew nothing. It was impressed upon him that his religion was in danger, and that his personal services and sacrifice were required by the Guru. It was, therefore, in a spirit of religious elation, fanatical, yet disciplined and law abiding, that the "Jathas" marched off every day from the Golden Temple. They would not have been human had they been able to resist the anti-Government influences of their surroundings.

Very few of the Akalis, however, who marched out to be arrested could be described as potential rebels. Their contempt of Government was not deep seated. It was a temporary obscurity of vision, the effect of the fanatical atmosphere into which they had been suddenly thrown. This spirit, however, did not persist beyond the stages of arrest and conviction, and when in custody the prisoners were inclined to be very truculent, their behaviour in jail being marked by a defiance of regulations and a surly pig-headedness.

Thus the impasse continued with the daily despatch of a "Jatha" and its inevitable arrest, until 5,000 Akalis had been captured; it only ended with the announcement that Sir Ganga Ram had secured the lease of the Mahant's land, and offered no objection to Akali intrusion thereon. The law-abiding public breathed again, and the "Guru-ka-Bagh" episode thus came to an unexpected end. The Akalis never-the-less proclaimed a victory and continued their agitation unabated, in spite of the fact that the Punjab Government was engaged in obtaining legislative sanction to the measure which, already referred to as the Gurdwara Bill, was virtually a complete surrender to Sikh aspirations in the matter of Gurdwara reform.

The chief effects of "Guru-ka-Bagh" struggle were vastly to increase the prestige and influence of the S. G. P. C., to impart renewed impetus to the agitation for Gurdwara reform, and to consolidate the Sikh community. The Parbandhak Committee had, for the time being, come to be regarded as the natural parliament, and practically the whole Sikh community accepted its decisions, and deferred to its authority. The only opposition was discernible among moderates and loyalists, who distrusted the Committee's ventures in political matters. In the rural areas the Akali cult again began to be universally popular, and, though the great majority of Sikhs still remained outside the Akali Dal, there were probably but a few who did not sympathise with their Akali brethren.

It is interesting to note that retired and demobilised Sikh soldiers were employed by the Akalis to inspect the mobilised jathas before they were despatched from Headquarters. Attempts were even made to raise special Akali jathas exclusively manned by ex-military men. It is also noteworthy that a few of the retired Sikh officers were persuaded to accept important offices under the S. G. P. C.

The Sikh question in 1923.—In the new year a policy of peaceful penetration supervened as regards shrine seizure. The mahants gave up the unequal struggle, and surrendered Gurdwaras wholesale. In January 1923 six were surrendered to the Akalis in Ambala, and by the end of March no less than 125 were in the hands of the Parbandhak Committee. Akali man-power, however, at the commencement of 1923 was unequal to the protracted demands made upon it during the Guru-ka-Bagh affair. The Parbandhak Committee, therefore, set itself to organise an Army of 50,000 under its sole control, with local units distributed according to "zails" and "thanas". For the first time the influence of a moderate element inclined to amicable relations with Government was noticeable. Internal differences had also arisen. The Udasis, some time previously, had adopted a posture of hostility towards the committee, in combination with the Nirmalas, a small sect of little financial or political strength, and the Kukas (a sect who affirm that religious instruction must be imparted by a living person, and who recognise three successors to the tenth Guru, of whom the last Guru Partap Singh is still the titular head). Their combined offensive had considerable success in discrediting Akali aspirations, but could make no headway after "Guru-ka-Bagh". The Nirmalas surrendered to the committee, and accepted its constitution, while the other sects abandoned all active opposition.

In July the Sikh League met in Amritsar at which a bitter controversy arose on the subject of Council boycott, which the League carried against the committee. The latter nevertheless included the strongest personalities individually of the committee, and Council entry was favoured by the mass of Sikh opinion.

The Nabha affair and Jaito.—In July 1923, Maharaja Ripudaman Singh, the Sikh ruler of the Nabha State, abdicated, and the administration passed into the hands of an officer appointed by the British Government. It is out of place here to go into the merits of this abdication, but it may be stated that it was looked upon in some quarters as a forced abdication, or deposition. A new Parbandhak Committee, which had come into existence in this same month soon began to interest itself in the reinstatement of the Maharaja. Resolutions were passed and a vigorous agitation in his favour was set on foot. His abdication could, by no stretch of imagination, be called a religious matter; he was no doubt a Sikh, he may also have been a supporter of the Akali cause, but that merely did not invest his personality with any religious sanctity. To give the policy a practical shape the committee made its first organised attempt to gain a foothold in the State territory at the end of August 1923. The place chosen was Jaito, where the Akalis announced that a Diwan would be held at the Gangsar Gurdwara on three consecutive days, the 25th, 26th and 27th. The State authorities permitted the Diwan to be held, on the condition that the proceedings would be strictly confined to religious matters, and that no political discussion would be indulged in. The Gurdwara building passed into the hands of the Akalis, and simultaneously with the Diwan held outside, they started an

"Akhandpath" (continuous recitation of the Granth Sahib). Having once got possession of the Gurdwara the Akalis were not prepared to leave. The three days were over, but the Diwan there was pursued from day to day, political speeches of an undesirable nature being freely made. Under the grave circumstances the duty of the authorities was clear. The Diwan outside was dispersed; the case of the Akalis inside the Gurdwara was not so easy to deal with. They were actually carrying on the "Akhandpath," any interruption to which constitutes, in Sikh faith, a gross insult to the Holy Book. It was decided to take regular charge of the "Akhandpath" without interrupting it, and this was effected by the Household Minister, (himself a Sikh) in a tactful manner, completely in accordance with Sikh tenets and custom: The Akalis in the Gurdwara made no protest, and offered no resistance at the time, nor was there the slightest mention of any interruption, or other disrespect in the "Ardas" (last prayer), which the Akalis before leaving were allowed to have. Nevertheless, all sorts of stories about the interruption were circulated, which made a direct appeal to the Sikh mind. The restoration of the Maharaja of Nabha was purposely thrown into the background. The Akhandpath had been interrupted, and it was the duty of every Sikh to resume it. The community freely offered their services, and, as a result, the S. G. P. C. soon began to despatch daily to the Gangsar Gurdwara at Jaito, a band of 25 Sikhs to resume the so-called interrupted Akhandpath, and to carry out a programme of non-violent passive resistance. On arrival at the State boundary, these bands were distinctly told that the Akhandpath which they wished to resume had long since been duly concluded, and they were offered permission to have another Akhandpath on the condition that they would leave the place after its conclusion.

The bands, however, had come under the orders of the Parbandhak Committee, and had not been authorised to abide by any conditions. It was really the big political issue that was at stake, and, for the successful decision of that issue, it was the stay of the Akalis within the State that mattered. On their refusal to accept the terms offered they were peacefully arrested, deported by train to Bawal, 150 miles distant, and there released.

This state of things commenced in September, and continued throughout the year.

The patience of the Government was now, however, exhausted, and the Parbandhak Committee, as well as the Akali Dal, were declared illegal associations on the 12th of October.

In January 1924, however, there was another development in the situation in that the Parbandhak Committee announced their decision to send occasionally new bands of 500 men to Jaito for the resumption of the interrupted Akhandpath. These bands were known as "Shahidi Jathas" bands of martyrs,—the choice of this expression containing as it does a pointed reference to Sikh history, and conveying a direct appeal to the Sikh mind, was significant. Their programme also was substantially different. The new bands were not to follow the same policy of voluntarily surrendering themselves to the authorities. While remaining non-violent, they were to offer resistance and start the Akhandpath at all costs.

The first of the Shahidi Jathas left Amritsar on the 9th of February, and was scheduled to arrive at Jaito on the 21st. These days would appear to have been carefully chosen to revive old associations. The 9th of February was Basant Panchmi day, a day dedicated to the memory of Haqiqat Rai, who is popularly known to have been killed for the sake of his religion, and attained martyrdom during Mohamedan rule. The 21st was the anniversary day of the Nankana tragedy. The departure of this Jatha was attended with considerable ceremony. The route lay through Sikh villages, mostly in British territory, and was thronged with worshippers and sightseers.

As far as the Jaito authorities were concerned there seemed to be no cause for perturbation. The larger Jathas were to be dealt with in the same way as the smaller ones. In order, however, to dissipate the widespread delusion about the interrupted Akhandpath, and also to demonstrate the genuineness and consistency of their policy of non-interference in religious matters, they decided to offer to admit to the Gangsar Gurdwara a prescribed number of the jatha at a time, on the execution of a written agreement containing certain conditions. These conditions were embodied in a written order, and passed by the Administrator; arrangements being made for its promulgation, during the march of the jatha, at various places.

The jatha, however, would not listen to reason. During the last stage it was joined by thousands of people, the whole crowd assuming threatening dimensions, all being variously armed; as such it advanced on the Gurdwara, covering a front of about 1,000 yards, and consisting of over 10,000 people. The Administrator went forward to meet this crowd, in the vain hope that wiser counsel might still prevail. His action was useless. Eventually, the inevitable occurred, and the State Forces fired on the crowd as a last resource, which resulted in a few casualties. After the crowed had partially dispersed the "Shahidi Jatha" voluntarily surrendered.

There was some revival of enthusiasm after this, and the sympathies, even of moderate Sikhs, were alienated for the time being from Government. Desperate efforts followed on the part of the committee to push home its programme of "Shahidi Jathas". No less than 13 were formed during the summer of 1924. and proceeded to Jaito for arrest, after circular tours in different Sikh districts; in general they were well behaved.

The decline of the Akali movement.—The enterprise, however, definitely and gradually failed, and for this several causes must be held responsible. In the first place the consistency of Government policy since the summer had a steady success in alienating popular sympathy The jathas met with gradually increasing indifferent receptions from the rural inhabitants in their wanderings as the novelty wore off. Attempts at intimidation or violence were countered with decision, and the mass of Zamindari opinion remained aloof.

Certain negotiations of April and May 1924 reached no definite conclusions, but had the effect of persuading moderate Sikhs of the sincerity of Government in attempting to find a remedy for the troubles which assailed the community, One result was to stimulate the formation of anti-Akali organisations which early attained a rapid and successful growth. In October a jatha composed of these moderates performed the Akhandpath at Jaito in accordance with the regulations prescribed by the Nabha State authorities. Plain speaking by H. E. the Governor of the Punjab at various centres put heart into those who had risked reputation by open advocacy of reason and moderation, while the intentions of Government were at the same time made clear beyond the possibility of doubt.

> "If I attempt to define our position, it is from a genuine desire to save the Sikhs and not to destroy them. We wish to save them from the discredit and loss of position which must be the fate of a community which yields to the advice of those who, for whatever motive, attempt to inculcate a mentality which is contemptuous of the rights of other communities, and subversive of the authority of the State. We desire to aid it to gain by legitimate and constitutional methods a full control over its religious institutions. We have never attempted in the past, nor shall we ever attempt in the future, to check it in the fullest exercise of its religious practices within the bounds of law and good citizenship. We have come into this matter, not because we were actuated by any feelings of hostility to the religious aspirations of any section of the Sikhs, but purely because it is our duty to maintain law and order, to prevent invasion of the rights of other communities, and to secure to individuals the peaceful enjoyment of any privileges secured to them by the verdict of our Courts. It has always been our policy and our tradition to stand aside in any matter affecting religious developments in any community; but we cannot stand aside when in the name of religion the rights either of individuals or of other sections of the public are invaded, or property is usurped, or the common law which must bind all communities is broken. We will not connive at what is called direct action in derogation of the rights of others and the claims of law; but we offer you our aid to obtain any legislation which will within reason and without undue prejudice of the rights of others, secure you the undisturbed right to manage your own religious institutions and endowments. Our immediate policy is not, as has been falsely represented, to divide the Sikhs, or for any purpose of our own to raise up one section against

another; our only object is to secure that all Sikhs equally and without distinction should come into the field to work for a solution on the lines and within the limits which I have indicated."

(*Sir Malcolm Hailey at Ambala, 29th August 1924.*)

With the growth of constitutional opposition inside the Sikh community, Akali aggression began to decline, and towards the end of 1924, opinion was united upon the necessity for a Gurdwara Bill which would determine once for all the course of future controversy on legitimate lines.

1925.—In 1925 all classes of Sikhs took a great interest in the proposed Gurdwara Bill, and though it was clear that the majority would welcome a settlement of the Gurdwara question, it was doubtful whether the passing of the bill would entirely stop the Akali agitation. In the meanwhile, friction between the S. G. P. C. and the Akali Dal existed, as many members of the latter openly expressed their dis-satisfaction with the conduct and policy of the former. There was a tendency on the part of the Akali Dal leaders to accuse the S. G. P. C. of having exceeded its powers in entering into negotiations at all, and suggested that it was betraying the cause of the Akalis if it agreed to any bill which left the Jaito question unsettled, and the prisoners still in jail. The moderate section was, however, in favour of coming to terms, but appeared to wish to avoid a definite split with the extremists.

Meanwhile the Sudhar Committees, which were being organised in all the Sikh Districts, were making headway in their attempts to combat Akali propaganda; the average villager was not closely concerned with the larger historical Gurdwaras (with the possible exception of the Durbar Sahib at Amritsar), the village Gurdwara being of far greater importance to him. Any attempt, therefore, to place the latter under a central committee, or to enforce subscriptions to a central authority was likely to be strongly resented.

It should be noted that these Sikh Sudhar Committees played a most important part in checking the tide of the Akali unrest throughout the province and helped a good deal in the restoration of law and order.

The secret of their success lay in the fact that being Sikhs themselves they could assure the ignorant Sikh masses that the whole Akali agitation was nothing but a "political pill" with a flimsy coating of sugar of religion over it, and thus saved the people from swallowing it. The "Sudharists" supported the general demand for Gurdwara reforms but advocated purely constitutional methods to attain them.

With the growth of this constitutional opposition within the Sikh ranks Akali aggression speedily declined, and the speeches delivered by H. E. the Governor of the Punjab at various places in reply to the addresses presented by the Sikh loyalists of the Sudhar Committees had a wonderful effect.

The continuance of the agitation, however, had inevitably a great effect on Sikh recruiting. Government had to adopt the policy of the closing to recruiting of Akali tainted villages. This implied that the supply of recruits was greatly curtailed. The ban on these villages was not finally removed until January of 1927, and the restrictions were very much felt, but undeniably did good in having the effect of discrediting the Akali movement among service families.

In May of this year a general meeting of the S. G. P. C. was held, and a resolution was passed that the Gurdwara Bill, to be introduced in the Punjab Legislative Council, met most of the requirements of the reform movement. It however, recommended that the successful working of the Bill would only be possible under the following conditions :—

(*a*) Release of Akali prisoners convicted, or under trial.

(*b*) Official recognition of the S. G. P. C. and the Akali Dal.

(*c*) Restoration to Sikhs of lands and pensions forfeited to Government.

On the 7th of May the Gurdwara Bill was introduced in the Punjab Legislative Council. It had an excellent reception, and was referred to a select committee. There was no doubt that the great majority of Sikhs would like to see the bill passed, and were prepared to accept it without substantial modifications. The Select Committee began its sittings on the 18th of May; it consisted of 7 Sikhs, 6 Hindus, 4 Mohamedans and 3 Europeans, a total of 13 unofficial and 7 official members, and the bill shortly afterwards was passed unanimously. Sir Malcolm Hailey in a speech at the end of the session remarked that the success of the Gurdwara Bill would be dependent on the spirit and temper in which the Sikhs themselves approached the administration of its provisions. He advocated a wide spirit of tolerance towards Hindus, and a discriminating liberality in dealing with the Udasis. The Punjab Government's share towards the smooth and successful working of the bill lay in the release of those who had been convicted (or were under trial), on charges which had arisen out of the recent agitation, with the exception of those convicted or under trial on charges of violence, or inciting to violance. Release would be conditional on the signing of an undertaking that they would obey the provisions of the law relating to Gurdwara Reform, and would not attempt to gain control of any shrine. Secondly, that the case of forfeiture of pensions and land would be dealt with by Government in a similar spirit. Thirdly, that Government would withdraw the notification declaring certain bodies to be unlawful when the Central Board, provided by the bill, was duly constituted.

He added, that, with regard to the Government of India's decision concerning the Nabha situation, that the Administrator of Nabha would release all Sikhs detained or imprisoned there, except those convicted, or under trial, on charges of violence : whilst secondly, bands of pilgrims would be permitted to proceed for religious worship to the Gangsar

Gurdwara at Jaito, under certain conditions, chief amongst which were abstention from holding political Diwans, or spreading propaganda in State territory.

Sir Malcolm Hailey concluded his speech by emphasising the fact that the Sikh community could not stand alone, and that its welfare and progress were bound up with the development of the Province as a whole, for which harmony, tranquillity and mutual trust were needed.

By August all the Nabha prisoners except those convicted for violence were released; there still remained, however, an under-current of Akali feeling that the whole of the prisoners should be similarly treated, no matter what the crime for which they had been convicted. Various Akalis throughout this year, and during 1926, continued to agitate for their release, and for the restoration of the Maharajah of Nabha. Meanwhile, however, several of those who were in jail declined to sign the undertaking that they would obey the provisions of the law relating to Gurdwara reform, whilst several of those who had been let free carried on an intensive anti-Government campaign in their villages, adopting the attitude that Gurdwara Reform was impossible under British rule. This, however, it may be stated, was the point of view of the extremists, who, whilst they did not actually wish to boycott the bill, hoped that the members of the Central Board would be largely Akali in character.

Early in October the S. G. P. C. held a meeting to discuss the Act, and a resolution was moved, and eventually carried, to accept and work the Gurdwara bill.

At the commencement of November the abandonment of a "morcha" at Bhai Pheru, which had been going on for some months, by a decision of a general meeting of the S. G. P. C., led to the hope on the part of the public generally, that the Akali agitation was at an end.

With effect from the 1st of November the Act came into force. Several meetings had been held by the S. G. P. C., which showed a great diversity of opinion between the extremist and the moderate views. At a meeting of the S. G. P. C. in November the main resolution reiterated the committee's approval of the act in principle, but called upon the Panth (Sikh community) to return such representatives to the Central Board, and other Local Committees, as would endeavour to secure the release of the prisoners at an early date. The majority of the rural class appeared to be in favour of working the Act, and it is doubtful whether they took much interest in the differences between the leaders. They undoubtedly desired to see the Gurdwara question settled, and were prepared to accept a settlement, if allowed by the extremist party. It was also doubtful whether the details of the bill were understood by the masses, and the release of the prisoners was the one point on which there was any real feeling.

Thus, following on the resolution of the S. G. P. C., efforts were made to work the bill. The registration of voters and the necessary election arrangements were commenced. These steps, however, proceeded but slowly, for registration was not generally understood by the masses, and it was not till June of 1926 that the elections finally took place.

The end of the year thus saw a very definite change for the better in the Sikh situation, the villagers had lost all faith in the Akali movement, and the whole tone had so greatly improved that many of the villages were removed from the Akali black list. and re-opened to recruiting.

There remains but little to add in this chapter to the History of the Sikhs. Events are of too recent a nature to warrant their inclusion in this handbook. The elections when they finally did take place in June of 1926, demonstrated that either the mass of the rural population were indifferent to the nature of the issue by declining to record their votes to the extent that had been anticipated, or that they were afraid to do so for fear of again becoming mixed up with the movement. The extremists, on the other hand, were well to the fore, and carried the day in the returning of an Akali leader as President. The main feature in the present Sikh situation is the break between the Arora-Khatri party and the Jat party, which, as regards the leaders means, the separation of the party of intrigue and the party of violence, and, as regards the masses has led to a general distrust of those whose aptitude for propaganda and skill in organisation were so largely responsible for making the Akali movement so dangerous. The principle of "live, and let live" might perhaps be made applicable to the outlook of the villagers in general, and when touring in the Districts British Officers were once more made welcome, and shown that hospitality to which they had been accustomed in pre-war days, and which had been temporarily withheld by a political outlook which had dominated all minds, unconscious though it had been by the majority of the masses, in the name of religion.

With regard to the future :—

Bolshevism may, rightly or wrongly, be considered to be the coming world peril. Its promoters at Moscow are said to have as their ultimate objective the peoples of the Far East and other Asiatic countries. Be this as it may—but, if India is their objective, then it is as well to note that the agricultural conditions of the Punjab much resemble those of the interior of Russia, and as such must attract the attention of their agents.

There is a further point and it is that of religion. In the Punjab if anybody's religion has got anything in common with the basic principles of Bolshevism it is that of the Sikh. To begin with his religion is democratic and preaches equailty and nobleness of labour. The dictum of Guru Govind Singh was to the effect that everything possessed by an individual Sikh belonged to the whole Panth and that the belongings of the Panth were to be equally shared by every individual Sikh. It has seldom been translated into practice. The authority of religion is however thin and the Sikh soil is likely to prove somewhat suitable for the growth of Bolshevism.

The symptoms of the disease are already visible to some extent amongst certain Sikhs although in most cases the would-be victims do not know themselves what diseases they are suffering from.

In view of this the "Kirti" movement organised by Sikh in the last decade agitators in the Doaba tract should be carefully watched, and Jat Sikhs who supply recruits for the Army should be warned in time to beware of the pitfalls.

The "Kirti" movement is a part of a conspiracy against the State which has been conducted since 1923—when the Akali agitation and Jatha activity were most intense—by a number of disaffected Sikhs in India sent in certain foreign countries. Their proposals included the formation of secret societies for revolutionary work under cover of religious or communal organizations, the presentation of trouble among the tribes of the N. W. F. P. and the usual institution of a campaign of terrorism and of assassination. A sum of Rs. 10,000 was received from the Kabul party with the object of setting up a press and in February the first issue of the publication appeared. In its contents it was explicit in the expression of its revolutionary aims, and has persistently advocated the cause and ideals of the Indian Ghadrites of 1914 and 1915 and glorified the Babbar Akalis as martyrs and heroes. The activities of the members have been potentially dangerous rather than actually dangerous and they openly preached communistic doctrines. The Pubjab "Kirti" party has become formally affiliated to the communist party, but their capacity for danger is at present restricted by the limitations of the leaders of the movement. The organization is however undoubtedly a real danger. Given a genuine agrarian grievance it could do great harm. The movement is closely associated with the Nau Jawan Bharat Sabha which was formed at Amritsar in March 1926.

CHAPTER III.

DISTRIBUTION OF SIKHS—ETHNOLOGICAL AND ETHNOGRAPHIC GLOSSARY OF CASTES.

It has already been mentioned in Chapter I that the Sikhs are concentrated mainly in the Ambala, Jullundur and Lahore Divisions, though they are also scattered in lesser numbers in the remaining ones of the Punjab.

This chapter will therefore be devoted to a description of their distribution, origin and classification; this should rightly have been previously described, but has purposely been omitted in order that the sequence of Sikh history, as outlined in the last chapter, should continue uninterrupted, and unobscured by additional detail, from its origin to the present day.

Distribution of Sikhs.

The map on page 63 shows the local distribution of Sikhs—according to the census return of 1911—though they vary greatly in density in different localities. The Ludhiana District and the Faridkot State have the highest proportion of Sikhs, *i.e.*, 400 and 425 respectively per thousand of the population. Ludhiana with the Phulkian (Patiala, Nabha, Jind) and Faridkot States forms the principal Sikh tract. The Patiala and Nabha States stand next in importance with a proportion of 300 to 400 Sikhs per thousand. Amritsar which is the centre of the Sikh religion, has only 280 Sikhs to every thousand. The Ferozepore and Jullundur Districts (including Kapurthala State) rank next in numerical order.

Sikhs are therefore recruited from almost all over the central Punjab which is generally divided for this purpose into two main areas called the "Malwa" and the "Manjha" respectively.

The "Malwa" consists of all the country lying south of the Sutlej river which stretches towards Rajputana and the Jumna. It includes the Districts of Ambala, Ferozepore, Hissar, and Ludhiana and the Indian States of Patiala, Nabha, Jhind, Malerkotla and Faridkot; it is considerably the largest.

The "Manjha" strictly speaking is the name given to the southern portion of the Bari Doab, or country lying between the Beas and Ravi rivers, in the neighbourhood of Lahore and Amritsar. A "Manjha" Sikh however is generally alluded to as one who is recruited from any of the districts north of the Sutlej. At the same time it may be mentioned that a term "Doaba Sikh" is frequently used. This denotes the Sikhs who live between the Sutlej and the Beas rivers, *i.e.*, those who inhabit the districts of Jullundur and Hoshiarpur and the Kapurthala State.

The ancestors of the Malwa Jats were mostly Hindu peasants, who, about the middle of the 16th century, emigrated from Jaisalmir and settled in the Central Punjab as peaceful subjects of the Mohamedan Emperors. The term Malwa, however, is now used in a far more extended sense, and it may be accepted as a rough rule, that a Malwa Sikh is any Sikh belonging to a district lying to the south of the Sutlej. Though essentially of the same race the two classes are distinguished from one another by certain well known distinctions of speech and a slight but mutual antipathy, which the course of time would not seem in any way to have removed.

Ethnological.—Sikhism, like Islam, being a religion, open to all classes includes amongst its adherents members of many races and castes. Of these by far the most important and numerous are the Jats, in fact more than two thirds of the Sikh population belonging to this tribe.

Perhaps no question connected with Indian ethnology has been more frequently discussed than that of the origin of the Jats. According to some authorities they are Aryans, of the same stock as the Rajputs and the name of their race is simply the modern Hindi for "Yadu" or "Jadu" the tribe of the famous "Kashatriya" clan to which the demi-god Krishna belonged. Others maintain that they are Indo-Scythians, identify them with the "Jati" and "Getae," or Goths, of the classical geographers, and even go so far as to assert that they are of the same race as the Magyars and Gypsies of Eastern Europe.

Crowther in his notes on Sikhs state "The strange resemblance of the Magyars to the Jats has led many ethnologists to believe that the two races are identical: not only are they alike in build, physionomy, and warlike-habits, but they brush their beards in the same fashion, and these little customs often endure longer than either manners or religion itself."

Denzil Ibbetson remarks that "It may be that the original Rajput and original Jat entered India at different periods in its history, but if they do not represent two separate waves of immigration, it is at least exceedingly probable, both from their identical physique and facial character, and from the close communion which has always existed between them, that they belong to one and the same ethnic stock. It is moreover, almost certain that the joint Jat-Rajput race contains not a few tribes of aboriginal descent, though it is in the main Aryo-Scythian."

Their exact origin therefore must remain in abeyance; the attention of the reader is, however, drawn to the appendix on the explanation of race tribe and caste which may assist in clarifying his ideas on this much discussed and difficult subject.

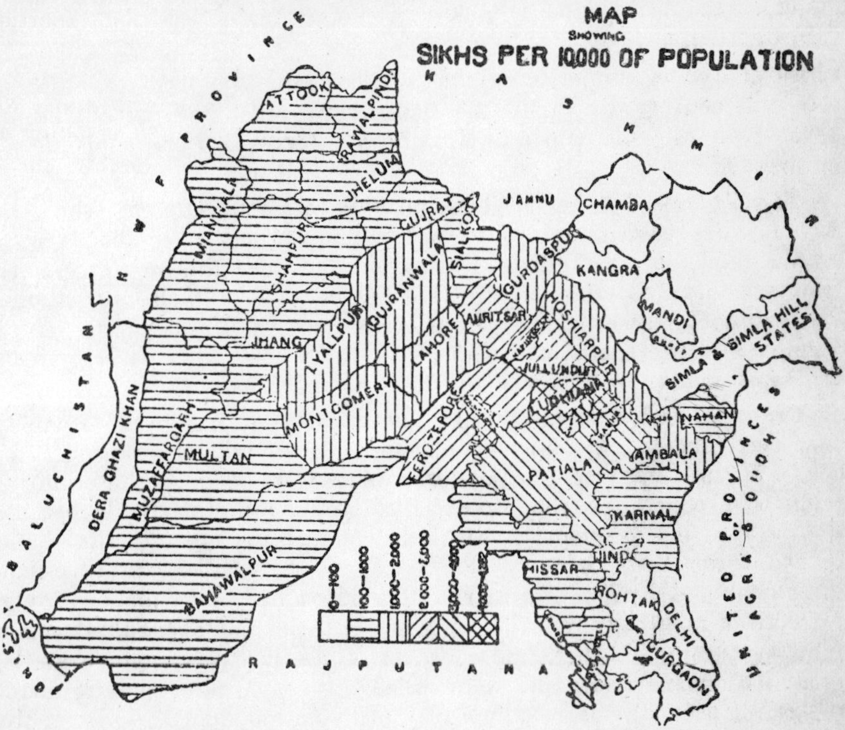

The races of ancient India.—The dawn of Indian history discloses two races struggling for the soil. One was a fair complexioned Sanskrit-speaking people of Aryan lineage, who entered the country from the north-west; the other a dark skinned race of lower type, the original inhabitants of the land, who were either driven by the Aryans into the hills, or reduced by them to servitude in the plains.

The cradle of the Aryan races.—The original home of the Aryan race is said to have been on the banks of the Oxus in Central Asia, though some authorities dispute this statement, and declare that the Aryans came from Central Europe. From there they migrated in two directions one branch moved north-westwards towards Europe, the other south-east towards Persia and India. It is with the latter that we are here concerned.

Crossing the Hindu Kush, the Aryans settled for some time in the valleys of Afghanistan; from thence they forced their way across the mountains into India, and gradually settled in the Punjab about 2000 B. C.

Early conditions of life among the Aryans.—We know very little of their manner of life. They roamed from one river valley to another with their cattle, making long halts in favourable situations to raise the crops required for their food. They were constantly at war, not only with the aboriginal tribes, but also amongst themselves. At the head of each tribe was a chief or Maharaja but each house-father was a warrior, husbandman and priest, offering up sacrifices to the gods direct, without the intervention of a professional priesthood.

The earliest records of the Aryans are contained in the Vedas—a series of hymns composed in the Sanskrit language from the 15th to the 10th century B. C. by the Rishis, an order of devout sages, devoted to religious meditation, whose utterances were supposed to be inspired.

The Vedas.—The early Vedas must have been composed while the Aryan tribes were marching towards India; others after their arrival on the banks of the Indus. During this advance the race progressed from a loose confederacy of various tribes into several well knit nations, and extended its settlements from the Himalayas in the north to the Vindhyas in the south, and throughout the whole of the river systems of Upper India, as far as to the East as the Sone.

Origin of the Brahmans or Aryan priests.—It has been explained that each head of a family conducted his own religious rites, but in course of time many ceremonial observances were added to the primitive religion, necessitating the service of a special priesthood. It became the custom to call upon the Rishis to conduct the great sacrifices and to chant the Vedic hymns. The art of writing was at this time unknown, and hymns and sacrificial phrases had to be handed down by word of mouth, from father to son. It thus came about that certain families became the hereditary owners of the liturgies required at the great national festivals and were called upon time after time to chant the tribal battle hymns, to invoke the divine aid, and to appease the divine wrath. These potent prayers were called Brahmas, and those who offered them were Brahmans. By degrees the number of ministrants required for a great sacrifice increased. Besides the high priests who superintended the ceremonies, there were the celebrants who dressed the alters, slew the victims, and poured out libations to the gods, while others chanted the Vedic hymns and repeated the phrases appropriate to particular rites. In this manner there arose a special priesthood—a class which was entrusted with the conduct of religious offices, while the rest of the community carried on their ordinary avocations of war, trade, and agriculture.

Origin of the warrior class.—As the Aryan colonists spread east and south, subduing the aboriginal races, they were to a large extent relieved from the burden of agricultural labour through the compulsory employment of the conquered people. In this manner there grew up a class of warriors freed from the toil of husbandry, who attended the Maharaja, and were always ready for battle. These kinsmen and companions of the kings gradually formed themselves into a separate class, and were referred to as Kshatriyas, *i.e.*, 'those connetced with the royal power', and eventually as Rajputs, or 'those of royal descent.'

Origin of the agricultural and trading classes.—The incessant fighting which had formed the common lot of the Aryans on their march eastward from the Indus, gradually ceased as the aboriginal races were subdued. Members of the community who from family ties, or from personal inclination, preferred war to the peaceful monotony of village life, had to seek for adventure in the hills and forests of the lower Himalayas, or the unknown country to the south of the Vindhyas. Distant expeditions were chiefly undertaken by those to whom war was a profession, while others, more peacefully inclined, stayed at home, devoting themselves to agriculture and the manufacturing arts.

The organisation into four classes.—Thus the Aryans and their retainers, by a process of natural selection gradually resolved themselves into four classes :—

1. The "Brahman", priestly caste, composed of the Rishis, their descendants and disciples, to whom was entrusted the expounding of the Vedas and the conduct of religious ceremonies.

2. The "Kshatriya," *i.e.*, or Rajput, or governing and military caste, composed of the Maharajas and their warrior kinsmen and companions, whose duty it was to rule, fight, administer justice, and protect the community in general. It is now represented by the Rajput and the Khatri.

3. The "Vaisiya" or trading and agricultural caste, which, assisted by the conquered aborigines, tilled the land, raised cattle, and manufactured the arms, implements and household utensils, required by the Aryan commonwealths. It is now represented by the Banya.

4. Besides the three Aryan castes, but immeasurably beneath them, there was the servile or Sudra caste, composed of captured aborigines whose lives had been spared, and of the progeny of marriages between Aryans of different castes and of Aryans and the women of the country, all of which, by the rigid exclusiveness of caste custom, came to be regarded as degraded.

It must be remembered, however, that in the early days of the Aryan settlements the line of separation between the three first named classes was far from being sharply defined. The transfer of individuals and their families from one to the other was not an uncommon occurrence, and numerous instances are recorded of kings and warriors terminating their careers as Rishis or sainty ascetics. Moreover, in very early times the Maharajas often combined the offices of the priesthood with kingly power, a custom which in rare instances has survived to the present day. In the same way it was not unusual for the more adventurous Vaisiyas to abandon agriculture, and join the ranks of the Kshatriyas. In course of time these occupational distinctions developed into separate castes, and as intermarriage became first of all restricted, and afterwards prohibited, each caste devoted itself more strictly to its own hereditary employment. All, however, were recognised as belonging to the twice-born or Aryan race, all were permitted to attend the great national sacrifices, and all worshipped the same gods.

Resistance of the Kshatriyas to the pretensions of the Brahmans.—But it must not be supposed, that Brahman supremacy was accepted without protest. Their claims to recognition as a distinct Levite class, of divine origin, and possessed of supernatural powers, were rejected by the Kshatriyas, who insisted, with perfect truth, that many of the Rishis who had composed the Vedas were kings and warriors rather than priests, and that no authority for the pretensions of the Brahmans could be found in the Vedic legends. There are traditions of a great struggle having taken place between the Brahmans and the Kshatriyas, in which the former were completely victorious. The details of this quarrel, however, are obscure, for the Brahmans, as exclusive custodians of the sacred writings took care to efface all reference to a struggle, which, from its very existence, cast a doubt on their pretensions to a divine origin.

The principle of caste not of universal acceptance.—It may here be noticed that many of the Aryan tribes rejected the theory of Brahmanical supremacy. Thus the earlier settlements west of the Indus never adopted the principle of caste; those between the Indus and the Jumna accepted it, but in a modified form; it was chiefly in the tract watered by the Jumna and the Ganges from Delhi on the west to Ajudhya and Benares on the east, that the Brahmans consolidated their authority; and became a conpact, learned, and influential body, the authors of the Sanskrit literature, and the lawgivers, scientists, and philosophers, of the whole Hindu world.

The change from Vedism to Brahmanism.—By the 5th century B. C. the original simplicity of the Vedic worship had been replaced by a philosophical creed, accompanied by an elaborate ritual. The early conception of a Supreme Being, made manifest through the physical forces of nature, gave way to the mystic triad of Brahma, Vishnu, and Siva, the Maker, Preserver, and Destroyer, with a tendency to create new gods, to worship the elements in various personifications, and to embody the attributes of each member of the Hindu Trinity in numerous avatars or incarnations. The new religion puzzled the people without satisfying them, while the growing arrogance of the Brahmans caused a universal desire for a return to more primitive beliefs.

The Buddhist reformation.—At this juncture, Sakya Muni, a Kshatriya prince of Behar, initiated the great reformation which eventually developed into a new religion. Universal charity, liberty, and equality, with the total rejection of caste, formed the fundamental principles of the new doctrine, and the personal cahracter of "Buddha," the 'Enlightened', as he was named by his disciples, immediately attracted a considerable following.

The growth of Buddhism was very rapid. By about 200 B. C. it had become the state religion in Hindustan. From thence it spread north into Nepal, and through Central Asia into China and Japan. At the same time Buddhist missionaries carried their faith into Ceylon, and from thence it was extended to Burma, Siam and Java.

The vitality of Brahmanism and the decline of Buddhism.—But though Brahmanism was undoubtedly modified by Buddhism, it was never displaced. Even in the 6th century Buddhism had commenced to decline, and before the Mohamedan faith had come fairly upon the scene, it had entirely disappeared from India. For more than a thousand years the two religions had existed side by side, and modern Hinduism is undoubtedly a combination of both.

The Dharma-Shastras. Institutes of Manu.—About 400 B. C., the Brahmans, finding in Buddhism a religious movement which threatened their spiritual authority, designed a code, which, besides maintaining their privileges, formed a definite authority on all points connected with Hindu law and ritual. This celebrated work, called the code of Manu, and known also as the Dharmashastras, is a compilation of the customary law current about the 5th century B. C. in the Aryan principalities on the banks of the Ganges and Jumna. The Brahmans claimed for it a divine origin, and ascribed it to Manu, the first Aryan man. In it the fourfold division of society is said to have been ordered by Brahma, the creator of the universe. The Brahmans are supposed to have emanated from his head, the Kshatriyas from his arms, the Vaisiyas from his thighs, and the Sudras from his feet. The code consists of a mass of precepts, religious, and secular rules for the administration of justice, and special enactments with regard to purification and penance. It was written with a view of stemming the tide of Buddhist reform by stringent rules against the intermingling of castes by marriage, and by forbidding the higher castes under severe penalties from eating drinking or holding intercourse with any of those ranking beneath them.

The Brahman revival.—The reaction in favour of Brahmanism began to have effect about 200 B. C. By the 8th century A. D. the Brahmans had completely re-established their authority. The simplicity of the Vedic faith was transformed beyond recognition. No efforts were spared to materialise religion. The gods were provided with wives. Caste was revived, no longer with the fourfold division of the Code of Manu, but with all the complicated occupational sub-divisions which exist to the present day. In all these changes we trace the efforts of an astute priesthood to establish a popular religion. No section of the community was forgotten. The smouldering enmity of the Kshatriyas was appeared by attributing a celestial origin to the ancestors of their ruling families. The Solar and Lunar races of Ajudhya and Mathura were flattered by the elevation of Rama and Krishna, their respective heroes, to the dignity of avatars, or incarnations of the divine Vishnu. Scythian invaders and aboriginal races were conciliated by the adoption of their tribal divinities. Their Totem*, tree, and serpent worship, though utterly at variance with the spirit of the Vedas was affiliated to the orthodox beliefs, and their princes and warriors were accorded the status of Kshatriyas as an inducement to accept the principle of caste.

Buddhism, in spite of the antagonistic nature of its doctrines, was disposed of in a similar manner; and Buddha, whose whole life and teaching had been a protest against the formalism of the Brahmans, was absorbed into the Hindu system, and, as an incarnation of Vishnu, was allotted a place in the pantheon of minor gods. Thus step by step, by diplomacy and adaptiveness, the Brahmans consolidated their authority, and established a religion which, having the Vedic faith of the Aryan races as its foundation, has absorbed and assimilated a portion of each of the religious systems which it has successively displaced.

Greek, Bactrian, and Scythian invasions.—During the period embraced by the rise and fall of Buddhism, *viz.*, from 242 B. C. to 500 A. D., India was subjected to a series of foreign invasions. The Greeks of Bactria, expelled by the hordes of Scythians, entered India in the second and first centuries B. C., and are said to have penetrated as far as Orissa. Meanwhile the Medi, Xanthii, Jatii, Getae and other Scythian races, were gradually working their way from the banks of the Oxus into Southern Afghanistan and the pastoral highland about Quetta, whence they forced their way by the Bolan Pass, through the Sulaiman Mountains into India, settling in the Punjab about the beginning of the first century. It is from these Scythian immigrants that most of the Jat Tribes are at any rate partly descended.

Geographical distribution of the Scythian races.—Starting from the banks of the Indus, which they occupied from Hazara to the coast of Scinde, the Scythians spread out in a fan-like shape from the Salt Range in the North, to the Aravelli Hills and the Chambal in the south, and as far to the east as the valley of the Jumna. They thus colonized the Punjab, Northern Rajputana, and the western half of the Gangetic Doab, and a considerable proportion of the inhabitants of these countries are undoubtedly of Scythian origin.

Conversion of the Scythian ancestors of the Jats to Hinduism in the 10th century.—Shortly after their arrival in India, the majority of these Scythian immigrants became converts to Buddhism; in course of time however, their religion was assimilated to that of their Aryan neighbours, and by the 10th century they had not only accepted the spiritual supremacy of the Brahmans but also in a modified degree, the restrictions and distinctions of caste.

---

*The ruder races of men are found divided into tribes, each of which is usually named after some animal, vegetable, or thing, which is an object of veneration or worship to the tribe. The animal, vegetable or thing is the Totem or god of the tribe. From the tribe being commonly named after its Totem, the word is also frequently employed to signify merely the tribal designation—Chambers Encyclopædia.

The ancestors of the four agnicular or fire tribes of Rajputs are generally considered to have been Scythian warriors who assisted the Brahmans in their final struggles with the Budhists, and were admitted into the ranks of the 'twice-born' as a reward for their services to Hinduism. Some sort of story being necessary to account for their origin and rank, the ready witted Brahmans bestowed upon them the title of 'fire born' to distinguish them from the original Rajput races which claim descent from Sun and Moon.

The distinction between Jats and certain tribes of Rajputs often social rather than ethnic.—As has before, been noticed the distinction between Jats and Rajputs is probably social rather than ethnic. "Those families of the Aryo-Scythian stock whom the tide of fortune raised to political importance, became Rajputs almost, by mere virtue of their rise, and their descendants have retained the title with its privileges by observing the rules by which the higher are distinguished from the lower castes in the Hindu scale of precedence; by refusing to intermarry with families of inferior rank; and by rigidly abstaining from widow marriage and refraining from menial and degrading occupations." Those who transgressed these rules fell from their high estate, and were reduced, some to the grade of a Jat or cultivator, others to that of a Gujar or herdsman.

One of the earliest Jat traditions, recorded by Tod in his 'Annals of Rajasthan' gives a striking example of the vicissitudes of Rajput families and the origin of their connection with the Jats. About 550 A. D. the Scythian King of Ghazni invaded the Punjab, and attacked Mansur Rao, a Yadu Rajput who was Raja of Salbahana or Lahore. The latter fled to the jungles with his heir leaving his five other sons concealed in the house of a Mahajan (a banker, and money-lender). Through the treachery of one of the Raja's subjects, the Ghazni king was informed of the children's hiding place, which he surrounded with a cordon of troops. The Mahajan, terrified by threats of immediate execution gave up the young princes, who were made to assume the peasant's garb, feed with Jats or husbandmen, and marry the daughters of their father's bhumias or cultivators. Thus it was that the Yadu princes fell from the rank of Rajput and assumed the designation of Jat, which has been retained ever since by their descendants. The truth of this legend is indirectly confirmed by the fact that the throwing of the discus or steel quoit, which, as an emblem of Vishnu, was the special weapon of the Yadu, is still a favourite pastime among many of the Jats of the Punjab.

This theory of a partially Rajput origin is further supported by the fact that the Jats were at one time regarded as belonging to the thirty-six rajkulas or royal tribes of India; and although the Rajput and Jat races are now entirely distinct, and intermarriage between them is impossible, there is evidence to show that Rajputs took Jatni wives as late as the fifth century, and there is no doubt that connections were frequently formed between them, though they may not always have been dignified by the name of marriage. From the earliest times the beauty and strength of Jat and Gujar women won the admiration of the Rajput princes, who received them into their Zananas as khawas or concubines; and it was more than probable that many Jat clans are descended from the offspring of such unions. "It is strange that many Jat tribes of this lineage concur in the same ridiculous story that their ancestress was a beautiful Jatni who, while going along with a water-pot on her head, stopped a runaway buffalo by pressing her foot on the rope tied to its neck, and did so without spilling the water. This feat of strength so pleased a Rajput chieftain who was looking on, that he immediately placed her in Zanana, and thus a new "got" or family sprang from the connexion.

But though the traditions of the Punjab Jats in almost all cases refer to a Rajput origin, and emigration to the Punjab from the Dekhan or Central India, others claim direct descent from the Scythian adventurers who forced their way into India from Ghazni and the Kandahar valley. Thus Man, Her, and Bhular Jats of the Central Punjab, sometimes call themselves Shibgotras, because they profess to be descended from the Jatta or matted hair of Siva, in contradistinction to the Kasabgotras who are the descendents of Rajputs by Jat women, or of Rajputs who have lost grade by the practice of "Karao," or widow marriage.

The Jats harass Mahmud's army in the Scinde desert in 1024.—We know little or nothing of the ancient history of the Jats. As early as the 7th century the Jats of Scinde were ruled over by a Brahman dynasty, and by the 11th century they had spread into the Punjab proper. We first hear of them in the annals of the Mohamedan historians, who tells us that in 1024 the Jats of Scinde cut up several detachments of Mahmud's army as he was returning across the desert to Ghazni, after the sack of Somnath in Gujarat. To punish these outrages Mahmud commenced operations against them in 1026.

Conflict between the Afghans and Jats.—The principal Jat settlements were then in the tract lying between the Indus and Sutlej. "Finding that the Jat country was intersected by large rivers, Mahmud, on reaching Mooltan, built a number of boats armed with iron spikes projecting from their prows to prevent their being boarded by the Jats who were experts in this system of warfare. In each boat he placed a party of ten archers, and men armed with naptha fire balls to burn the Jat fleet. The Jats sent their wives, children and effects to Sind-Sagar, and launched a flotilla of well armed vessels to meet the Ghaznians. A terrible conflict ensued, but the projecting spikes sank a number of the Jat boats, while others were set on fire. Few escaped from this scene of terror, and those who did, met with the more severe fate of captivity. Many Jat tribes must have been taken away as captives to Ghazni, which would account for the vague traditional connexion with that place which is claimed by so many of the clans.

Conversion of the Jats of the Western Punjab to Islam in the 15th and 16th centuries.—The growing power of the Jats was so crippled by this disaster that we hear nothing more of them, or of their military exploits, until 1658, when they reappeared as valuable alies of Aurangzeb in the troubled times that followed the deposition of Shah Jahan. We cannot ascertain with any precision when the Jats of Western Punjab adopted Islam, but when Babar invaded India in 1525, he found that in the Salt Range they had been subdued and converted by the Gakkars, and by the Awans, Janjuas and other tribes of Rajput rank which had adopted the Mohamedan religion. About the same time the Jats of the Scinde were driven back from the foot of the Sulaimans to the banks of the Indus by the advance of the Pathan and Baluch.

The Mohamedan Jats of the Western Punjab.—West of the Indus and the Ravi the Jats became Musalmans, and being a conquered people, of no political importance were looked down upon by the Pathans, Moghals, and Muslims of Rajput descent, who seized their lands, and thus drove them to seek a living as nomads wandering with their herds over the grazing grounds of the western plains of the Punjab. To this day, in Scinde, and the Doab of the Indus and Sutlej, 'Jat' is the usual term for a grazier or herdsman, and is applied indiscriminately to a congerie of various tribes, Jats proper, degraded Rajputs, and mongrels of every race, who have nothing in common save their Mohamedan religion, their agricultural occupation, and their subordinate social position. In the same way the Baluchis who came into the lower frontier district as a dominant race, contemptuously included all cultivating tribes who were not Baluch, or of some race such as the Sayed or Pathan, whom they had been accustomed to look upon as their equals, under the generic name of Jats and the people themselves lost the very memory of their origin. The proverbs of the Pathans and Baluchis are full of contemptous references to the Jats or 'Hindkis' as they are perhaps more commonly called. The Jat is such a fool that only God can take care of him "Get round a Pathan by coaxing, but heave a clod at a Hindki.". In short the Mohamedan Jat of the Indus valley and the Salt Range is looked down upon as a member of an inferior race, and the position he there occupies is very different from that which is held by his Sikh and Hindu brethren of the Central and Eastern Punjab, and the Northern and Eastern portions of Rajputana.

The Jat Sikhs.—The Jats* of the Punjab proper have been truly described as "the backbone of the province" by character and physique, as well as by numbers and locality. They are stalwart sturdy yeomen, of great independence, industry and agricultural skill, and collectively form perhaps the finest peasantry in India**. It is probable that many

---

*In the North-West Province and the Eastern Districts of the Punjab, Hindu Jats are called Jats, pronounced Jaats; in the Central Punjab they are mostly Sikhs and are called Jats pronounced Juts. This is a mere dialectic difference.

**Ethnography of the Punjab. Denxji Ibbetson.

of their ancestors came up the Sutlej valley into the Central Punjab from the country bordering on the mouth of the Bolan Pass, but the great majority derive their origin from Rajputana, which, about 800 years ago, was abandoned by their forefathers in favour of the fertile plains of the Malwa, and the latter, in fact, may now be regarded as the true home of the Jat Sikh.

The republicanism of the Jats.—From the earliest times Jats have been remarkable for their rejection of the monarchical principle, and their strong partiality for self-governing commonwealths. One of the names by which they were known to the ancients was Arashtra, or kingless; and the village community, an institution which from its organisation forms a typical example of the primitive agricultural commonwealth, has always been most flourishing in districts inhabited by Jats.

The Jats of Rajputana, previous to their conquest by Rajput fugitives from Kanouj in 1184, on the defeat of the latter by Muhammad Ghori, were divided into small republics which extended into the Central and Eastern Punjab. One of these petty commonwealths, that of Phul or Maharaj, survived to within recent times. It was afterwards broken up into the principalities of Patiala, Nabha and Jhind, which are known to this day as the Phulkian States.

The rise of the Jats due to the Mohamedan persecutions and the weakness of the Moghal Empire.—Like the Mahrattas, the Jats owed their independence party to the religious persecutions of the Musalmans which drove them to revolt; partly to the internal dissensions of the latter days of the Moghal Empire which gave them a favourable opportunity of consolidating their power and assuming a national character; and partly to religious fanaticism and the undying hatred of Mohamedans stirred up by the teachings of Govind Singh the last and most famous of the Sikh Gurus.

Ethnographic Glossary of Castes.

The castes falling under the category of Sikh cultivators are as follows:—*viz.*, Jat, Rajput, Kamboh, Saini, Mali, Lobana, and the minor castes of Ror and Mahton.

It must not be inferred that every one of the members of these castes and tribes live upon the land or that none of them follow any other occupation. The grouping only implies that cultivation of land is the traditional occupation of each of the above mentioned castes and that the majority of the members of each still pursue it.

By far the most important of all these from the point of view of recruitment for the Indian Army is the Jat Sikh, for it is from this class, with the exception of our Pioneer Battalions who enlist Mazbhis, that almost the whole of our recruits are enlisted. Such being so, the numerous clans or sub-divisions of which this class is composed is explained in considerable detail separately in Chapter VI, whilst a summary for ready reference in tabulated form is given in the Appedices.

Brahman Sikhs.—The renunciation of caste which formed the fundamental principle of Guru Govind Singh's teaching, was naturally inimical to the ideas of the Brahmans, whose intelligence taught them that they had little to gain from Sikhism. Their enlistment is not generally desirable, though individually they often make good soldiers, the reason being that their influence over Sikhs of lower castes is apt to be detrimental to discipline and to destroy the "raison d'etre" of Sikhism; furthermore they are comparatively few in number. The Brahmans of the Punjab nearly all belong to the Sarsut or Saraswat division, and more especially to one of its clans called Mujhal. These military Brahmans have, as a rule, given up their sacerdotal character, cultivate lands, and either enlist in the police or become clerks. Their intelligence and education generally enables them to rise to the higher grades. They are found all over the Punjab, but are most numerous in the cis-Sutlej districts.

Rajputs.—In the Punjab, Jat and Rajput tribes are often so closely connected, that it is sometimes extremely difficult to determine to which of these races a tribe really belongs. Most authorities agree that Rajputs and Jats belong to an Aryo-Scythian stock which entered India from the plains of Central Asia, and that they probably represent at least two separate waves of immigration. "But admitting this theory to be true, it is at least exceedingly probable, both from their almost identical physique and social character, and the close communion which has always existed between them, that they belong to one and the same enthnic stock; while whether this be so or not, it is almost certain that they have been for many centuries, and are still, so intermingled and so blended into one people, that it is practically impossible to distinguish them as separate wholes" (Ethnography of the Punjab; Denzil Ibbetson).

Under the Sikhs, the Rajput was overshadowed by the Jat, who resenting his assumption of superiority, and his refusal to join him on equal terms in the ranks of the Khalsa, deliberately persecuted him wherever and whenever he had the power. Under the circumstances it is not to be wondered at that the number of Rajput Sikhs is but small. The few who have adopted the faith of Guru Govind are met with in Gurdaspur (485), Hoshiarpur (1,087), Sialkote (1,050), Jullundur (3,000), Lahore (2,400), Ferozepore (2,000), where they have adopted agriculture and lost the extreme pride of race which is generally their most prominent characteristic. They are accorded a high social position, and make excellent soldiers though the number now serving is but small; considerable numbers enlisted during the Great War.

Khatris.—The Khatris are Hindus and Sikhs with a total population of 514,847 and are found all over the Punjab. It is a well known caste of high status amongst the Hindus.

The Khatris claim a Rajput or Kshatriya descent, but nowadays their principal occupation is commerce, though many cultivate their own lands. Besides monopolising the trade of the Punjab and Afghanistan and doing a good deal beyond those limits, they are, in the Punjab, the chief civil administrators, and clerical work is largely in their hands. So far as the Sikhs have a priesthood, they are, moreover, their priests and Gurus. Both Nanak and Govind were, and the Sodhis and Bedis are, Khatris. They are not usually military in their character, though considerable numbers enlisted during the Great War, they have not, however, the same military qualities as the Jat Sikh to whom, like the Aroras, they are greatly socially inferior. Diwan Sawan Mal, Governor of Mooltan, and his notorious successor, Mulraj, were Khatris; and Hari Singh, who was considered one of the best generals in the Khalsa army, also belonged to this class. In the Punjab no village can get on without its Khatri who keeps the accounts, does the banking business, and buys and sells the grain. In Afghanistan, among a rough alien people, the Khatris are, as a rule, confined to the position of humble dealers, shopkeepers and money-lenders; but in that capacity the Pathans seem to look on them as a kind of valuable animal and a Pathan will steal another man's Khatri not only for the sake of ransom, as is sometimes done in Peshawar and the Hazara frontier, but also as he might steal a milch-cow, or, as Jews might, I dare say, be carried off in the middle ages with a view to render them profitable. The Khatris are staunch Hindus. and it is somewhat singular that, while giving a religion and priests to the Sikhs, they themselves are comparatively seldom of that persuasion.

There are colonies of Khatri Sikhs in the Miranzai, Swat and Tirah valleys, where they live as hamsayas or retainers of the Pathans amongst whom they have settled. They are supposed to be descendants of refugees who, about 1756, sought an asylum in the hills from the tyranny of Ahmad Shah* and his son Timur. They have not dropped any of their Sikh customs. A few have been enlisted from time to time in the army and border police, where their knowledge of Pushtu and local topography makes them valuable soldiers when employed on Frontier service.

The Khatris are divided into four principal clans, as follows :—

Bunjahi	Bahri.
Sarim	Kohkran.

Besides the above, there are numerous social divisions, such as the Dhaighar, Charzati and Chhezati, which are again split up into various families and septs.

---

*This was Ahmed Shah Abdali, a Saddozai Afghan, who, in 1747, on the death of his master Nadir Shah, was crowned King of Kabul, with the title of Durri Durrani or "Pearl of Pearls."

He repeatedly invaded India, and by marrying his son Timur to the daughter of the Delhi Emperor, gained as her dowry the whole of the Punjab and Lahore. (The Races of Afghanistan.—Bellew).

The Bunjahi Khatris owe their influence and importance to the fact that they include the Bedi and Sodhi clans, to which belonged the founders of the Sikh faith. Guru Nanak was a Bedi, while the remaining Gurus, from Ram Das onwards, were Sodhis.

The Khatris are most numerous in the Lahore (61,500), Amritsar (50,000), Jullundur (25,500), Rawalpindi (22,000), and Jhelum (21,000), districts, though they are to be found in lesser numbers in nearly all the Districts of the Punjab.

Khatris, being the hereditary priests of the Sikhs, are strict in the observance of the ordinances of their religion, and make excellent regimental Granthis. They have a high social position by caste, and make good soldiers if recruited from the agricultural class, as they were during the Great War.

Aroras.—The Aroras claim to be of Khatri origin and say that they became outcastes from the Kshatriya, or Rajput stock during the persecution of that people by Parashu or the 'axe-armed Rama', the last incarnation of Vishnu and the special protector of Brahmans. To escape his wrath, the Aroras denied their caste, and described themselves as 'aur' or 'another', hence their name. It is probable, however, that the name Arora is really derived from Aror, now Rori, the ancient capital of Scinde. The tribe is divided into two principal branches—the "Uttaradhi" descended from families who fled northwards, and the "Dekhana" from those who escaped to the south. The "Uttaradhi" branch is sub-divided into two minor septs called "Bahri" and "Bunjahi", which correspond with similarly named Khatri clans, and thus confirm the theory of the Arora connection with that tribe. The "Dekhana" are split up into two sub-divisions—The "Dehra" and "Dakhanadhian". The "Bahri" and "Dhakanadhian" claim social superiority over all other septs of the tribe.

The Arora is the trader "par excellence" of the south-western portion of the Punjab. More than half of the Aroras dwell in Mooltan and Derajat. The remainder are scattered throughout the Doaba and Manjha districts. Like the Khatri, and unlike the Banya, the Arora is no mere trader, but his social position is far inferior to theirs, chiefly no doubt, because his special habitat is among the frontier Mohamedans by whom all Hindus are held in the greatest contempt. He is commonly known as a Kirar, a word which is almost synonymous with 'coward'. The word Kirar, indeed, appears to be applied to all Punjabi traders whether Khatris or Aroras, to distinguish them from the Banyas and Mahajans of Hindustan. The occupational distinction between a Khatri and an Arora is that while the former is usually a contractor, official or accountant, the latter, as a rule, is only a petty trader. The Arora is active, enterprising, industrious, and thrifty, and will turn his hand to any work. He is found throughout Afghanistan and even in Turkistan, and is the Hindu trader of those countries. The proverbs of the Punjab peasantry are full of allusions to the cowardice and treachery of this tribe. Aroras are of inferior physique and their character is thus summed up: "a cowardly secretive, acquisitive race, very necessary and useful in their way, but possessed of few manly qualities and both despised and envied by the great Musalman tribes of Bannu". About 9 per cent. of the Aroras are Sikhs, the remainder being Hindus. Some of the latter however, especially on the Sutlej and Lower Indus, are really "Munna", *i.e.*, shaven Sikhs, or followers of Baba Nanak, while others either worship the Krishna incarnation of Vishnu, or the Indus river itself, under the names of Khawaja Khizr and Zinda Pir. The Arora, whether Sikh or Hindu, is generally unsuited for military service, and men of this class should never be enlisted except under special circumstances.*

Labanas.—Labanas are Sikhs, Hindus, and Mohamedans and are distributed all over the Punjab, the total population in 1911 being 58,000.

They enjoy among Sikhs much the same status as Mahtons whom they closely resemble. The Labanas of the Punjab correspond to the Banjaras of Hindustan and the Dekhan, and were formerly largely employed by Khatris and Aroras as carriers of grain and merchandise. The spread of railway communication has now dealt a death blow to their carrying trade, and many have now settled on the land as rope manufacturers, merchants, and agriculturists. Trey have been declared an agricultural tribe in the Ambala and Gujrat Districts and the Lahore and Jullundur divisions. The Banjaras were formerly great suppliers of carriage, and Indian armies, from the time of the Moghals to that of Lake and Wellesley, were largely dependent upon them for supplies and transport. Physically and intellectually there is but little to choose between Labanas and Jats. They possess great courage and endurance and their hereditary connection with the carrying trade renders them very knowledgable in matters relating to transport. The esteem with which the Labana is regarded by the Jat is greater than that which his social position would warrant. Labanas are enlisted, and are far better at looking after animals than the average Jat Sikh; those who are Sikhs are imbued with a spirit of martial ardour and possess most of the qualifications required in an infantry soldier; they enlisted freely during the Great War and made excellent soldiers. They are found chiefly in the Lahore (3,500), Gujranwala (8,000), Sialkote (7,000), Gurdaspur (5,000) and Gujrat (8,000) districts, and have a large colony in Bahawalpur, where they are mostly "Munnas", *i.e.*, followers of Baba Nanak.

Mahtams and Mahtons.—Mahtams are by religion Hindus, Sikhs and Mohamedans. Their total population in the 1931 census was 65,000. They are met with mostly in the Ferozepore, Lahore,

---

*It is only fair to add, however, that it is stated by one authority that "the Aroras who reside in the Punjab proper make very fair soldiers and are not the despicable people above described".

They could, if required, be enlisted with Khatri Sikhs, with whom, however, they would compare as a rule unfavourably.

Amritsar, Sialkot and Gujranwala Districts, and Bahawalpur State. The status of the caste is low. They are partly vagrants and hunters and partly agriculturists, found chiefly on the banks of the Punjab rivers, more especially the Sutlej where they pick up a living by snaring animals. They have been declared an agricultural tribe in the districts of Ferozepore, Lahore, Montgomery and Multan. The Mahtam is also known as "Rassibat".

It is to be noted that the Mahtons of Hoshiarpur and Jullundur are quite distinct from the Mahtams with whom they were classed as recently as 1901. In appearance they are short and dark and of sturdy build; in character they are said to be quarrelsome and litigious. About one-third of the tribe profess to be Sikhs and have occasionally been enlisted, though this procedure is not advocated.

They make fair soldiers but are looked down upon by the Jats. Their principal clans or gots are as follows :—

Dupaich.	Khatti.	Barar	Sakrel.
Puri.	Sasharvai.	Karsudh.	Babat.
Matiai.	Khattan.	Gaihind.	Shafan.
Gughial.	Thindal	Papla.	Jhalwal.

Mahtons have been returned from the Hoshiarpur, Jullundur, Ferozepore, and Lyallpur Districts. Their real home, however, is in the Hoshiarpur and Jullundur Districts. Their total population is only 65,000 of whom approximately one-half are Sikhs. The Mahtons were originally Rajputs of a fairly high status, and the term was one of distinction equivalent to Mehta; but they lost the Rajput status some time ago in consequence mainly of the adoption of agriculture as their occupation in preference to military service, and the introduction of widow remarriage, which, to this day, is vigorously tabooed by high class Rajputs, not only among the Hindus, but also among the Mohamedans. They were thus degraded into a separate group or caste.

Sainis.—In 1931, the total population of Sainis was 157,203 and except for 400 Mohamedans, were Hindus and Sikhs. They chiefly inhabit Delhi, Karnal, Amballa and Lyallpur Districts, the Jullundur and Lahore Divisions and the Kalsia, Nahan, Nalagarh, Mandi, Kapurthala and Patiala States.

They are hardy cultivators akin to malis but of a better social standing as they own land and are seldom mere market gardeners. They were enlisted in considerable numbers during the Great War and proved good soldiers, orderly and well behaved; they do not, however, possess the military qualities of the Jats who are very much their social superiors.

The following are the names of their principle clans :—

Boli.	Pawan.	Gaddi.
Salarhri.	Hamarti.	Badwal.
Alagni.	Mangar.	Badyal.
Baryal.	Baigal.	

Kalals, Karals or Ahluwalias.—The Kalals or Karals are Hindus, Sikhs and Mohamedans with a total population of 33,500.

The Kalal or Karal, as he is generally called in the western Punjab is a hereditary distiller and seller of spirituous liquors. But since the manufacture and traffic in spirits has been subjected to Government regulation, a large proportion of the clan, and more especially the Sikh and Mohamedan sections, have abandoned their proper calling, and taken to other pursuits such as agriculture, service—both civil and military—trade, shopkeeping, etc. Kalals are renowned for their energy and enterprise. Their obstinacy is referred to in a well-known proverb—"Death may budge, but a Kalal won't". The original social position of the clan was an extremely humble one, but in the Punjab it has been raised by special circumstances. The reigning family of Kapurthala is descended from one Sada Singh, Kalal, who founded the village of Ahlu near Lahore. The family gradually rose in the social scale, and Badar Singh, the great grandson of Sada Singh, Kalal, married the daughter of a petty Sardar of the district. From this union sprang Jassa Singh, who was the most powerful and influential chief that the Sikhs possessed until the rise of Ranjit Singh. He adopted the title of Ahluwalia from the name of his ancestral village, and it is still retained not only by the Kapurthala family, but very generally by all Sikh Kalals. There are about 33,500 Kalals in the Punjab, of whom over 9,000 are Sikhs. Men of this clan are physically and intellectually but little inferior to Jats, and they generally make good soldiers. The Kalals of the Manjha, Kapurthala, and Patiala are probably the best. They are sometimes called Neb.

Tarkhans or Ramgarhias.—Tarkhans are Hindus, Sikhs and Mohamedans with a total population in 1931 of 652,000.

The Lohar or blacksmith, and the Tarkhan or carpenter, are closely allied, and rank highest among the village artizans. Though separate caste, they are probably of the same origin, and in most parts of the Punjab intermarry. The Tarkhan manufactures and repairs the agricultural implements and household furniture required in his village. Though practically of the same caste, the social position of the Tarkhan is distinctly superior to that of the Lohar. Sikh Tarkhans always call themselves Ramgarhias in remembrance of a famous ancestor called Jassa Singh, who was the leader of the Ramgarhia Misl or confederacy, and the builder of the Ramgarh or citadel of Amritsar. Many Ramgarhias are cultivators and hold respectable positions. The tribe is distributed throughout the Punjab and includes in its total population some 158,000 Sikhs. Tarkhans seldom enlist as they can earn better wages by working at their trade. The following are the principal septs of the clan :—

Dhaman.	Khatti.	Siasan.
Matharu.	Gade.	Tharu.
Netal.	Janjua.	Kokhar.

Nais.—The Nai is the village barber. His occupation is a menial one, his duties being to shave and shampoo the villagers, and attend upon the village guests. But he is really much more than barber. He is the hereditary bearer of formal messages from one village to another such as news of auspicious events, formal congratulations and letters fixing the dates of weddings, etc. News of a death is never carried by him, but always by a Chuhra. He, in company with a Brahman, acts as the lagi or 'go between' in the negotiations which precede a betrothal. At marriage ceremonies too, he plays an important part, next indeed to that of the Brahman himself, and on all these occasions receives suitable gratuities. Notwithstanding all this, the Nai is essentially a kamin or village servant, of much the same social standing as the Dhobi, far above the Chamar, but somewhat below the Lohar, for his occupation as a barber proper is considered degrading. The outcaste tribes have their own Nais, for a Nai who has shaved a Chuhra would not be permitted to touch a Jat. The Nais are popularly regarded as extremely astute. "The Jackal", says the Punjab villager, "is the sharpest amongst beasts, the crow among birds, and the Nai among men". The tribe is found throughout the Punjab and has a population of about 376,000, of which over 39,000 are Sikhs. A Sikh barber would appear to be rather an anomaly, but it must be remembered that in addition to his more usual functions he shampoos, cuts the nails, and cleans the ears of his clients. His village name, in fact, is Naherna, the 'nail cutter'. The Nai Sikh was frequently enlisted as a soldier in former days, but, in common with other humble classes of Sikhs, has been gradually displayed by the Jat, though considerable numbers were enlisted during the great war. The following are the principal gots of the tribe :—

Gola.	Bhanbheru.
Basi.	Bahgu.
Bhatti.	Kokhar.

Chhimbas (*Namabansis*).—The Chhimba or calico-printer is closely associated with the Dhobi or washerman; both belonging to the same tribe, though the occupation of the former is considered slightly less degrading than that of the latter. The Dhobi is a true village menial in the sense that he receive a fixed share of the produce in return for washing the clothes of the villagers wherever he performs that office.

He only occupies this position, however, among the higher castes of landowners; for among the Jats, and classes of similar standing, the washing is generally done by the women of the family. His social position is very low, for his occupation is considered impure, and he alone of the tribes which are not outcasted, will imitate the Kumhar in keeping and using a donkey. He stands below the Nai, but perhaps above the Kumhar. The Chhimba is properly a stamper of coloured patterns on the cotton fabrics of the country, but, as has before been remarked, he can hardly be distinguished from the Dhobi. Besides being a printer, he dyes in madder, leaving other colours, more especially indigo, which is an abomination to all Hindus, to his Musalman confrere the Lilari or Rangrez. The patron saint of the Sikh and Hindu Chhimbas is a worthy named Baba Namdeo, who lived at Batala in Gurdaspur towards the end of the 15th century. The Chhimba or Namabansi Sikh, as he is occasionally called in his village, was at one time freely enlisted, and made a tolerably efficient soldier. Care should be taken not to confound him with "Chima" who is a Jat of very good standing. The following are the principal septs of the tribe :—

Sippal.	Bhatti.
Khakhar.	Kamboh.

There are about 91,000 Chhimbas in the Punjab, but only approximately 17,000 are Sikhs. Chhimbas are also known by the names of Chipi, Chhibu and Chapagar. Many Chhimbas have now taken to tailoring and Sikh darzis are generally of this class.

Jhinwars, Jhiwars Kahars, or Mehra.—The Jhinwars are Hindus, Sikhs and Mohamedans and in 1931 totalled 275,000.

The Jhinwar, who is generally called Mehra among the Sikhs, is a carrier, waterman, fisherman, and basket-maker. He also carries palanquins, and all such burdens as are borne by a yoke on the shoulders. He is especially concerned with the cultivation of waternuts, the netting of waterfowl, and the sinking of wells. He is a true kamin or village menial, receiving customary dues in return for customary service. In this capacity he supplies all the baskets needed by the cultivator, and brings water to the men in the fields at harvest time, to the houses where the women are secluded, and attends to the guests at weddings and on similar occasions. His social standing is in one respect high; for all will drink at his hands, and all will eat the food he has cooked. He is nevertheless a servant, though perhaps the highest of that class. The Jhinwar seldom works in the fields except for pay at harvest time, or on other special occasions. Besides the occupations already described, the Jhinwar, is the cook, and his wife the "accoucheuse" of the Punjab proper. Dais and wet-nurses are nearly always of the Jhinwar caste. Moreover the common oven, which forms so important a feature in the village life of the Punjab, and on which the peasantry have their bread baked in the hot weather, is almost always in the hands of a Jhinwar, who is also the village wood-cutter. Sikhs of this class have been known to make good soldiers. In Sikh Regiments the Jhinwar is employed as a Langri or regimental cook in preference to any other class. If he carries water in a skin he is called a Sakka, and if in earthern or brass vessels a Kahar. The primary occupation of the Kahar is carrying litters. From this and from the fact that they are 'clean' Sudras, Kahars are employed as servants by all respectable Sikhs and Hindus, and are largely enrolled by the Indian Hospital Corps for service in Indian Hospitals.

Ramdasias.—The Ramdasia is now generally a weaver, but is of the same tribe as the Chamar or leather dresser. The open adoption of a definite faith by outcaste classes such as the Chuhra and Chamar is, as a rule, the first step made in their upward struggle, and is very commonly accompanied by the abandonment of their old occupation for one which stands higher in the social scale. Thus the Chuhra scavenger on becoming a Musalman will refuse to remove nightsoil, and on becoming a Sikh will take to tanning and leather work. The tanner and leather worker on becoming a Mahomedan will give up tanning, and on taking the Sikh "pahul" will turn his hand to the loom and so forth. The Hindu reformation which produced Sikhism, also produced many Bhagats, or religious leaders of low caste origin, who taught the people the principles of religion in their own vernaculars, instead of in the unintelligible Sanskrit of the Brahmans. Among these Bhagats were Kabir (a Julaha), Nam Deo (a Chhimba), and Ravi Das (a Chamar). Their writings are constantly quoted in the "Adi Granth". One of the reforms contemplated and partially carried out by Sikhism was the abolition of caste, carrying with it a general permission to study the Hindu scriptures, a privilege which was extended even to such outcastes as Chuhras and Chamars. Taking advantage of this concession, some of the lowest classes became Sikhs. They gave up their degrading occupations and took to other means of livelihood. They also changed their name, and gave up social intercourse with the unconverted members of their tribe as far as they possibly could. Thus the Chamars on their conversion to Sikhism took the name of Revi Das the first Bhagat of their race, to show that they followed his example. Ramdasia is only a corruption of Ravdasia the correct form of the word. Similarly Chhimba Sikhs called themselves Namabansis after their great leader, Nam Deo. In the present day if a Chamar takes the "pahul" and becomes a Sikh, he at once joins the Ramdasias. The latter will only marry the daughters of ordinary Chamars, conditionally on their taking the "pahul". A Ramdasia would not drink from the hands of an ordinary Chamar, unless the latter became a Sikh. Some authorities are of opinion that Ramdasias take their name, not from the Bhagat Ravi Das, but from Ramdas, the 4th Guru of the Sikhs, who was the first to accept Chamars as converts. Ramdasias are found chiefly in the Doaba and Malwa districts, where they are mostly field labourers. They have proved good soldiers in spite of their lowly origin, but are seldom of robust physique. Many Ramdasias are Nanakpanthis, few are but true Pahullas.

Mazbhis, Rangretas, or Chuhras.—The Chuhra of the Punjab corresponds to the Bhangi of Hindustan and is par excellence the sweeper and scavenger of the village community. In the 1931 census of a total of 670,000, one hundred and fifty seven thousand were returned Sikhs. He is found throughout the province, being most numerous, however, in Ferozepore, Lahore, Amritsar and Faridkot, where much of the agricultural labour is performed by men of this caste. As one of the regular village menials, he receives a customary share of the product of each harvest, and in return performs certain indispensable offices for his clients of higher castes. In the eastern Punjab he sweeps the houses and villages, collects cowdung, kneads it into cakes and stacks it, works up the manure, helps with the cattle, and takes them from village to village. In the Sikh districts he adds to these functions actual hard work at the plough and in the fields. He claims the flesh of such animals as to not divide the hoof the cloven-footed belonging to his humble confrere the Chamar. The religion of the Chuhras is a very flexible one. They are supposed to be of aboriginal descent but accretions by degradation have, in any case, been so large that it is impossible to distinguish Aryan from aboriginal blood among them.

The civilising effect of Sikhism in raising the social position of the lowest classes has already been noticed under the heading of Ramdasia and finds an admirable illustration in the person of the Mazbhi or Chuhra convert to Sikhism. As a simple Chuhra, the Hindu sweeper occupies the lowest place in the social scale; he is avoided by all, and his merest touch is regarded as pollution. He is still a village menial, but he is no longer the remover of night-soil. He takes the "pahul," wears his hair long, abstains from tobacco, and strives by a rigorous and punctilious observance of all Sikh customs and ritual, to blot out the memory of his former degradation.

The highest classes of Mazbhis profess to be descended from three Chuhras who gallantly rescued the body of Tegh Bahadur from a Mohamedan mob after the Guru had been cruelly executed at Delhi by the fanatical Emperor Aurangzeb. The three sweepers, on their return to Amritsar with the martyr's corpse, were at once baptized into the Sikh faith by Guru Govind Singh, who, in recognition of their valour and devotion, gave them the title of Mazbhi or 'faithful'. Many Mazbhis, however, are supposed to be descended from Mohamedans who were forcibly converted to Sikhism in the time of Ranjit Singh. Owing to the intense hatred of the Sikhs for Islam, most of these converts were classed with Chamars and Chuhras; and as the first Chuhras admitted to the faith of the Khalsa had been given the title of Mazbhi, the same title was also applied to their converted Mohamedan associates. True Mazbhis are generally short, with black shiny skins, high cheek bones, flat noses, and a distinctly aboriginal type of face. The Mazbhis are entirely Sikhs and numbered 21,500, in 1911.

We hear little of the Mazbhi Sikhs during the troubled times following the decline of the Moghal Empire, but during the reign of Ranjit Singh they were extensively enlisted in the Khalsa army, being generally stationed on the Peshawar border where constant fighting gave them ample opportunities of showing their bravery and endurance.

After the British occupation of the Punjab, the Mazbhis degenerated into a criminal tribe of thugs, robbers, and dacoits. About 1851 the Maharaja Gulab Singh of Kashmir established a corps of Mazbhis, which he employed in overawing his Mohamedan subjects. About the same time two Mazbhi coolie corps were raised, one for employment on the construction of the Grand Trunk Road, and another for similar work in Ceylon. On the outbreak of the Mutiny, the Mazbhis were still regarded as a criminal class and it was thought advisable to send them out of the Punjab by forming them into pioneer regiments for service against the mutinous sepoys. Their extraordinary bravery, endurance, and patience under great and protracted privations, soon won for them a high reputation as soldiers—a reputation which has increased by their subsequent achievements in China, Abyssinia, Afghanistan, numerous campaigns on the Frontier, and on various fronts during the Great War.

The descendants of the Chuhra converts of Govind Singh sometimes describe themselves as "asl" Mazbhis, to distinguish them from their Chuhra brethren whose conversion to Sikhism is more recent. In some districts, more especially in Ambala and Ludhiana, certain Mazbhis call themselves Rangretas and profess to be socially superior to the rest of the tribe. These distinctions, however, are more theoretical than real, for the "asl" Mazbhi, once satisfied as to the genuineness of a Chuhra's conversion, accepts him as a brother, and will eat and drink with him without objection. Moreover, it is generally admitted by the Mazbhi Granthis themselves that a Chuhra family which has embraced Sikhism and scrupulously adhered to its tenets, is, after the second generation, unquestionably entitled to rank with the best of the crignal Mazbhis.* In some Pioneer Regiments Chuhra converts to Sikhism are called Malwais,† a somewhat misleading term, as it really means an inhabitant of the Malwa. It is probable that this practice arose from the fact that those first enlisted came from the cis-Sutlej districts, but the term is now applied indiscriminately to all who are Mazbhis by conversion, in contradistinction to those who are Mazbhis by descent. As a matter of fact Chuhras and Mazbhis, like any other Sikh, may either be Manjhails or Malwais, according as they are recruited from the districts west or east of the Sutlej.

---

*This statement is, however, open to question, for many authorities declare that the "asl" Mazbhi holds aloof from the Chuhra, and that the latter's conversion to Sikhism makes little difference in his social condition for some generations.

†It has been suggested that the Malwai is a corruption of 'Malai,' 'admitted, in allusion to the story of their origin.

Until recently Mazbhis were not found in large numbers in any particular locality, being scattered in groups of two or three families through the Jat villages, where they worked as labourers for the owners of the soil. Government, however, recognising the advisability of separating them from communities where their position was menial and degrading, formed colonies of Mazbhi pensioners in the Gujranwala district, near the Chenab, where grants of lands enable them to practise agriculture and thus escape from a release to the humble position which they would hold among the Jats.

This arrangement is not only of advantage as a means of rewarding, deserving soldiers, but is also calculated to result in the formation of a really valuable recruiting ground.

Dekhani Sikhs.—Reference has been made on page 10 to the Sikh Colony at Naderh on the Godavery, where Govind Singh met his death in 1708. The total number of Sikhs in the Dekhan is 4,637, and they are found chiefly in Naderh itself and in Hyderabad, Aurangabad, Digloor, and Mundnoor. These Dekhani Sikhs are mostly the descendants of Sikhs pilgrims from the Punjab who first came to Naderh as worshippers at the Gurdwara erected over Govind Singh's Samad, and, obtaining employment in the Dekhan, eventually formed colonies. They are now entirely localised, and they intermarry among themselves.

The Dekhani Sikhs are initiated by taking the "pahul", and share in the "parshad" or communion. They are accepted as true Sikhs by their brethern of the Punjab, but are considered as of an inferior class. About 1,200 of these Dekhani Sikhs are in the service of the Nizam—some in the police and some in the infantry. A certain number enlisted in the Central India Horse during the Mutiny.

The Dekhani Sikh is distinguishable from his Punjabi confrere by his dress, which is still much the same as it was in the time of Govind Singh. They wear the Kachh or short drawers, and their head-dress is the small tightly tied pag such as the Sikhs of the Punjab now wear under the turban. As true Govindi Sikhs they are careful observers of the five kakkas, and conform strictly to the ordinances of the tenth Guru.

Aheris.—Aheris are found mostly in the Hissar, Gurgaon, Karnal, and Ambala Districts and the Patiala and Jind States. They are all Hindus except in the Phulkian States where they follow the Sikh and Mohamedan religions as well. In 1911 the total population of this caste was 19,000 of whom only a very small proportion are Sikhs. They generally work in reed and grass and move about in gangs in search of employment as labourers or as reapers at harvest time. They live outside the main village homesteads.

Bahrupias.—Bahrupias are a very small caste of Sikhs with a population in 1911 of 841 only. They chiefly inhabit the Gujrat district. Bahrupia means a disguised man, *i.e.*, an actor or mimic. It is a functional caste made up by accretions from other castes.

Banjaras.—Banjaras belong to all religions *viz.*, Hindu, Sikh, and Mohamedan and are found in all parts of the Punjab. Their total population in 1911 was under 9,000. They are itinerant traders and carriers and go about, piercing noses and ears of children and selling ear and nose rings and other cheap ornaments.

Bazighars.—Bazighars are mostly Hindus but contain a certain number of Sikhs. They had a total population in 1911 of 36,000, and are scattered all over the province. They are a gypsy tribe of vagrant habits who wander about practising acrobatic feats.

Bhatras.—Bhatras are both Hindus and Sikhs with a total population of about 1,000. They claim Brahman origin but would appear to be degraded Bhats. They receive offerings at eclipses, tell fortunes, and go about begging in the garb of Sadhus.

Julahas.—Julahas are Mohamedans, Hindus and Sikhs totalling 667,500 and are scattered all over the Province. Julaha means weaver and was originally a purely functional term which has crystallised into a new caste. He is called Paoli in the Western Punjab and is an important artizan there, especially because no weaving is done by the leather working or scavenger castes. The Julaha is despised not only on account of his proverbial stupidity, but also because of his amphibious life, the indigenous handloom necessitating work with the lower half of the body in a pit. He is reputed to be a coward of the worst type.

Khalsa.—Khalsa is an old term, which denotes the true followers of Guru Govind Singh, but in the past it has been used merely to signify the persuasion of members of various castes who belonged to the orthodox Sikh religion. In the 1911 census, it was returned for the time as a caste, *i.e.*, as a social group numbering 16,000. In the census of 1921, the Sect numbered 530,000. The advocates of the "Khalsa" or "Tat Khalsa" movement, disregard the restriction of caste and inter-dining and aim at establishing a universal brotherhood among the Sikhs. They have thus preferred to call themselves by the common title Khalsa instead of stating the caste to which they belonged. When receiving his "pahul" a Sikh is instructed to regard Guru Govind Singh as his father, Mai Sahib Devan as his mother, Patna Sahib as his birthplace, and "Sodhbans" as his caste.

Kumhars.—Kumhars are Hindus, Sikhs, and Mohamedans. They numbered in 1931 upwards of 620,000 and are found almost everywhere in the Punjab. They are the potters and brick burners of the Province. They are indispensable to agriculture, in the well-irrigated tracts of the western and central Punjab, where they supply earthen pots for the well-gear. In other parts the demand for earthen pitchers, etc., keeps them engaged to a certain extent, though, with the gradual increase of modern substitutes and conveniences, they are seeking employment in other branches of industry.

Meghs.—Meghs are practically all Hindus and, of a total population of 23,000, under 1,000 are Sikhs. They inhabit the district North of the Sutlej River. The Megh is a low caste, considered untcuchable by the orthodox Hindu, but the Arya Samaj has purified numerous numbers of the caste and raised them to the status of touchables. By occupation the Meghs are largely weavers, but they also follow other pursuits such as field labourers, grass cutters, etc.

Rors.—There are very few "Sikh" Rors; they number only 400 out of a total population of 40,000. They deserve mention as they claim a Rajput origin and their social status is the same as the Jat. Their chief occupation is agriculture, they inhabit the Rohtak, Ambala and Karnal Districts and the Jhind State, though their real seat is in the great Dhak jungles South of Thanesar in the Karnal District.

Saiqalgars.—A Saiqalgar is a purely functionary term used for armourers and burnishers of metal. They are looked upon as a low caste, but claim to be Lohars. They are very few in number, in all only 1,500 and are Hindus and Sikhs as well as Mohamedans. They mostly inhabit the Ambala Division, the Jullundur, Multan, Lahore, and Rawalpindi districts and Patiala State.

Sunars.—Sunars are Hindus, Sikhs and Mohamedans and are scattered all over the Punjab. They number in all 160,000. They are the gold and silversmiths as well as the jewellers of the Province. Sunar is undoubtedly a functional term, although for generations the group has been treated as a separate caste. The members are endeavouring to obtain Rajput and Khatri status.

Thatthiars.—Thatthiars number 4,000 and are Hindus, Sikhs, and Mohamedans, scattered generally all over the Punjab.

A Thatthiar is a functional term and is used for one who makes vessels of copper, brass and other mixed metal, as distinct from the Kasera, who sells them.

CHAPTER IV.

Salient features of the lives of the Gurus.

The origin of Sikhism has already been made clear in the earlier chapters.

In this chapter it is proposed to deal with the subject in somewhat greater detail, in regard to that portion of its formation and growth which is connected with the lives of the Gurus.

Guru Nanak, 1469-1539.—The first "Guru", or spiritual leader of the Sikhs, was a Khatri, named Nanak, who was born in the year 1469 in the neighbourhood of Lahore, at a place called Talwandi. He appears to have been naturally of a pious disposition and of a reflecting mind, and there is reason to believe that in his youth he made himself familiar with the popular creeds of both the Mohamedans and the Hindus, and that he gained a general knowledge of the Koran and Brahmanical Shastras. In a moment of enthusiasm he abandoned his home and strove to obtain wisdom by penitent meditation, by study, and by an enlarged intercourse with mankind. With this object he is stated to have constantly travelled, and, returning to his native land, he threw aside the habit of an ascetic and passed the remainder of his seventy years in calling upon men to worship the one invisible God, to live virtuously, and to be tolerant of the feelings of others. He combined the excellencies of preceding reformers and avoided the more grave errors into which they had fallen. Instead of the circumscribed divinity he loftily invoked the Lord as the one, the sole, the timeless being, the creator, the self existent, the incomprehensible and the ever-lasting. He told all creeds and persuasions whether Mohamedans or Hindus that "virtues and charities, heroic acts and gathered wisdom, are nought of themselves, that the only knowledge which availeth is the knowledge of God (*vide* "Adi Granth" towards the end of the portion called "Asa").

He asserted no special divinity, although he may possibly have considered himself, as he came to be considered by others, the successor of these inspired teachers of his belief, sent to reclaim fallen mortals of all creeds and countries within the limits of his knowledge. He rendered his mission applicable to all times and places, yet he declared himself to be but the slave, the humble messenger of the Almighty, making use of universal truth as his sole instrument. He did not claim for his writings the merit of a direct transcription of the words of God. "Fight with no weapon", said he, " Save the word of God; a holy teacher hath no means save the purity of his doctrine".

Thus Nanak extricated his followers from the accumulated errors of ages. He left them unfettered by rules, to become an increasing body of truthful worshippers. His reform was in its immediate effects religious and moral only. He left the progress of his people to the operation of time; his care was rather to prevent them contracting into a sect and his comprehensive principles narrowing into monastic distinctions. This he effected by excluding his son, a meditative and perhaps a bigoted ascetic, and chose instead one of his disciples, Lahna, who with a name changed to "Angad" was acknowledged as the teacher of the Sikhs.

Nanak died at Kartarpur, on the Ravi, about 40 miles above Lahore, where there is a place of worship sacred to him. One of his two sons Sri Chand, referred to above, justified his father's fears and became the founder of the Hindu Sect of "Udasis".

Essence of Nanak's teachings.—The essence of Nanak's teaching thus was that all men are alike in the eyes of the Almighty. The authority of the Brahmans and the virtue of their incantations and sacrifices were rejected, whilst salvation was taught as lying in repentance and in pure and righteous conduct. At the same time he did not despite or attack the Hindu or Mohamedan teachers; he held, indeed, that they too had been sent from God, but he preached a higher and purer religion embracing all that was best in both. He respected the Hindu veneration of the cow and the Mohamedan abhorrence of the pig, but recommended as a higher rule than either, total abstinence from flesh. In short he attacked nothing, condemned nobody; but he sought to draw men's minds from the shadow to the substance, to glorify what was highest and best in the religion of each, and was content to leave to all men, at least for a while, the outward and visible signs to which they were traditionally accustomed.

Nothing in fact could have been more gentle or less aggressive than his doctrine; nothing more unlike the teaching of his great successor Govind.

The followers of Nanak were called Sikhs, and as the creed spread, this appellation became that descriptive title of the whole people. It must however be remembered that the term Sikh is a religious and not a racial designation, and that it belongs only to those who have accepted the faith of the Khalsa. The followers of Nanak at the present time are the "Nanak-Panthis" or "Sajdharis", who are "Sikhs", as opposed to "Singhs" the name by which the followers of Govind Singh, the tenth Guru, are particularly distinguished.

Guru Angad, 1539-1552.—Guru Angad was born at Sarai Naga close to Mukhtsar in the Ferozepore District in 1504. He was a Khatri of the Tihan sub-division. Little is related of his ministry, except that he committed to writing much of what he had heard about Nanak from the Guru's ancient companion Bala Sindhu, as well as some devotional observations of his own, which were afterwards incorporated in the "Granth Sahib". Angad was true to the principles of his great teacher, and, not deeming either of his sons worthy to succeed him, appointed Amar Das as his successor.

Guru Amar Das, 1552-1574.—Amar Das was a Khatri of the Bhalla sub-division and was born at Basarke in the Amritsar District in 1479. He was active in preaching and successful in obtaining converts. The immediate followers of Sri Chand, the son of Nanak, had hitherto been regarded as almost equally the disciples of the first teacher with the direct adherents of Angad; Amar Das, however, declared passive and recluse "Udasis" to be wholly separate from active and domestic Sikhs, and thus finally preserved the infant church from disappearing as one of many sects.

Amar Das died in 1574 after a ministration of twenty-two years.

Guru Ram Das, 1574-81.—Guru Ram Das, the son-in-law of Amar Das, was a Khatri of the Sodhi sub-division and was born in Lahore in 1534. He was a man of considerable merit and of a quiet and peaceful disposition. He is said to have been held in esteem by Akbar, and restored an old tank at Ramdaspur, which he renamed Amritsar, or the tank of immortality. He played a considerable part in promoting the faith of Guru Nanak and in founding the town of Amritsar, which, as the most convenient and fertile centre, he laid as the foundations of the future greatness of the Sikhs as a nation. Nominating Arjan Dev, his youngest son, as his successor, Guru Ram Das died in 1581.

Guru Arjan Dev, 1581-1606.—The succession of Guru Arjan Dev to the Gadi was the introduction of a new era in the history of Sikhism. His manifold activities infused public spirit into the community. Places of worship were built wherever Sikh influence was felt. Large tanks were dug and lands were set apart, the proceeds of which went to defray the expenses of their upkeep. Arjan was perhaps the first who clearly understood the wide import of the teachings of Nanak, or who perceived how applicable they were to every state of life and to every condition of society. He made Amritsar the proper seat of his followers, the centre which should attract their worldly longings for a material bond of union. He also introduced a regular form of organised taxation and thus the Sikhs became accustomed to a regular form of government. He next arranged the various writings of his predecessors, adding to them the best known, or the most suitable, compositions of some other religious reformers, and completing the whole with a prayer and some exhortations of his own, he declared the compilation to be pre-eminently the "Granth" or book of Sikh scriptures, a rule of faith for his disciples.

Arjan may in fact be described as the Luther of the Sikh reformation. Like the latter he insisted that the scriptures should be read to the people in the vulgar tongue instead of in an extinct and classical language.

True to his Khatri instinct, he was a keen and successful trader and by utilizing the services and money of his disciples in mercantile transactions, he gradually accumulated considerable wealth for his sect.

Arjan became famous amongst pious devotees, but to the orthodox Hindu priests the idea of compiling the Granth Sahib in a language other than Hindi or Sanskrit was abhorrent. The organization of Sikh dissenters, further, into a strong commonwealth, which aimed at casting off the irksome influence of many time-honoured institutions, spread a feeling of alarm through orthodox circles. The leaders represented to the rulers of the day that the Guru was preaching a revolt against the paramount power, and that the Granth he had compiled contained references derogatory to the founder of Islam.

This effort to discredit him however failed, but the fact of his giving shelter to Jahangir's son, Khusro, who had rebelled against his father, and who had fled to the Punjab, infuriated Jahangir, and he was summoned to his presence, and after incarceration, was submitted to torture, which hastened, if it did not actually cause his death in 1606.

With the arrest and death of Arjan began that Mohamedan persecution which was so mightily to change the spirit of the new faith. It was in fact the turning point in Sikh History, and the effect of the persecution became immediately apparent.

Guru Har Gobind 1606-1645.—Har Gobind was not more than eleven years of age at his father's death, yet in a short time he became a military and political leader as well as a spiritual teacher.

Nanak had enjoined secular occupation, Arjun carried the injunction into practice, and the impulse thus given speedily extended and became general. The temper and circumstances of Har Gobind both prompted him to invovation. Arjun had trafficked as a merchant, but, Har Gobind grasped a sword, and marched with his devoted followers among the troops of the Empire, or boldly led them to oppose and overcome provincial governors or personal enemies. He encouraged his followers to eat meat as giving them strength and daring. He substituted zeal in the cause for saintliness of life, and added a military system to the civil organization which had already been established by Arjun. He became a follower of the Emperor Jahangir on his death in 1628 he continued in the employ of the Mohamedan Government; but he appears soon to have been led into a course of armed resistance to the Imperial officers in the Punjab, and after various incidents he retired for a time to the wastes of Bhatinda, only to come forth again to raid and foray as opportunity offered against the Mohamedans. He thus became very popular amongst his down trodden Hindu neighbours, and his camp was the chosen rallying place for the oppressed and fugitives from justice.

He died in peace in 1645 at Kartarpur on the Sutlej and was succeeded by Har Rai.

During the ministry of Har Gobind, the Sikhs increased greatly in numbers and already formed a kind of separate State within the Empire.

Guru Har Rai, 1645-1661.—The ministry of Har Rai was mild, yet such as won for him general respect. He remained at Kartarpur for a time, when he moved eastward into the district of Sirmoor and became involved in 1658 in the struggle between Dara Shikoh and his brothers for the Empire of India. He died at Kartarpur in 1661 and his youngest son, Har Kishen, was recognised as head of the Sikhs.

Guru Har Kishen, 1661-1664.—Har Kishen was only six years of age when his father died and before he had even left Delhi he was attacked by small-pox and died in 1664.

Guru Tegh Bahadur.—Tegh Bahadur was now generally acknowledged as the head of the Sikhs. He seems to have been of a pious but moody character, and to have lacked both the general temper of his father Guru Har Gobind, and the lofty mind of his son, Govind, who succeeded him. Yet his own example powerfully aided in making the disciples of Nanak a material as well as a devotional people. His reverence for the sword of his father and his repeated injunction that his disciples should obey the bearer of his arrows show more of the kingly than of the priestly spirit.

Early in his career this supremacy and his life were both endangered by the machinations of Ram Rai, the elder son of Har Rai, and he was summoned to Delhi as a pretender to power and disturber of the peace, but was allowed to go free. After a time he returned to the Punjab and settled at Makhowal on the Sutlej, where he appears to have followed the example of his father, Har Govind, with unequal footsteps. He is reported to have subsisted himself and his disciples by plunder in a way that rendered him unpopular with the peasantry. He was appealed to by the Brahmans of Kashmir for aid against the Moghal oppression. The Imperial troops were sent against him and his followers were defeated and made prisoners.

When Tegh Bahadur was on his way to Delhi he sent for his youthful son, and girding upon him the sword of Har Govind, he hailed him as the Guru of the Sikhs. He told he was himself led to death and enjoined upon him the necessity and merit of revenge.

All the accounts agree that Tegh Bahadur was ignominiously put to death in 1675, and that the stern and bigoted Aurangzeb had his body publicly exposed in the streets of Delhi.

It was on this occasion that the famous prophecy, on the ultimate sovereignty of the white race in Delhi is said to have been uttered "I see", he said dauntlessly to the Emperor, "a power rising in the west which will sweep your Empire into the dust". His body was quartered and hung before the city gates; but the Sikhs never forgot his prophetic words. "They have accounted largely for Sikh loyalty to British rule; and they are on the lips of the gallant Punjab Regiments before Delhi in 1857, when at last they avenged in blood the martyrdom of their leader" (Rawlinson, Indian Historical Studies, p. 177).

The Guru's place of martyrdom bears the name of Sis Gang and is situated in Chandni Chowk. Before his death he begged that an effort might be made to rescue his body from his enemies. Three sweepers were despatched to Delhi for the purpose, and at great personal risk bore off the mutilated corpse of their master from the midst of a fanatical Mohamedan crowd. As a reward for their fidelity and devotion they were immediately admitted into the community of the Khalsa by Guru Govind Singh who bestowed upon them the title of "Mazbhi" or faithful. It is from the descendents and converts of these Mazbhi Sikhs that our Pioneer regiments are now chiefly recruited.

Guru Govind Singh.—Guru Govind Singh was the last and at the sametime the most famous of the ten Gurus. Under him the freternity which had sprung into existence as a quiet sect of a purely religious nature, and which had become a military society of a doubtful character, developed into the political organization which was to rule the greater part of Northern India, and to furnish the British Armies with their stoutest and most worthy opponents.

His life has already been dealt with in considerable detail in Chapter II of this book and there remains but little further to add thereto.

During the period of his early manhood he finished his education, which was far more complete than any of his predecessors. Lepel Griffin in his "Ranjit Singh" states:—"It does not appear that this remarkable man, who, in intelligence, capacity, and fixity of purpose, was infinitely the superior of all his predecessors, undertook what he considered to be the mission of his life, in the formation of the scattered Sikh people into a formidable confederacy, and the destruction of the Mohamedan power in the Punjab, until he was well advanced in manhood; certainly over-thirty years of age. Till then he devoted himself to study and preparation for his self-imposed duties. At the same time, not neglecting the accomplishments of a well-born youth of his age, he became a keen sportsman, and skilled, in all feats of arms. When he emerged from his seclusion, he was at once accepted by the Sikhs as their natural and hereditary leader, and they were quite ready to follow the murder of his father on their Mohamedan oppressors.

Before commencing his work, he desired to obtain the blessing of the Hindu goddess Devi, one of whose shrines was on a hill near his home at Anandpur. After the practice of the necessary preliminary austerities, numerous and long continued, the goddess appeared, demanded a human sacrifice as the price of her protection, and informed him that the most acceptable offering would be the head of one of his sons. The mothers of the children naturally refused to surrender them to such a fate, so Govind Singh appealed to his friends, of whom it is recorded that five offered themselves as the sacrifice, and one, whose name is not given, as accepted and slain before the shrine. The goddess was pleased with the offering and the subsequent career of Govind Singh and his violent death seem to have been preshadowed in its bloody inauguration.

Meanwhile the son of the Guru was filled with a passionate longing for revenge. He realised, however, the necessity for a larger following, and, imitating the example of his Mohamedan enemies, determined to make use of religion as a stepping stone to political power.

History is apt to repeat itself and in the events of the 20th Century we see the same procedure adopted in the history of the movement of Gurdwara Reform.

Thus emerging from his retirement he preached the "Khalsa", the faith of the "pure", the "elect", and the "liberated". He openly attacked all distinctions of caste, a point in his doctrine it is important to remember, if later developments are to be understood, and insisted on the equality of all who would join him. He resuscitated the old baptismal rite of the Sikhs, and proclaimed it as the "pahul", or "gate", by which all might enter the fraternity, while he gave to its members the "parshad", or communion, as a sacrement of union in which the four orders of Hindu Society (the Brahman, or priest; the Kshatriya or warrior; the Vaisiya or trader; the Sudra or menial) should eat from the same dish.

Perceiving that great national weakness resulted from the disunion caused by caste, he proclaimed the social equality of all who were members of the Khalsa.

The higher castes naturally murmured at these reforms, and many of them left him, but the lowers orders rejoiced at the new dispensation and flocked in numbers to his standard. These he inspired with military ardour, with the hope of social freedom and national independence, and with abhorrence of the hated Mohamedan.

CHAPTER V.

The Sikh Religion.

About the time of the Protestant Reformation in Europe, and before either the Moghals or Portuguese had appeared in India, a number of Hindu reformers, whose ideas had been largely influenced by Islam, strove to reform their religion by disowning caste, and by insisting on the unity of the Godhead in lieu of the idolatrous doctrines of the Brahmans.

In the 12th Century, Ramaniya taught that Brahma was the omnipotent and omnicient ruler of the universe. Three hundred years later Vallabha, a disciple of the same school, taught that the human soul was like a spark from the supreme spirit, and though separate, was identical with its essence. From these sects sprang various theistic movements of which the most important are Ramanand, Kabir, and the latter's famous disciple—Baba Nanak.

Kabir himself lived at the beginning of the 15th Century and is believed to have been Mohamedan. Unable to endure the intolerence of his own relegion, he became a disciple of Ramanand, and, like the latter was a true worshipper of Vishnu. He conformed to no rites and denounced idol worship. The gist of his doctrines was that every man was bound to search for a true spiritual guide or "Guru" and having found one, to submit his mind, conscience and body, to his orders.

Nanak, the founder of Sikhism, was an admirer of Kabir, whose utterances are constantly found quoted in the "Adi Granth". Nanak's main idea was the deliverance of Hinduism from its incubus of caste, superstition, and idolatry, while he took exception to much of the ritual and doctrines of the Mohamedan religion. He welcomed persons of all ranks as his followers and taught that the Supreme Being was no respector of persons, and he endeavoured to show a middle way for salvation. He criticised both religions freely and did not attempt, as is so often believed to be the case, to reconcile Hinduism to Islam. He preached that there is only one true God, he condemned idol worship, proclaimed the futility of pilgrimages and declared that the path to salvation lay through good deeds combined with devotion to the Supreme Being. Thus he strove not to found a separate religion as a revolt from Hinduism, but to reconcile the ancient beliefs with the purer creed.

The most important doctrine of the Adi Granth is that of reverence and obedience to God and after Him comes the Guru, whose qualifications are mentioned in it. The practices of ablution, of giving alms, of abstinence from animal food are enjoined. While as ethical teaching, evil speaking, unchastity, anger, covetousness, selfishness, and want of faith, are specially denounced. Nanak taught that the position of a householder as head of a family and engaged in the business of the world was a most honourable one, and strongly discouraged the idea that any special virtue was to be gained by leading an ascetic life.

The Adi Granth is equally hostile to Brahmanism and Islam, yet Nanak did not enjoin the abolition of either his docrine was that all should live as brothers, yet remaining in their own respective faith. This was scrupulously adhered to by his five successors until the sixth, Guru Govind, changed the aspect. He put on two swords, the first as "Piri" indicative of spiritualism, the second as "Miri" or worldly power.

It is unnecessary to follow in great detail the course of the Sikh religion at this period, for it has already been explained in the Chapters on Sikh History and in the lives of the Gurus. Sikhism, in short, continued to exist as a pacific cult until about the end of the seventeenth Century, when the political tyranny of the Musalmans and the social tyranny of the Hindus converted it into a militant creed.

The momentous change was accomplished under the direction of Guru Govind Singh, the tenth and last of the Gurus.

His teaching did not affect any material change in the Sikh creed so far as religious principles were concerned, but he tried to organise the Sikhs into a separate nation, to consolidate their power, and to bring them more completely out of the ranks of Hinduism so as to launch them with greater effect against Islam. With this object he ordained on them the observance of certain rules of conduct and insisted on a definite ceremony of initiation in the baptism or "pahul". Briefly speaking Govind Singh added five points to the religion of Nanak. Firstly, the ceremony of baptism was changed from the "charan ghawal" to that of "Amrit", *i.e.*, the Sikh no longer drank the water in which the feet of his Guru had been placed, but was solemnly initiated in the presence of five believers by drinking a mixture of sugar and water which had been stirred with a steel dagger. Secondly the "Singh" which he had now become, had to carry about his person the five marks beginning with the letter "K" known as the five "kakkas", which has already been described. Thirdly the Singh had to abstain from smoking tobacco. Fourthly he could only eat meat which had been killed by "jhatka", or decapitation. Fifthly he was not to observe distinctions of caste or pay special reverence to Brahmans.

Govind Singh also enjoined upon his followers the necessity for eating the "kara parshad", or communion from a common dish, as an indication that they had abandoned the principles of caste. He forbade the worship of shrines or temples, and the observance of Mohamedan and Hindu rites, such as circumcision, and the wearing of the Brahmanical thread. The use of caps and saffron coloured garments was also forbidden, the former because they were worn by Musalmans, and the latter because saffron was, and still is, the favourite colour of Hindu ascetics. He urged the necessity for wearing steel and a "safa", for bathing in cold water, for combing the hair twice a day and for repeating portions of the Granth Sahib morning, evening, and before meals; infanticide was strictly forbidden and daughters were never to be sold in marriage.

Towards the close of the last century some of these observances were falling into disuse, but latterly owing to various factors there has been a great revival in Sikhism which has made a very marked advance. In 1881 there were 1,706,165 Sikhs as opposed to 4,072,000 in 1931.

The birth status of a Hindu is unalterable of whatever caste he may be; with the Sikh however the reverse is the case. Born of a Sikh father he is not himself counted of the faith until he has received the batism of the "pahul".

To the women who are still largely uneducated, the abstract faith of Sikhism is less attractive than Hinduism with its innumerable Gods and childish legends, which are easily understood, and give to religious exercises a colour and life that the recital of the Granth Sahib can never impart. They are more susceptible to such influences than men and they will thus visit Hindu temples as well as the village Gurdwara. Joining in the Hindu worship a Sikh woman has her share in the outdoor life of the women of the village. Moreover the influence of the Brahman priest weighs more heavily on the women than on the men. He promises her children and that the proper observance of Hindu ritual will secure to her her husband's love, and guarantee her good fortune hereafter. Thus she will do anything and everything for the sake of her child, and it cannot be gainsaid that the men also in some cases are not entirely exempt from the influences of the same sentiments.

The pricipal Sikh prayer are as follows :—

The Asa Di War; *Sukhmani Sahib*; *Japji Sahib*.—Early morning.

Rahras.—Evening.

Keertan Sohla.—At the time of retiring.

Sikhs generally go through their devotions alone, either in the village dharamsala or Gurdwara, or on the banks of any tank or stream in convenient proximity to their homes.

The most important centre of Sikh religious activity is the Golden Temple or Darbar Sahib at Amritsar. The causeway leading to this shrine is approached from quadrangle facing the "Akal Bunga" or "Pavilion of Immortality", through an arched gateway called the "Darshan Darwaza" or "Gate of Prayer". A copy of the "Granth Sahib" is kept in the Temple, watched over by attendants, and from which passages are read morning and evning to the assembled worshippers. These attend in large numbers especially at the great festivals. On the opening of the Sacred Book by the Granthi, silence is maintained. On the conclusion of the reading every man bows his head to the ground as a sign of respect and will repeat "Wah guru ji ka khalsa sri wah guru ji ki fateh—Sat sri Akal". The book is then closed and reverently covered with silks.

The initiation of Sikhs by the administering of the "pahul" is carried out in any Gurdwara of anywhere where 5 Sikhs can be collected together to administer it.

It should be noted that the tendency of modern Sikhism is rather away from Hinduism and not towards it. In theory the Sikh religion enjoined on all Sikhs to rise above all the prejudices and superstitions prevalent amongst Hindus. The Akali movement of Gurdwara reforms has actually suceeded in separating Sikhs from Hindus. There is now evident a general healthy change in the rural Sikh life as far as these old prejudices and superstitions are concerned. This is so far the only bright side of the Akali propaganda. The reason for the relatively more rapid growth of Sikhs during the last decennum undoubtedly lies in the realisation by the Sikhs of the fact that their religion is quite independent of Hinduism, and the conversion to Sikhism of many of the depressed classes who formerly swelled the ranks of the Hindus. An examination of recent statistics reveals that Hindus have decreased in Districts and States which shows a high percentage of increase amongst Sikhs. Statistics of conversion are not available but the figures of Sikh Churahs and Mazhbis registered in the Districts of Ferozepur and Amritsar suggest that the lower classes are being fast absorbed into Sikhism as the result of the efforts of Sikh preachers. Other contributory causes are possibly by frequency of widow remarriage, less disparity in the ages of husband and wife and consequently a higher birth-rate.

The Sikh is free from worship to the village godlings and the sun to which the Hindu is so addicted.

The most important of the village godlings is the "Seetla", or Goddess of "Small pox", every peasant woman will worship her merely for the sake of her child. The Ganges River is worshipped by the Jat peasant but not by the orthodox Sixh; neverthless it comes in for a share of the peoples offerings. It is supposed to flow from Vishnu's feet and to fall on Siva's head and is considered sufficiently sacred as to atone for any sin committed by a person who bathed therein. The River Jumna is also bracketed with the Ganges, but generally speaking bathing in either of these two rivers is a Hindu custom and not a Sikh.

"Khwaja Khizir", or the God of water is worshipped by the Jat cultivator for obvious reasons as water is most necessary for the agriculturist. Small offerings are thus frequently thrown into the village tanks or well. Of the minor divinities the "Bhumra", or God of the homestead is worshipped, for as often as not he is the spirit of the founder of the village; his shrine can be recognised by its domed roof either just outside the village site or close to the village dharamsala.

Once a year the Zamindar will worship the "Jathera", or common ancestor of the clan, to whom a large shrine is erected in the neighbourhood of the village. Villagers who have migrated will periodically make long pilgrimages to worship at the shrine of their ancester, or, if the distance is too great, will bring away a brick from the original shrine and use it as the foundation of a new one.

"Guga Pir" or the serpent deity is worshipped in the month of September ("Naumi") by the Jat cultivator against snake bite, and the efficiency of prayers to his saint in case of snake bite is much believed in. His symbol is a pole, with a tuft of peacocks feathers at the summit.

Of trees and plants the only one that is reverenced by the Jat Sikh is the "pipal", this again is from a common sense point of view owing to the shade which it gives, it is therefore never cut and is often carefully watered.

Among minor religious observances is the reverence for the cow. This is far more highly reverenced by the Hindu than by the Sikh, to the former of whom it is indeed sacred. In the case of the Sikh the reason for this reverence is primarily an economic one. Originally India was an agricutural country; there was no other occupation or industry for the masses but cultivation, and the only animal that existed for their purpose of tilling the land was the bullock. It was therefore considered advisable, by the sages of the time, to preserve the cow for the purposes of breeding, thus serving the double object of maintaining the supply and of keeping down the price of the bullock so that it should be within the reach of every husbandman. In order to ensure that this was done the cow was given a religious sanctity which it maintains to the present day.

The Hindu regards the monkey and peacock as sacred, the former because it is the representative of Hanuman, the monkey God, and the latter because it is the protege of Shanda, one of the minor Hindu divinities. Neither one nor the other of these are sacred to the Sikhs nor should they technically have any objection to their being killed, but the fact remains that they do not do so as a rule themselves. Large numbers of peacocks are frequently met with round and about Sikh villages.

Small pox and kindred pustular diseases are supposed to be caused by a band of seven sisters of whim "Seetla" or "Mata" is the greatest and most virulent. There is generally a shrine to "Seetla" in every village; certainly women and children, as opposed to the men, worship her.

During an epidemic of small-pox no offerings are made, and if the disease has once seized upon a village all offerings are discontinued until it has disappeared, as otherwise the evil will spread. So long, however, as she stays her hand, nothing is too good for the Goddess.

"Bhuts" and "chorels" are the spirits of men and women who have died violent deaths either by accident, suicide or capital punishment without the subsequent performance of proper funeral ceremonies. A bad man when dead, is said to have been a "Bhut", while a woman who dies in childbirth is said to be born a Churel. A very ugly woman is nicknamed a "churel" while a similarly afficted man is called a "Bhut" in general talk. Sweepers if buried mouth upwards are said to be sure to become "Bhuts". The small whirlwinds that raise pillars of dust in the hot weather are supposed to be Bhuts going to bathe in the Ganges. They are mostly feared by women and children.

"Pret" is practically another name for "Bhut" and is supposed to be the spirit of those who are reformed or crippled, or of persons who have not been dead for a year.

There are many petty superstitions of the Punjab which are more or less in vogue amongst the Sikh population, but they are tending to die out and orthodox Sikhs do not believe in them. To sneeze is auspicious, for it implies that you are unlikely to die for some time; at the same time it is not considered auspicious for a man to move or go when he hears a sneeze as it is considered that the one who sneezes will not get the object of his desire, and that he will be unlucky.

Odd numbers are lucky with the exception of three and thirteen. "Terah tin" is the Punjab equivalent for sixes and sevens.

As is natural there are many superstitions connected with agriculture. These vary with Districts and are believed into a greater or lesser extent according to each individual, in exactly the same way as in the West, and it is not considered necessary to deal with the subject at greater length.

CHAPTER VI.

SIKH SECTS AND SUB-DIVISIONS OF JAT SIKHS.

Explanation of Kesdhari and Sajdhari Sikhs.—It has already been explained that Sikhism is of two kinds—the simple theism of Nanak which was marked by no outward signs, and the warlike faith of Govind, which was indicated by the long hair and certain customs, such as abstinence from tobacco and the assumption of the title "Singh".

The "Nanak Panthis" of to-day are known roughly as Sikhs who are not Singhs, *i.e.*, they are followers of the early Gurus who do not think it necessary to follow the ceremonial and social observances inculcated by Guru Gobind. Their characteristics are mainly negative. They do *not* forbid smoking; they do *not* insist on long hair, or the other four "Kakkas", they are *not* baptised with the "Pahul" and they do *not* even in theory reject the authority of the Brahmans.

The chief external difference between the "Nanak Panthi" or "Sajdhari" Sikhs and the followers of Guru Govind Singh, is in the disposal of the hair; the former, like the Hindu, shaves all but the scalp-lock, called "Bodi" or "choti", and hence is often known as a Mona, or shaven Sikh, or a Sajdhari, to distinguish him from Gobind Singh, or true Sikh, who always wears long hair and is known as a Keshdhari. The "Nanak Panthi" in fact, is little more than a lax Hindu who has been influenced by the teaching of the Sikh Gurus, and pays reverence to the sacred book the "Granth".

Even amongst the Keshdhari however, a large number allow their sons to have their hair cut, up to about 15 years of age, when they take the "Pahul" and begin to wear the "Kes", but all the time the boys are as good Sikhs as the parents. Then again in the same family, one brother may be a Keshdhari, another a Sajdhari, and the third while wearing the Kes may be a sarwaria who smokes the hukka. In numerous cases the father is a Keshdhari, the son does not wear the Kes, and the grandson is again initiated and becomes a follower of the precepts of Guru Govind Singh. There are several instances in which the wife of a Sajdhari Sikh vows to make her first son Keshdhari. The younger sons remain Sajdharis. A Keshdhari marries the daughter of a Sajdhai and the daughters of Keshdhari marry Sajdharis. Indeed intermarriages between Keshdhari and Sajdhari Sikhs and ordinary Hindus are still matters of everyday occurrence, although the modern movement has succeeded to a considerable extent in confining the followers of Guru Gobind Singh in a water tight compartment, restricting intermarriages with non-keshdharis and enforcing the initiation on all male descendants of Keshdharis. To this day however, instances of Sajdhari sons of Keshdhari fathers, particulaly in the educated community, are fairly numerous.

In an interesting book written by an authoritative author on the principles of the Sikh Gurus, he has collected references from the Adi Granth to show how the belief in Hindu incarnations and in Hindu mythology pervades the utterances of Guru Nanak, Tegh Bahadur, and of Namder and Kabir, of which the book is full. References to all shades of belief from the trinity (Brahma, Vishnu and Shiva) to the deeds of the Avataras, the appearance of Bhagwan in response to the prayers of devotees, the restoration to life of the "King's Cow", and the injunction to recite the name of Rama are found in abundance. The "Japji Sahib" is full of Hindu ideas and the "Chandipath", composed by Guru Gobind Singh, shows how staunch a devotee of the Goddess Durga he was.

Difficulty in differentiating between Sikhism and Hinduism.—The above facts are quoted to show why it is so difficult to differentiate Sikhism from Hinduism. In considering the question, the fact must not be lost sight of that in the religious life of a Hindu there two fundamental principles, namely (1) the belief in a set of doctrines and (2) the adherence to the instructions of a Guru. The Guru need not be alive.

If he has left a set of instructions and rules of conduct as a legacy, the followers of those become the disciples of that Guru. Baba Nanak is very strong in vindicating the greatness of the Guru and identifying him with God (Japji Sahib), for his "Guru" was "Bhagwan" Himself.

To the Sikhs the words of the "Satguru" (true Guru) are the scriptures. But so is the case with the Hindus, who maintain "Guru Brahma, Guru Vishnu, Guru Sakshat Maheshwarah, Gurureva Jagat Sarvam Tasmai Shri Gurave Namah" (The Guru is Brahma, Vishnu and Shiva manifested, he is the whole universe Homage to that exalted Guru).

This explains the apparently double relegious adherence of Hindus who also profess to be Sikhs.

Census Variations in numbers of Sikhs.—The following figures indicate the variations in the numbers of Sikhs from one census to another.

Year.	Males.	Females.	Total.
1881	964,436	741,729	1,706,165
1891	1,036,525	812,846	1,849,371
1901	1,182,296	920,600	2,102,896
1911	1,651,595	1,232,134	2,883,729
1921	..		3,110,060
1931	2,270,946	1,800,678	4.071,624

The increase between 1901 and 1911 was quite abnormal, particularly in view of the fact that there was a general decline in population in consequence of the excess of death rate over birth rate. A considerable portion of the difference was however due to a more extensive scope of the term Sikh in the census held in 1911.

For the purpose of comparison with the figures of previous censuses, Keshdharis and Sajdharis should be saparately dealt with, the former figures corresponding to the statistics of 1901 and the latter representing the section of Sikhs, which was in the census of 1901, included in Hindus. The Keshdharis aggregate 2,415,478, and the Sajdharis number 468,251. So the increase compared with the figures of 1901 is Keshdharis 15 per cent., total Sikhs 37 per cent.

The gain would appear to have occurred by acretions from the Hindus. It was not possible to ascertain the number of people who took the "Pahul" in the decade ending 1911, but the Singh Sabhas were very active in enforcing the tenets of Guru Gobind Singh on all followers of Guru Nanak, whether Sikhs or Hindus, and they were greatly assisted in the Army. The separatist movement also succeeded to a considerable extent in dictating the observance of Guru Gobind Singh's tenets, which greatly raised the status of Keshdhari Sikhs.

The sects of Sikhs according to the census returns (1921) are as follows :—

Sects.	Keshdhari.	Sajdhari.
Unspecified	1,992,386	209,770
Gobind Sing	42,678	..
Hazuri	246,384	1,613
Kuka Namdhari	4,037	..
Mazbhi	2,305	..
Nihang	3,954	..
Nanakpanthi	22,486	14,179
Panjpiria	4,592	..
Ram Dasi	10,568	209
Ram Rai	605	..
Sarwaria (Sultanis)	14,259	2,383
Jat Khalsa (including Khalsa)	531,290	..
Udasi	776	66
Radhaswami	..	378
Baba Jowahir Singh	1,437	440*
Baba Kalu	966	..
Nirankari	574	995*

Sects.	Keshdhari.	Sajdhari.
Jogi	..	333*
Kaladhari	..	187*
Namder	..	434*
Baba Gurditta	1,741	206*
Nirmala	378	..*
Basant Sahi	655	..*
Niranjam	778	..*
Mahader	251	..*
Barbhag Singh	..	6,383*
Arya	..	63†
Balmiki	..	1,120†
Lalbegi	..	1,595†
Sanatan Dharm	..	4,425†
Dev Dharm	..	25†
Devi Upasak	..	94†
Sewak Darya	..	11†

Details by Sects.—Gobind Singhis.—The followers of Guru Gobind Singh. All Sikhs wearing the Kesh and observing the other restrictions enjoined by Guru Gobind Singh who do not belong to any other specified sect. describe themselves as Gobind Singhis. In 1891 their strength was 839,138 but in 1901 only 396,056 returned themselves as such; in 1911 this had further still fallen to 107,827 but these figures were for British territory only. The decrease is accounted for by the large number of unspecified Keshdhari Sikhs, and the Tat Khalsa or Khalsa.

Hazuris.—At the same time many of the followers of Guru Gobind Singh have put themselves down as Hazuris. They are those Sikhs who have paid a visit to Hazur Sahib in Hyderabad (Deccan) where Guru Gobind Singh breathed his last, and have been initiated there. It is really a title of religious merit similar to that of Haji amongst the

* Miscellaneous Sikh Sects.
† Sects analogus to other religious.

Mohamedans. The initiation at Hazur Sahib is supposed to confer great religious sanctity, at the same time imposing certain restrictions. The orthodox Hazuris are supposed to go about in yellow or blue garments and very often cook their own food, eating from nobody else's hands. The orthodox type is however on the wane.

Kukas.—The Kuka movement appears to be on the decline owing to the disfavour with which the followers of this sect are looked upon in political circles and the opening created by the Tat Khalsa movement for religious zeal

The "Kuka" or "Shouters were founded by an Udasi Arora named Bulaka Singh of Hazro in the Attock District about the middle of the last century. His principle object appears to have been to break the power which the Brahmans had acquired over the Sikhs. After his death the doctrines of the sect were disseminated by a carpenter named Ram Singh who proclaimed he was the incarnation of Govind Singh the latter was the only true Guru; that no Brahmans were ever to be employed; and that all worship save the reading of the Granth was prohibited.

Establishing his headquarters at Baini in the Ludhiana District, disciples began to flock to him and from the proceeds of their offerings he was able to erect a large "Dehra" and to travel about in considerable state. Early in 1872 a gang of his followers, after working themselves up into a state of religious frenzy started off on a raid in the Patiala and Malerkotla States. The State troops pursued and surrounded them after some desultory fighting, in which several men were killed. Ram Singh was deported to Rangoon, where he died in 1887, being succeeded by his brother Budh Singh.

This sect is known as Kukas because unlike ordinary Sikhs they permit themselves to fall into a state of frenzy during their religious exercises, shaking their heads and reciting their prayers in a loud voice. They finish their devotions with a loud cry of "Sat Sri Akal"—God is true—. Their religious meetings are said to end sometimes in disgusting orgies. They sometimes try to conceal the fact of their belonging to this sect by calling themselves "Naindharis". They are found chiefly in the Jullundur, Ludhiana, Ferozepore, Amritsar, Gujranwala and Sialkot Districts and the Patiala State. Kukas are supposed to avoid meat and spirits; many refuse to believe in the death of Ram Singh, and live in expectation of his early reappearance. In 1900 they totalled 10,000. In other respects they are only Puritans of the school of Govind with a more marked hatred of Mohamedans and tobacco than most other sects of the Sikhs. Their enlistment, needless to say, is strictly prohibited . They may be regarded as a puritanical Sikh sect and differ from ordinary Sikhs in the manner of wearing the turban, and in carrying a necklace or woollen cord, divided into knots which serve as beads for prayers.

Nihangs or Akalis.—These owe their origin to the express patronage of Guru Govind. The name means 'immortal' because they are followers of the "Akal Purkh" or "Immortal God" They generaly recevied account of their origin is that Guru Govind, seeing his infant son playing before him with his turban peaked in the fashion adopted by the Akalis, blessed him, and instituted a sect which should follow the same custom, though some say that Ajit Singh was the founder. The "Akalis" first came into prominence during the reign of Ranjit Singh. Their headquarters were at Amritsar where they constituted themselves the guardians of the temple and the faith. They were the bravest and the most unruly soldiers in the Sikh Army, and their qualities were skillfully turned to account by Ranjit Singh who employed them with success against the Pathan enemies across the Indus. The Akali is distinguished very conspicously by his blue dress and peaked turban which is often surmounted with steel quoits. He is most particular with regard to the "five Kakkas" and in preserving every outward form prescribed by Govind Singh. They do not eat meat or drink spirits, but are immoderate in their consumption of "Bhang". In other respects they are such purists that they will avoid Hindu rites even at their marriage ceremonies. The sect is found chiefly in Amritsar and at Kiratpur in the Hoshiarpur District where there is a shrine to the memory of their leader Phula Singh.

Mazbhis.—Are Sikhs proper. A description of their origin appears under castes. The Mazbhis in the past have proved themselves, and are, at the present time, extremely good soldiers. The Pioneer Regiments—old designation, 23rd, 32nd, 34th—into which they recruited have a proud record of service in many campaigns. An authoritative writer remarks "The general reluctance of the low caste Hindu to elevate himself by becoming a Sikh may perhaps be explained by the historical exception of the Mazbhis". These Sikhs the descendants of converts from the despised sweeper caste were welcomed by the Khalsa at a time when they were engaged in a desparate struggle with the forces of Islam. But when the Sikhs dominated the Punjab they found that the equality their religion promised them existed in theory rather than fact. They occupied much the same position among the Jat and Khalsa descended Sikhs, as their ancestors the sweepers enjoyed among Hindus. According to the census report of 1921 the Mazbhi population numbered 2,305 (but this in view of the 1911 census is presumed an error for 22,305). They have taken to husbandry and have been declared as a separate agricultural tribe in the Districts of Gujranwala and Lyallpur.

Nanak Panthis.—The followers of Guru Nanak are called Nanak Panthis; and persons designating themselves such are found among both the Hindus and Sikhs. In one way all Sikhs are Nanak Panthis, as the religion originated with Guru Nanak, but those who have attached themselves particularly to the tenets of Guru Gobind Singh, call themselves Gobind Singhi, as described above, while the adherents of the other Sikh Gurus, or their descendants, or the followers of certain religious orders among the Sikhs, have adopted specific titles. The following figures with regard to Nanak Panthis are given as an illustration of the difficulties attached to classifying the various sects and to the changes in numbers of the various sects which are constantly taking place.

Comparative Table.

Nanak Panthis.		1921.	1911.	1891.
Hindu		..	21,756	542,621
Sikh	Sajdhari	14,179	176,036	..
	Keshdhari	22,486	99,601	438,653

In 1911 most of the Hindus, following the teachings of Guru Nanak who are known roughly as Sikhs other than Singhs, have now classed themselves as Sikhs, and, consequently, the number of Nanak Panthis who have preferred to give Hinduism as their religion, has fallen as shown above. At the same time the term appears to have come into disfavour among the Keshdhari Sikhs who have appeared under other titles reducing the strength of Nanak Panthi Sikhs from 438,653 to 26,665.

Panj Pirias.—In the census of 1891 seven hundred and three Sikhs were returned as belonging to this particualr sect. In that of 1911, 10,372 were so shown, while the number fell to 4,592 in 1921.

Ram Dasia.—A Ram Dasia means a follower of Guru Ram Das, the fourth Sikh Guru. Most of the followers of this sect are Chamars.

Comparative table of strength.

Ram Dasias	1911.	1921.	1931.
Hindu	199,465	Untraceable.	12,235
Sikh	10,312	10,777	67,080

The large decrease is due partly to a confusion of the name with Raidasias (the appearance of the two names being identical in Urdu) and largely to the fact that the tract where the followers of this sect abound, has suffered heavily from epidemics. It is also stated that a large number of Ram Dasias are going over to the tenets of Guru Gobind Singh and joining the ranks of the Khalsa Panth. The sect is strongest in the Eastern Punjab, where the Chamar weavers are in abundance.

Ram Rai.—The founder of this sect was Guru Ram Rai. The Ram Rais came from all classes of society, but the sect is disappearing gradually, as its adherents who differ little from other Sikhs are being absorbed into the Khalsa Panth.

Comparative table of strength.

Ram Rais.		
	Hindus.	Sikhs.
1891	52,317	30,376
1911	2,001	26,576
1921	..	605

The decrease in this sect is phenomenal. The Ram Rais are confined chiefly to the Districts of Hoshiarpur, Jullundur and Ludhiana.

They are followers of Ram Rai, the elder brother of Guru Har Kishan, who was excluded from the office of Guru on account of his tendency to keep on good terms with the Moghal authorities, for which he was awarded a "Jagir" in Dehra Dun. As the breach between the Mohamedans and Sikhs widened the relations of Ram Rai and his followers towards other Sikhs became more and more strained and in the days of Gobind Singh the mutual hatred of the two parties become very intense.

The Ram Rais, while acknowledging the other Gurus, refused to recognise Gurus Hargobind and Gobind Singh, and although they appear to lay some emphasis on the fact of their being Sikhs, they do not preserve the Kesh, and are expressly disclaimed by their orthodox Khalsa brethren.

Members of this sect belong chiefly to the labouring and agricultural classes.

Sarwaria or Sultanis.—The most common name of this sect is Sarwaria but it is also known as Sultani, and in some places by other names such as Nigahia, Lakhdata, Dhunkalia, etc.

The comparative strengths are as follows :—

	Hindus.	Sikhs.		
1891	689,772	34,789		
1911	230,988	Sajdharis	25,880	79,085
		Keshdharis	53,205	
1921	Not traceable	Sajdharis	2,383	16,642
		Keshdharis	14,259	

This sect comprise the followers of Sakhi Sultan Sarwar. The worship of Sultan Sarwar is one of the numberless signs of Musalman influence which we come across in the daily life of the Hindu peasant of the Punjab. The traditions regarding his birth are rather vague, but the saint's family is believed to have emigrated from Bagdad to the Punjab early in the 12th Century, where, though himself a Mohamedan, he is said to have enlisted the Hindu. God Bhairon as his messenger.

The cult of the Sultanis is unsectarian in its creed, plastic in its observances and is in fact a sort of compromise between Hinduism and Islam. The shrines are known as 'Pirkhanas' or 'Thans'. The unpretending little edifices are to be seen outside many hamlets in the Central and Eastern Punjab. They generally consist of a hollow plastered brick cube, covered with a small dome with low minarets at the four corners. The Guardians of the shrines called 'Bharais' are generally Mohamedans and go round on Thursday beating drums and collecting offerings. The principle "Sultani" shrine is at Nigha in the Dera Ghazi Khan District and thousands of Sikh, Hindu and Mahomedan pilgrims flock to that fair which is held there annually, many of them in the hope of, or in gratitude for, the birth of a son, the boon which is supposed to be specially the gift of the saint.

The two religions of the Hindu Jats, *viz.*, Sikhism and the worship of Sultan Sarwar do not really differ very much in practice. "Sultanis" are constantly taking the "Pahul" and the conversion makes no difference to them except that they have to give up smoking. A "Sultani" will generally call himself a Sikh (which is here used in its original sense of "discipline" and means that the Sultani Jat is a disciple of Sakhi Sarwar, just as a Nanak Panthi Sikh is a disciple of Baba Nanak) and does not seem to recognise much difference between himself and the follower of Govind, except that the later cannot enjoy his pipe.

The only observance which distinguishes Sarwar's followers from ordinary Hindus is that they will not eat the flesh of animals killed by "Jhatka". The Sultani if he eats meat at all must eat animals whose throats have been cut in the orthodox Musalman manner.

Tat Khalsa.—(Including Khalsa). The term Tat Khalsa dates back to the time of Baba Banda, one of the trusted disciples of Guru Govind Singh, who, after the latter's death, proclaimed himself as the eleventh Guru.

Those who accepted his pretension came to be known as "Bandai-Khalsa" but others who adhered to the command of Guru Gobind Singh that the "Granth" was thereafter to be their Guru gave themselves the name "Tat" (pure)—Khalsa.

With the fall of Banda Bahadur his following gradually melted away and the term Tat Khalsa also fell into disuse. It was revived at the beginning of the present century by the class known as the Neo-Sikh Party (a term disliked by the Sikhs of that class, but which was hit upon by those, who, in the absence of any better term, had to find one to denote the reformed section of the Sikh community). This party are wholly devoted to the tenets of the 10 Gurus and do not like their religions to be corrupted by association with any non-Sikh belief.

The term "Tat Khalsa" appears to have been taken up by the Hindus who are opposed to the separatist movement of the Sikhs, as a nickname, which is resented by the reform movement.

The members of this group, who numbered 531,290 in the 1921 census, diregard caste and restrictions of eating and drinking, and aim at establishing a universal brotherhood amongst the Sikhs, with views, liberal in some respects, orthodox in others, based mainly upon convenience. The movement is more or less reactionary and although averse to fanaticism it enjoins a very straight "esprit-de-corps". The chief centre of the movement is Amritsar which alone supplies a membership of 125,000 males and 91,000 females out of the whole total.

Udasi.—This sect is an ascetic order which was founded by Sri Chand, the eldest son of Guru Nanak. It is recruited from all classes and has its principal shrine of Dera Baba Nanak in the Gurdaspur District. Nevertheless Udasi initiates are becoming rare. The influence of modern times militates very strongly against taking up religious orders. They pay special attention to the "Adi Granth", are generally celibate, and will eat food from any Hindu. The initiation is simple. The prentice has to wash the great toes of five Udasis assembled for the purpose and drink the water so obtained. They are taught the "Bani" (instructions) of Baba Sri Chand son of Guru Nanak. The Guru changes the disciples name and thenceforth he is called by the new name. Their service consists of a ringing of bells and the blare of instruments, chanting of hymns and waving of lights before the "Adi Granth" and portrait of Nanak. They are by no means uniform in their customs. Some are Kesdharis and others Sajdharis and some wear caste marks. They generally burn their dead and subsist on voluntary offerings. This is one of the reasons of their decline in numbers as begging is becoming less profitable, compared with the lucrativeness of professions, for the charitable disposition of the Hindus is now finding other outlets. The large institutions supported mainly by private charity now find it difficult to maintain large numbers of Sadhus, owing partly to high prices and partly to the curtailment of pecuniary assistance.

In the Malwa Districts the "Udasis" are mostly Jats by origin and are found in possession of the "Dharmsalas" where they distribute food for such as come for it, and read the "Granth" both of Nanak and Govind Singh. The head of each "Udasi" brotherhood is called a "Mahant" and his disciples "Chelas". The ordinary dress is "Bhagwa" (salmon coloured) clothes; many however go entirely naked except for a waist cloth, and rub ashes all over their body. The majority are ascetics, but some engage in secular pursuits.

"Udasis" are most numerous in the Jullundur, Rohtak, and Ferozepore Districts and only totalled about 832 in the 1921 census.

Radhaswami.—This sect is one of very recent growth and its followers are very few in number. Nevertheless it is unique and deserves mention.

The sect was founded by Seth Shiv Diyal Singh in 1861, who was known as "Swamiji Maharaj". He was succeeded in 1878 by Rai Bahadur Salig Ram and called Hazoor Sahib by his devotees. It was under the latter's leadership that the sect came into prominence. He died in 1898.

The strength of the sect was not ascertained in 1901. The figures of 1891 compared with 1911 and 1921 are as follows :—

	Sikhs.
1891	4
1911	424
1921	378

The teaching of the sect are esoteric and three planes (Pind, Biranand and Dyaldis) are recognised instead of five in the Hindu philosophy. The school derives all knowledge in the astral and higher planes through the highly developed sense of hearing instead of through the sixth sense—mind—of the Hindus. The attempt of the school is to justify all its teachings on a scientific basis. They consequently reject all revealed books and profess that the doctrines and practices taught by them are completely new and not contained in any other faith. They believe in re-incarnation and hence in "Karma". Exaltation to the abode of the supreme spirit (Radhaswami) is salvation which implies separate existence of the liberated spirit on that highest plane. The practice taught is that the elevation of the spirit is achieved purely by meditation.

The sect appears to be growing and the assurance that all the teachings are based on rational grounds and not on mere hearsay forms a great attraction to the educated classes.

Miscellaneous Sects.

Baba Jowahir Singh.—Baba Jowahir Singh, a Sikh saint, has numerous followers in the North Eastern Punjab amongst both Hindus and Sikhs.

Comparative Table of Strength.

	Sikhs.
1891	3,204
1911	1.877

The sect appears to be on the decline.

The saint was one of the disciples of Guru Amar Das, the third Sikh Guru. There is a temple at Khatkar Kalan in the Jullundur District, dedicated to his name, and a pond in the Ajmergarh Pergunnah of the Patiala State is held sacred to his memory. This pond known as Joharji is said to be of great sanctity, and was supposed to be associated with the death of Sarwan at the hands of Dasharatha, father of Rama. The pond was possessed by a man-eating Rakshasa (Demon) named Mahiya. The Baba killed him and rid the place of his oppression. The "Phauri" (wooden instrument for removing litter) with which he struck the demon is preserved in the temple built by the late Maharaja Narendra Singh of Patiala. But Mahiya the demon is said to have prayed to the Baba Sahib for a blessing, and this was granted, the Baba assuring him that all the pilgrims would worship him as well. All pilgrims therefore, after making their obeissance at the temple of Baba Jowahir Singh offer a goat in the name of Mahiya.

Nirmalas.—The Nirmalas though Govindi Sikhs have by degrees rid themselves of the main distinguishing marks of the Khalsa faith, and are gradually returning to a pure form of orthodox Hinduism. The Nirmalas like the Akalis, date from the time of Guru Govind Singh, though they allege that their order was founded by Guru Nanak himself. It is said that the Guru sent three followers to Benares to acquire a knowledge of Sanskrit, and that, on their return, he blessed them as being the only learned men amongst the Sikhs, and called them Nirmala (spotless). They were allowed to take the "Pahul" and founded the order of Nirmala Sadhus. The fraternity had at first great influence amongst the Sikhs, but their taste for Sanskrit literature led them to re-adopt many of the customs of the Shastras. They gave up the use of meat and spirits and assumed the ordinary ochre coloured dress of the Hindu "fakir" which was strictly prohibited to the followers of Govind Singh, and some of them are now only distinguishable from Udasis by wearing the "Kesh" or uncut hair.

The headquarters of the sect are at Hardwar. Their numbers appear to be steadily declining. They are regarded as unorthodox by most classes of Sikhs, and are especially disliked by the Akalis with whom they have a standing quarrel with regard to the right to worship at the great Sikh shrine at Naderh or Abcharnagar in the Dekkan.

Niranjani.—This sect was founded in the 16th Century by Baba Handal, who was cook and tax collector to Amar Das, the third Guru, and worshipped the Almighty under the name of Niranjan, or "The Bright One". His followers are styled Niranjanis. They are rapidly declining in numbers. Those who still exist are found chiefly in the Jullundur, and Amritsar Districts and Kapurthala State.

Their chief claim to notice is their rejection of the ordinary funeral customs of Sikhs and Hindus. They reject all "Kiria Karams" and funeral rites, and do not send the bones of their dead to the Ganges. They have special marriage rites of their own and do not reverence Brahmans. Their principle shrine is at Jandiala.

Nirankari.—The Nirankaris are believers in one God. They are nothing more or less than staunch followers of Guru Nanak.

This sect was founded by a Khatri of Peshawar named Bhai Dial, who settled in Rawalpindi about 70 years ago. He died thereabout 1870, and was succeeded in the office of Guru by his two sons. The word "Nirankar" means properly "The Formless One" and was a term commonly used by Nanak for describing the Deity. In addition to being believers in one God, the Nirankaris avoid the adoration of idols, make no offerings to Brahmans or to the dead, abstain strictly from flesh and wine, and are said to pay strict attention to the truth in all things. Their sacred book is the "Adi Granth" of Baba Nanak. Their marriages are not performed according to the Hindu "Dharma Shastras" and the bride and bridegroom, instead of circumambulating the sacred fire, walk round a copy of the "Adi Granth". The ceremony is conducted by a Granthi instead of a Brahman, and "widow marriage" is not only allowed, but often takes place among them. At funerals they dispense with all Hindu ceremonials, and instead of mourning look upon death as an occasion for rejoicing. Besides the usual places of Sikh pilgrimage the "Nirankaris" look with special reverence upon a pool in the park at Rawalpindi to which they have given the name of Amritsar. The sect however appears to be fast disappearing judging by the returns, as follows :—

	Sikhs.
1891	46,610
1911	1,569

Mahadev.—This sect is a rapidly declining one and totals only 251 in the census report of 1911.

Mahadev means "Shiv Upasak" *i.e.*, a worshipper of Shiva.

This sect may be regarded as one of those analogous to the Hindu religion.

Jogi.—In the 1911 census this sect numbered only 333 Sajdhari Sikhs. As a sect they worship "Bhairon" and appear to be at a considerable discount. One seldom hears of additions to the order except at Bohar in Rohtak.

Kaladharis.—This sect also appears to be rapidly on the decline; in the 1911 census they only totalled 187 Sajdhari Sikhs. They are the followers of the Bairagi Mahants of that designation belonging to the Hoshiarpur District.

Sects analogous to other religions.

The sects analogous to other religions are as follows. Their strengths in the 1911 census were :—

Arya	63
Balmiki	1,120
Lalbegi	1,595
Sanatan Dharm	4,425
Dev Dharm	25
Devi Upasak	94

It is not proposed to enter into detail with regard to these; put briefly the "Balmiki" and "Lalbegi" Sikhs are Chuhras, who also read the "Granth Sahib" or respect the teachings of Guru Nanak in consequence of residence in the Sikh villages. The Sikh "Sanatandharmis" are those, who, although true Sikhs still observe the Hindu customs and at times (particularly of marriage and death) worship the Hindu Gods and follow Hindu ceremonies.

Some of the staunchest "Devdharmis" are Sikhs and have returned their faith as a sect of Sikhism rather than that of Hinduism.

The Devi Upasak Sikhs practice Devi worship but are rapidly declining due partly to the fact that they are regarded with some contempt by the stricter Sikhs of the Punjab.

CHAPTER VI.

PART II.

SUB-DIVISIONS OF JAT SIKHS.

To those who have no experience of Sikhs, a Sikh is just a Sikh. and no differentiation is made between the cultivating class, *i.e.*, the Jat Sikh, and the non-cultivating class such as the Arora, and Khatri, or trading classes, of Sikhs, and the Chamars, Chhimbas, Chuaras, Jhinwars, etc., who are the menial classes of Sikhs, and who are not enrolled as combatants in our Indian Army.

In the present chapter it is intended only to deal with the Jat Sikh.

It is, however, also perhaps not generally realised that this tribe is divided into innumerable sub-divisions, or clans ("Gots"), who are scattered all over the main recruiting areas of the "Malwa", the "Manjha" and the "Doaba"; it is the object of this chapter, therefore, to try and make clear who all these are, with the salient features of their origin and characteristics, and their distribution by Districts in the Punjab.

This method has been adopted in order to give information in a more easily accessible form to those who enlist their recruits from a certain area, than if each clan was taken as a whole for the Punjab.

Figures from various censuses have been quoted in order to show the numerical importance of each clan, and to assist those recruiting, and other regimental officers who may proceed on this duty, as to what they may expect to find in the various tehsils. Numbers will vary slightly with each census in future, but the figures quoted will always form a sound working basis.

It should not be lost sight of that each individual takes the greatest pride in his clan, and a comparison of the various merits, demerits and peculiarities of the various clans form an interesting study by itself.

The multitude of "Gots", or clans, among the Jat Sikhs is a very remarkable feature. Not only do adjoining villages belong to different "Gots", but inside each village will generally be found two or three sub-divisions of distinct origin. This is accounted for by the manner in which the country was colonized. In the history of each village it will be seen that the founders came, in comparatively recent times, from different parts of the country, or at all events from different parent villages, and belonged to different "Gots"; they united merely for their own convenience, the common tie of belonging to the same tribe being sufficient. To the south and west of the Ludhiana District as an instance, we find that the Jats came in bodies, and villages belonging to the same "Got" lie either in groups, or within short distances of each other. Thus the "Sidhu" and "Gils" appear to have come eastward in large parties, and to have settled down in adjoining or alternate villages in the western part of Jagraon. In the Amritsar

District the "Sindhu" Jats, which are the strongest clan in the district are found in detached villages, at different points of all three tehsils composing this district, but muster specially strong in the S. W. corner of Tarn Taran. The central village of this clan is Sirhali Kalan, and from this they founded and peopled the ring of villages which lie round it.

It may generally be stated, however, that the rule throughout the Sikh area is variety of "Gots", and the few groups that occur of villages belonging to one "Got" are the exception. The reason for this apparently is that throughout the eastern parts, especially in the neighbourhood of Sirhind and Ludhiana, the Imperial authority was always strong enough to protect its subjects, who settled down in small villages as they came; while in the west it was less felt, and people of one "Got" had to collect in large villages for protection.

The Malwa.

Ludhiana District.

The leading "Gots" in this district, and in particular to the Ludhiana and Jagraon tehsils, are the Garewal, Gil, Sidhu, Dhaliwal, Dhillon, Sekhon and Bhander.

The Garewal Jats.—First in rank are the Garewals. This "Got" holds about 75 villages, of which some are very large, near Ludhiana, in a group, and members of it are also to be found scattered over the district. They trace their descent to a Rajput Raja, Rikh, who, according to the tradition, came from the south and settled in Kalur in the hills. "Bairsi", son of Rikh, left Kalur. and settled at Nayabad to the south of Ludhiana, where he contracted a marriage with a Jatni, called "Rupkaur", and had to start a "Got" for himself, as his brothers would have nothing further to do with him. His son was "Gare", whence the name of the "Got", but another fanciful name was "Karewal" from "Karewa". The descendants of Bairsi gradually spread over the country to the south-west of Ludhiana. The "Garewals" are admitted by the other "Gots" to be at the top of the social scale, and are known as "Sahu" log, *i.e.*, "superior". Their women do not take part in field work, in which respect they are unique amongst all the other Sikh "Gots", whilst their girls are sought in marriage by the best families of Sirdars. The Garewal families of Kila Raipur, Gujarwal and Naurangwal had a sort of local authority at the close of the 18th Century, and are in consequence the proudest of the Jats. They are good cultivators, but their holdings are very small, which induces them to take freely to military service, where they make excellent soldiers, and perhaps are amongst the few who in the changing conditions of modern times still look upon it as a matter of "izzat". The area which they inhabit might almost be said to be an entirely military one. Nearly every family has one or more pensioners, or serving soldiers amongst its numbers, and the complete changes from mud huts to "pukka" houses which has taken place in the last ten years, testifies to the money which the sepoys' savings has brought to their villages. A widow can marry her "dewar" (husband's younger brother) or "jeth" (husband's elder brother) only. This is also the rule amongst the Gils and Sidhus.

The Gils.—The Gils are the next best "Got" to the Garewal, and indeed between the two there is very little to choose. They own about 50 villages, mostly in the Jagraon tehsil. They also enlist very freely, and rendered excellent service during the War, coming forward almost to a man. The Gils claim descent from "Surajbansi Rajputs", their ancestor being a king of "Gharmela" in the South, whose son Akaura took to agriculture. His son again, named Gil, founded the Got which moved northward by degrees, and came into the district 250—300 years ago, it is said, in the reign of Shah Jehan. The Gils are first rate agriculturists, but their habits are generally extravagant.

The Sidhus.—The Sidhus have a good many villages in the Jagraon tehsil and here are of the "Barar" section. They are a well-known "Got" throughout the Lahore and Amritsar districts also, and a further description of them appears under Amritsar. They originally came from the south-west, it is believed, from Faridkot, about 200—300 years ago.

The Dhaliwals.—This is also a good clan of high social standing, and possesses a large number of villages lying about Pakhowal, and are found in the Jagraon tehsil mostly. Their ancestor was a Rajput who came from Jaisalmir, and settled in Kangar in Nabha territory becoming a Jat. From Kangar his descendants came into the Ludhiana District under the Rais and their Sikh successors. They are scattered about all over the Phulkian States, and extend as far eastward as Ferozepore.

The Bhanders.—The Bhanders are centred chiefly in the small zamindari of the Raja of Malaudh, where they own upwards of 20 villages. They are the descendants of "Bhander", who was reported to be the off-spring of the union of a Rajput and a woman of inferior caste. He settled in Bhatinda in Patiala territory, and thence his descendants migrated to Rao Siana in Malaudh. They make excellent soldiers, and as a rule enlist freely.

The Sekhons.—The Sekhons are scattered over the district, and are to be met with all over the Malwa area. They had a similar origin to the Bhanders, and are reported to have come from Bhadour in Patiala territory.

The Dhilons.—The Dhilons are scattered all over the district, coming originally from west of the Sutlej, further particulars of this clan are given under Amritsar District.

Minor sub-divisions.—Minor sub-divisions of Jat Sikhs found in the Ludhiana District are Gandhu, Man, Sandhu, Mangat, Chima, Rathi. They are found scattered over the district, usually holding single villages, or sub-divisions thereof.

The other sub-divisions which are found in this district are as follows :—

Ludhiana District.

Jat Sikh Sub-divisions.	District Total 1911.	Distribution by Tehsils.		
		Ludhiana.	Samrala.	Jagraon.
Aulak	685	49	68	568
Bains	247	129	39	79
Bal	1,261	977	..	284
Bhangu	1,144	505	639	..
Bopa Rai	1,477	604	36	837
Bhullar	1,770	1,051	106	713
Chahil	4,538	3,598	300	640
Chima	2,972	1,676	248	1,048
Deo	634	205	317	112
Dhaliwal	10,818	6,311	486	4,021
Dhillon	3,286	1,505	543	1,238
Dhindsa	1,511	740	403	368
Garewal	15,112	12,751	622	1,730
Gil	9,367	5,378	602	3,387
Her	1,201	287	128	786
Kang	299	93	206	..
Man	3,521	1,391	989	1,141
Mangat	2,221	1,159	951	111
Main	881	13	..	868
Saroi	2,036	475	..	1,561
Sidhu	8,247	2,659	..	5,588
Sindhu	3,243	833	1,284	1,126

N. B.—This list omits those sub-divisions whose members are below 500.

Malerkotla State.

Jat Sikh Sub-divisions.	District Total 1911.
Aulak	609
Baddechha	285
Bagri	448
Bhandher	163
Bath	259
Bopa Rai	410
Chahil	1,826
Chima	695
Dhaliwal	1,029
Dhillon	648
Garewal	476
Jhalli	460
Mendahar	996
Opal	541
Sindhu	645
Waraich	794

Ambala District.

The Jats of the district cover two widely different classes. In the two northern tehsils of Kharar and Rupar they are a fine set of men of the type common in neighbouring Punjab districts. All over the east and south they are of poorer physique, and not nearly so strongly marked with the persistent energy and fertility in resource which are the usual characteristics of the race. The Jat Sikh in this district is split up into "Gots" innumerable. It is comparatively rare in Ambala to find a cluster of villages owned by Jats of one "Got", or even a single village in which one "Got" largely predominates, but as exceptions, the strong "Baidwan" communities of tehsil Kharar may be mentioned, holding among others the large and flourishing villages of Sohana, Kumra and Mauli; the Chahil villages of tehsil Ambala, and the Her, Kang and Sindhu villages of Rupar. The "Baidwan Got" is the most important Jat "Got" in the district. They are a somewhat turbulent lot of men, but strong and prosperous cultivators, and unlike the ordinary zamindars of Ambala they readily enter Government service in the Army and Police.

Sub-Divisions of Jats.

Baidwan	2,000	Dhindsa	1,200
Bains	1,200	Gil	2,800
Chahil	1,950	Her	2,200
Dhillon	530	Kang	1,500
		Man	1,900
		Pawania	1,150
		Sindhu	5,400

The only two possible tehsils for Sikh recruiting are Rupar and Kharar; it is significant that whereas of all classes there were only 2,851 in the Army on the outbreak of war, the district could only produce a total of 7,000 during the period of its four years to the Armistice, inclusive of all Sikhs other than Jat.

Patiala State.

Patiala derives its name from its capital city which was founded by Raja Ala Singh, about 1762 A.D. It is the most eastern of the three Phulkian States, and with a total area of 5,412 square miles is considerably the largest and most wealthy of the native states in the Eastern Punjab.

Nearly every caste in the Punjab is represented in Patiala, but the Jats who comprise 30 per cent. of the population are by far the strongest element.

The Jats of Patiala mostly claim Rajput origin, and appear to have migrated from Jaisalmir into the Malwa about the middle of the 15th Century, though the "Asli", or original "Gots", Man, Bhullar and Her, which are of the Shiv "Gotra", were probably settled in the Malwa before the other Jats.

The Sidhus.—(45,000) are the most numerous and important subdivision of the Jat Sikhs in Patiala. Besides the ruling families of the Phulkian States and Faridkot, many families of note belong to the Sidhu clan. They claim descent from a Bhatti Rajput, Jaisal, of Jaisalmir. They are strongest in the Anahadgarh "Nizamat". They form an exogamous section and avoid one "Got" only in marriage. Important families are the Jagirdars of Bhadaur, and of Talwandi, Kotli Sabo and Jiundan.

Harike.—This is one of the Siddhu septs, and is called after Chaudhri Hari its ancestor. He and his descendants founded 15 villages on both banks of the Sutlej, whence the name "Harike Pattan"; Buddha Singh, one of his descendants, settled at Sekha in the Barnala pargannah.

Mehta.—This is also a "Munhi" or sept of the Sidhu "Got". It is named after its ancestor Mehta, who founded the village of Mehta near Marnala. Several of this sept held the post of Commander-in-Chief in the State.

Chahil.—These claim that Chahil, their eponym, was born of a hill fairy. They are numerous in Bhikkhi, in which tehsil they own many villages, and they also hold scattered villages in the tehsils of Narwana, Amargarh, Bhawanigarh and Fatehgarh. Sardar Partap Singh, Chahil, was Bakhshi to the State. He was in command of the Patiala contingent at Delhi in 1857.

The Dhaliwals.—These claim to be Chandra Bansi Rajputs by origin, through Dhaliwal Bhatti, who migrated from Jaisalmir and settled at Kangar in Nabha territory in the 12th or 13th Century. In the time of Akbar the Chief of the Dhaliwalis, Mihr Matha, is said to have given a daughter in marriage to that Emperor, whence the Dhaliwals and the 35 Jat Tribes which concurred in the bestowal of a Jat girl on the Emperor, acquired the title or status of Darbari. The Darbari Jats in this State are the Tiwanas of Chinarthal, the Jhalli Gils of Dharmot and Siawara, the Manders of Jarg and the Mangats of Rampur and Jatani. Darbari Jats pay special fees to their Mirasis at weddings. The Dhaliwals, after the decline of Mihr Matha's family, dispersed, and some migrated into the State, where they are mainly found in the tehsils of Bhatinda and Bhikkhi, and also in stray villages in Sunam, Amargarh and Sahibgarh. The main Dhaliwal septs are the Mani, Udi, Rureka, Dina and Ramana.

The Man Jats.—These say they migrated from the North, and claim descent from Mandhata, a Rajput, by a "karewa" marriage. Mandhata settled in Sadowa in Ferozepore, and thence in Akbar's reign the Mans migrated into the present "nizamat" of Anahadgarh, in which they own many villages. Their chief sub-septs in this State are Maur, Sandar, Khawala and Paroga, and they give their names to the villages of Maur, Manwala, Man Khera and Mansa. They avoid only the one "Got" in marriages, and form no alliances with the Bhulars or Sher Gils. The Mansahia Jats regard themselves as superior to other Mans. Tradition says they owe their name to the fact that the head of the family paid the revenues due to the Emperor punctually.

The Dhillon Jats.—These claim descent from Raja Karn. The Dhillons are said to have migrated from Delhi under the Moghals, and are now mainly found in tehsil Govindgarh, and in scattered villages in Bhikkhi and Fatehgarh tehsils. Their chief sub-septs in this state are the Mahna, Bangria, Gat, Jandi, Saraya, Garah and Mutal. They only avoid the father's "Got" in marriage, and make no alliances with the Dhindsa and Wal (a sub-sept of the Sekhons) on account of some old dispute.

The Gils.—These have been described under the Ludhiana District. The founder of this clan Gil, settled in Bhatinda, where he married a Dhaliwal. Thence in the time of Shah Jehan, they migrated to the Sahibgarh and Sunam tehsils in which they are now numerous. They are also found in the Rajpura and Bhikkhi tehsil. They have 11 sub-septs, Sher, Kak, Landra, Sihai, Bhadon, Jhagar, Barala, Karora, Kand, Jaji and Jhala, the last of which is strongly represented in the tehsil of Sahibgarh, where it holds 11 villages.

The Dhindsas.—These claim descent from Raja Karn. They migrated from Sirsa in the time of the Moghal Emperors, and settled in Chaunda Manvi in tehsil Amargarh, round which place they own a number of villages. They are also found in scattered villages in the tehsils of Rajpura, Ghanaur and Patiala.

The Randhawas (or Radhawas).—Hold only two villages in Sahibgarh and Minsa village in Amargarh tehsil. They offer, however, one or two points of interest. Their ancestors settled at Mimsa, near which on their migrating thither, the axle of one of their carts broke, and its owners took it as an omen that they should settle at that spot. The others went on, and failing to pursuade their comrades to accompany them, they uttered a curse upon them that they should be compelled to seek a new home every 12 years. Every twelfth year they take a cart to the spot and worship it, and an uncle cuts a lock of hair from his nephew's head. On their return home, it is said, the axle of the cart invariably breaks on the road.

The Sarahs (or Sarais).—These are mainly found in "nizamats" Anahadgarh and Karmgarh. The Kaleke Sirdars belong to the "Sarae Got". They trace their descent from the Bhatti Rajputs of Jaisalmir, and are named after their ancestor Chaudri Kala, who founded the village of Kalanwali in Sirsa; his grandfather Maluka founded Kaleke near Dhanaula where his descendants still hold land. Sirdars Gurbaksh Singh and Haria Singh, brothers-in-law of Maharaja Ala Singh, were fifth in descent from Chaudhri Kala. The former was Maharaja Ala Singh's Diwan, and accompanied him in all his expeditions, and is best remembered for his services when Maharaja Ranjit Singh came to Patiala to visit Maharaja Sahib Singh. Mai Fatto, wife of Maharaja Ala Singh belonged to this family, and Maharaja Karu Singh also married into it.

The Pawanias.—These are of Shiv "Gotra", like the Man, Bhular and Her with the two latter of whom they do not intermarry. They migrated from Hissar, and own 4 villages in the Sunam tehsil.

The Ghumans.—These also claim Rajput descent. Migrating in the time of Jehangir from Rajputana, they settled at Sajuma in the Jind State, and now hold 11 villages near Bhawanigarh, Ghumana in Rajpura, and a village in Patiala tehsil.

The Wains.—These claim to be Tur Rajputs by origin, they are said to have migrated from Delhi. Their ancestor Mainpal married a widow, and his son Wain is their eponym. They hold many villages in the Bangar (tehsil Narwana) and stray villages in the Sunam and Patiala tehsils.

The Mangats.—Are only found in the Sahibgarh tehsil, where they hold 6 villages.

The Sindhus.—These appear to have immigrated into the State from the Manjha in the 16th Century, and are found in scattered villages in the Ghanaur, Rajpura, Amargarh, Bhatinda and Barnala tehsils.

The Bhudars.—These are said to have been driven from Man in Ferozepore by the Siddhus, and then to have dispersed. They own nearly the whole of 7 villages in Barnala and 4 in Sunam. Their sub-septs are Kosa, Munga, Dahr and Bhatia.

The Sekhons.—These claim descent from the Ponwar Rajputs. They are named after their ancestor Sekhon, who had seven sons after whom were named seven "munhis" or septs. Mai Akaur, mother of Maharaja Karm Singh, whose life sheds a lustre over Patiala history, belonged to this family, and her brother Sardar Diwan Singh was Commander-in-Chief. They hold Bakshiwala in (Sunam tehsil), Kaulgarh (in Pail), Kishangarh and Kanhgarh (in Bhikkhi) and Karmgarh (in Anhadgarh tehsil).

The Mahils.—These trace their descent from the Tur Rajputs and came from Delhi. The clan holds Shahpuri Khurd and Kalan, also Namol in the Sunam tehsil and Khanpur in Dhuri.

The remaining sub-divisions of Jat Sikhs which are to be found in this State, are as follows :—

Patiala State.

Jat Sub-division.	1911 Total.	Jat Sub-division.	1911 Total.
Jat Athwal	514	Jat Biling	1,500
„ Aulak	2,540	„ Birk	1,200
„ Autal	973	„ Bole	1,000
„ Awjle	1,380	„ Bope Rae	1,600
„ Bains	1,004	„ Bore	660
„ Bagar	600	„ Chahil	21,500
„ Bachal	280	„ Chattha	1,600
„ Baidwan	550	„ Chandi	750
„ Bachta	370	„ Chima	1,300
„ Bandechhe	1.180	„ Chohan	1,800
„ Bajwa	940	„ Chopare	350
„ Bandhel	750	„ Dallu	950
„ Bansi	830	„ Dangi	60
„ Basati	370	„ Doraian	250
„ Bandar	1.060	„ Dehia	250
„ Banwaria	760	„ Dhariwal	18.000
„ Bhatthal	1,870	„ Dhanoe	1,100
„ Batoe	630	„ Dhanor	1,500
„ Beri	670	„ Dhandian	300
„ Bhainiwal	1.480	„ Dhanake	6,500
„ Bhangu	3,550	„ Dhandhana	550
„ Bhuller	4,100	„ Dhawe	1,600
„ Bhatti	470	„ Dhallian	300
„ Bhuttar	460	„ Dhandiwal	4,000

Jat Sub-division.	1911 Total.	Jat Sub-division.	1911 Total.
Jat Dhillon	10,500	Jat Jhund	1,350
„ Dhindsa	2,650	„ Kahlon	70
„ Dholu	15	„ Kail Rauni . . .	2,800
„ Dhota	800	„ Kandoe	90
„ Dullat	1,300	„ Kang	950
„ Gadra	700	„ Kankar	50
„ Gandhu	6,000	„ Kharand. . . .	2,600
„ Gangore	1,300	„ Khangas. . . .	270
„ Garewal	3,560	„ Kharral	550
„ Ganghas	620	„ Khera	560
„ Ghumman. . . .	5,200	„ Khatre	550
„ Gil	15,300	„ Khire	710
„ Godara	730	„ Koharia	790
„ Gosal	560	„ Lahar	530
„ Gurne	1,300	„ Lamba	40
„ Hari	710	„ Lohchap. . . .	160
„ Her	880	„ Mahil	723
„ Hinjha	1,400	„ Mahvi	750
„ Jakhar	[illegible]00	„ Maindal	1,150
„ Janjh	1,700	„ Man	16,000
„ Janjhar	1,200	„ Mandahar . . .	1,850
„ Jaria	310	„ Mander	2,300
„ Jassar	870	„ Mandi	1,150
„ Jatana	1,400	„ Mangat	2,700
„ Jawinda	500	„ Maur	1,100
„ Jhalli	530	„ Nagre	570

Jat Sub-division.	1911 Total.	Jat Sub-division.	1911 Total.
Jat Nain	350	Jat Sarao	1,850
" Nalla	700	" Sarah	6,600
" Narani	1,550	" Sarai	220
" Narwan	1,290	" Sari.	2,600
" Nat	620	" Saroe	7,600
" Punder	1,350	" Sarware	1,800
" Pawania	1,520	" Sekhon	3,500
" Punia	1,800	" Sihumar	30
" Randhawe	2,320	" Sidhu	46,000
" Ranwan	500	" Sindhu	11,500
" Raparia	15	" Siri	620
" Rathaul	650	" Sohal	600
" Rathi	850	" Suhi	3,000
" Rattiwal	480	" Suraj	670
" Sahrawat	390	" Tarka	130
" Salu.	80	" Tawana	3,200
" Sangwan	280	" Thind	600
" Samrao	1,300	" Uppal	800
" Songhare	1,200	" Varaich	650

Nabha State.

The State of Nabha is the second in population and revenue, though the smallest in area, of the three Phulkian States, with 966 square miles. Its rulers, however, as the descendants of Chaudri Tilok Singh—the eldest son of Chaudri Phul, claim that they represent the senior branch of the Phulkian family. As a separate and sovereign State Nabha may be said to date from the fall of Sirhind in 1763. Prior to that year its chiefs had been merely rural notables, whose influence was overshadowed by that of the cadet branch which was rising to regal power under Ala Singh, the founder of the Patiala State.

A description of the particular sub-divisions of Jat Sikhs call for no special mention, as having been already described elsewhere. The list of those that are to be found in the State, omitting those whose numbers are under 500, are as follows :—

Jat	Aulok	1,000	Jat	Dhinsa	500
"	Bhangu	503	"	Gil	3,700
"	Bhullar	1,400	"	Man	3,000
"	Bhuttar	600	"	Randhawa	500
"	Chahil	2,000	"	Sarai	1,300
"	Dhariwal	6,000	"	Sidhu	10,000
"	Dhillon	3,750	"	Sindhu	3,000

Jind State.

Jind, though the second in area, is the smallest in population, containing as it does the sterile Bagar tract of the Dadri tehsil. It has a total area of 1,268 square miles, and consits of three tracts, *viz.*, Sangrur, Jind and Dadri.

The history of Jind as a separate and ruling State dates from 1763, in which year the Confederate Sikhs having captured Sirhind town from the Governor, to whom Ahmed Shah Durani had entrusted it, partitioned the old Moghal province of Sirhind. Prior to that year Sukhchen, grandson of Phul, the ancestor of all the Phulkian families, had been a mere rural notable.

The Sikh Jats are only found in the tehsil of Sangrur. The principal sub-divisions are Sangwar, Redhu, Chahil, Sidhu and Man. Of these the only ones that require mention in detail are the first two.

The Sangwars.—The clan claims descent from Sardha, a Rajput of Sarsu Janglu. Sangu, son of Naini his descendant, migrated from Ajmer and founded Baghanwal, near Khari Buttar, and became a Jat. The clan is a very small one, and, in fact, numbers under 50.

The Redhus.—This clan is similarly a very small one, and is descended from a Jat, Redhu, who founded Kandela in Jin tehsil.

Details of the other sub-divisions which are to be found in this State, are as follows :—

Jind State.

Sub-division.	Total in 1911.	Sub-division.	Total in 1911.
Jat Sikhs Basi	410	Jat Sikhs Man	2,400
" " Bhogar . . .	1,200	" " Mandhar . . .	700
" " Bhullar . . .	830	" " Pawania . . .	180
" " Bora	30	" " Redhu . . .	15
" " Chahil	380	" " Sahrawat . . .	25
" " Dhaliwal . . .	650	" " Sangwar . . .	20
" " Dhillon . . .	510	" " Sarao	520
" " Ghangas . .	25	" " Sidhu	2,450
" " Gil	600	" " Sindhu . . .	780
" " Kali Rawan . . .	250	" " Sohi	450
" " Mahil	380		

Ferozepore District.

The Sikh Jats are preponderant in all the tehsils of the Ferozepore District, namely

Moga	98,000
Zira	2 ,600
Ferozepore	12,000
Mukhtsar	38,000
Fazilka	20,000
Total .	191,600

In 1931, the total population of Jat Sikhs in this district was 231,532.

The Sidhus.—This tribe is the largest of all the sections of the Jats, and number approximately 69,000. It occupies the entire west and south of Moga, the Mahraj villages, the greater part of southern Mukhtsar, and numerous villages in the sandy tracts of the Ferozepore and Zira tehsils, and in the east of Fazilka Rohi.

This tribe has already been referred to under other districts, and for a full account of it, Sir L. Griffin's Punjab Rajas' should be studied.

There are 21 sections or "muhins" of Sidhus, which are named as follows :—

> Rathaia, Khilria, Mahramia, Darake, Mahrajke, Ratia, Bhulin, Harike, Bandhate, Bhukun, Jaid, Barar, Pahloke, Sara, Manoke, Khokarke, Ugarke Sahuke, Amunke, Achal, Aspal.

After the Barar and Mahrajke sections, the most important are the Jaid, Sara, Mahrami, Darake and Harike. The Sara intermarry with the other "muhins" showing that the "Got" is practically too large and is beginning to sub-divide. The process will probably go further in time, for the Sidhus occupy so large an area of the Cis-Sutlej country, that if they rigorously regard the whole tribe as a single "Got", many of them would be unable to find a wife at all.

The Gils.—This clan is also scattered throughout the district. Moga tehsil holds a total of 18,000, Ferozepore being next with 6,000, whilst Mukhtsar, Zira and Fazilka contain nearly 2,000 each. They are the only important section of the Jats who do not trace their origin to a Bhatti stock. They say they come from a Raja of the Variach clan of Rajputs. The name Gil is explained by a story to the effect that the Raja had no children by his Rajputni wives, and therefore married a Jat woman. She bore a son, but the other wives, moved by jealousy, exposed it in a marshy spot in the jungle. The infant was accidentally found by the King's minister, and called Gil, from the place where he was found, "gil" meaning moisture.

Another version is given at page 352 of Sir L. Griffin's "Punjab Chiefs", according to which the child who was exposed was the son of Gil, and he was found being licked and fondled by a tiger ("sher"), whence he received the name of the Sher Gil. The Sher Gil are one section of the Gils. Other large sections are the Wadan Gils and Vairsi Gils. There are 12 sections all together. The Wadan Gils say that one of their ancestors was Raja Bhainipal, who built the fort at Bhatinda, so named, it is said, because he buried a bania called Bhatia in the foundations.

The Wadan Gils were settled about the beginning of the 17th century in the south and west of Moga. They were driven from here by the Barars further north, where they established themselves about Chhirak, Ghal and Moga where they are now.

The Sher Gils are mostly to be found in the Manjha and in the south of the Zira and Ferozepore tehsils.

The Dhaliwals or Dhariwals.—These are the next most important clan in the district, and were the earliest of the Jat tribes to settle themselves in it. They inhabit chiefly the Moga tehsil, where they number 12,000; each of the other tehsils contain 2,000. Their origin is uncertain; all they can tell is that they came from Dharanagri, which they say is somewhere in the south of India. They are divided into 2 sections, the Udis and the Manis. The principal villages of the Udis are Badhni, Lupon, Lohara, Ransih, Salabatpura and Raoki. Bilaspur, Saidoke, Mackhiki, Dholpur and Himmatpur belong to the Mani section.

The Khosas.—These are a strongly marked tribe, though holding only about a dozen villages, mostly near the junction of the three tehsils of Moga, Zira and Ferozepore. They say that they are Tunwar Rajputs from Delhi, and that they have a story resembling that of the Gils, of their ancestor Randhir having been exposed as an infant and miraculously preserved being sheltered by a kite. The Khosas had formerly a character for crime. They have an independent bearing, whilst as cultivators they do not take a very high place. They number 3,000.

The Sandhus (Sindhus).—The Sandhus of Ferozepore District have, mostly come into it from the Manjha. They number about 10,500. Their principal villages are Sarhali, Waltoha, Chabba, Bharana and Manwan, though they own others in the south of Ferozepore.

General.—In general, the foregoing are the only tribes that require any extended notice in this district; there are, however, many miscellaneous clans scattered throughout the district, as follows :—

—	Total in 1911.	—	Total in 1911.
Jat Aulak	1,400	Jat Khosa	4,300
,, Bath	600	,, Korutana	920
,, Bhullar	3,300	,, Mahi	580
,, Bahar	500	,, Mahil	370
,, Bhuttar	1,200	,, Man	7,000
,, Chahil	2,100	,, Pannun	110
,, Chima	830	,, Rai	900
,, Dhillon	7,500	,, Randhawa	310
,, Garund	1,110	,, Sang	1,500
,, Her	650	,, Sangi	520
,, Jakhan	100	,, Sarai	4,300
,, Johal	860	,, Shekhun	1.800
,, Kaler	720	,, Sindhu	10,800
,, Kang	800	,, Sumra	550
,, Kargha	550	,, Wandar	1.520
,, Khera	800	,, Wirk	500

Faridkot State.

Faridkot is a State lying in the south of the Ferozepore District, with an area of 643 square miles. It is almost surrounded by the Ferozepore District. Moga tehsil lying on the east, Ferozepore on the north and northwest, Muktsar, on the west. On the south lies a portion of the Patiala State. It consists of two "pargannahs", Faridkot in the North, and Kot Kapura in the South. The pargannah of Jaito which belongs to the Nabha State forms an island in the Kot Kapura pargannah.

The most important Jat Sikh clan is that of the Sidhus (20,000). The ruling family of the State belongs to this clan. They own 3/5ths of the Kot Kaprua, and 2/5ths of the Faridkot tehsil. Their history is that Ahlu and Mahma, the sons of Barar (grandsons of Sindhu), settled in this neighbourhood about 1706 A. D. They are known as Sidhu Barar Aspal after their ancestor Aspal. The descendants of Mahma live in six villages, Mahma Siwai, Mahma Sirhari, Mahma Larja, Birj Mahma, Mahma Bhagwana and Mahma Balahar. The decendants of Alu live in 5 villages Ahlu, Dhanewala, Ganga, Bhissiana and Kaiai. The ruling family belongs to the Kapurik branch.

Another branch of the Barar family is descended from Wanju who settled in the Bukhri "Ilaqa" 260 years ago.

Minor clans of the Sidhu Jats are as follows :—

Harike	Khanche . . . . . .
Maharmae	Bhaike . . . . . .
R.sah	Bhabuke . . . . . .
Merajke	Malhana . . . . . .
Dewanke	Jituke . . . . . .
	Warahah . . . . . .

The Gil Jats (3,500) come next in importance in the State, and own a dozen villages. They came originally from Sangu in the Amritsar District, and settled in Chur Chak, a village in the Zira tehsil of Ferozepore. Thence they moved to the waste land north of Faridkot.

The Sandhu Jats (3,000) are descended from Kirbe who came from Mamdot 300 years ago, and they now own 17 villages.

The Dhillon Jats (2,800) came from the Amritsar District to Kot Kapura City 200 years ago, and are found in the State in 9 villages.

The last clan of any size and importance is the Dhaliwal (1,750), who came from Patiala about the same time to Kot Kapura.

Hissar District.

The Sikhs of the Hissar District are confined entirely to the Sirsa tehsil and the northern part of the Fatehabad tehsil, and immigrated mostly from the Malwa country in the north, and from Patiala.

The Jat sub-divisions which are to be found in this District are as follows :—

Sub-Division.	Number (1911).	Sub-Division.	Number (1911).
Jat Bhainiwal	130	Jat Lonba	80
„ Bara	50	„ Man	600
„ Bola	950	„ Nian	70
„ Chahil	1,700	„ Pangal	20
„ Chanhan	40	„ Punia	250
„ Dedwal	1,450	„ Saharan	120
„ Dhillon	400	„ Sahag	50
„ Dhariwal	800	„ Sadu	2,000
„ Dhundwal	60	„ Sara	2,500
„ Dodi	30	„ Sawaich	80
„ Gil	650	„ Sidhu	5,250
„ Godara	175	„ Sindhu	600
„ Kaswan	75	„ Hiri	25

The Maniha.

The "Manjha" is a term which is sometimes loosely used to denote the whole of the upper part of the Bari Doab, as distinguished from the Malwa, the country lying south of the Sutlej. But a Jat Sikh of Amritsar in speaking of the Manjha refers more particularly to that part of the Tarn Taran tehsil which lies below the old road from Atari to Goindwal and to the Kasur and part of the Chunian tehsils of Lahore. Ajnala is not counted as the Manjha, nor, properly speaking, is the Amritsar tehsil. Since the old "Badshahi" road above mentioned was superseded by the metalled Grand Trunk road, the limits of the Manjha have, in common speech been extended, and the whole of that part of the Amritsar district which lies on the right of a traveller going towards Jullundur on the Grand Trunk road is spoken of as the Manjha. Jullundur and Kapurthala are spoken of as the Doaba, anything beyond that is vaguely termed the Malwa; the Sialkot district is "darya par", or "Ravi par" and different parts of the Amritsar tehsil are referred to by mentioning the name of some central village, such as "Majitha ki taraf". The Gurdaspur district, though in the upper part of the Bari Doab, is never held to be part of the Manjha. In short, the Jat of Amritsar in speaking of the Manjha, may be understood as referring to that part of the district which is peopled almost entirely by orthodox followers of Guru Gobind Singh excluding the tract once extensively held by Sultani Hindu Jats (the Bangal of Amritsar tehsil), by Narajani Sikh (the Jandiala sandridge), the "nahri" country round Amritsar where Kambohs and miscellaneous tribes become most numerous, and the Ajnala tehsil, where there is a strong admixture of Mohamedans, Arains, and Rajputs, who are so numerous in the Ravi side tracts. Certainly the Sultanis have now largely become orthodox Sikhs, and the Gil Sikh Jats near Majitha, and the Aulaks and others of Ajnala, are as devoted followers of Guru Govind Singh as the men of the Manjha, but the distinction is still kept up, and the dividing line may be roughly taken to be the Grand Trunk **road.**

SUB-DIVISION OF JAT SIKHS IN THE MANJHA.

Amritsar.

The sub-divisions of greatest numerical strength in the Amritsar district are the Sindhu, Gil, Randhawa, Sidhu, Dhaun, Dhillon, Bal, Aulakh, Pannun, Chahil, Sohal, China, Mahil, Bhullar, Kang and Man. Of these the first three mentioned far exceed in numbers any of the others.

The Sindhus.—The Sindhu Jats, it will be seen, are the strongest clan in the district. They are found in detached villages at different points of all three tehsils but muster specially strongly in the south west corner of Tarn Taran. The central village of this group is Sirhali Kalan, and from this they have founded and peopled the ring of villages which lie round it. Here they hold 32 villages. This part of the tehsil was formerly known as the "Khara Manjha," a bleak tree-less tract with deep brackish wells, a soil sometimes poor and sandy, but generally hard and unpromising, and an uncertain rainfall. Canal irrigation has now changed the appearance of the country, and the system of cultivation to some extent, but still the soil yields a small return, and holdings being small the Sindhus have always eagerly taken to military service. Hardly a family but has one or more memebrs in the Indian Army, the Burma Military police, or in service in the Straits Settlements, or in China. Military employ is traditional amongst the Sindhus, and from this tribe the Sikhs draw many of their best men. They are the best specimens of the Manjha Jat which the district can show. The way they hold the land is perplexing, for most of those who own land in the later founded hamlets round Sirhali, are still recorded as owing land in Sirhali itself, and it often happens that a family owns land in three or four estates.

It is difficult to cultivate each one of these separate holdings, consequently exchanges and tenancies are common, and often give rise to disputes, which, as land is scarce, are keenly fought out. Men on service find it easy to mortgage their land during their absence. It is easily redeemed out of savings on their return, and in every village there are pensioners who are only too ready to take it up, and advance money on it. The clan is found in some strength in the neighbouring corner of the Kasur tehsil, and also across the Sutlej in the Malwa area, chiefly in Ferozepore, but there is no other collection of Sindhu villages in Amritsar. The Sindhus of the Sirkali "ilaqa" have an ancient feud with the Pannuns of Naushera and Chaudriwala said to have arisen out of a murder by a Sirhali man of a Pannun connection by marriage. The two clans are good enough friends, but still intermarriages never take place between the Pannuns of these two villages and the Sindhus of the Sirhali neighbourhood. Neither clan will give, or take a bride from the other. There is no well known family belonging to this clan. The Sindhus are independent, and not much given to abide by the law, and their headmen have little authority.

The Gils.—The next strongest clan is that of the Gils. They are known as excellent and hard working cultivators. They hold about 25 villages in whole or in part in Tarn Taran, but they are scattered all through the tehsil. They muster strongest in the Amritsar tehsil, near Majitha, and it is said to this clan that the Majitha Sirdars, the descendants of Sirdar Desa Singh, belong. Majitha, and part of Sohiyan Kalan in the Amritsar tehsil, and Dhotian in Tarn Taran are the largest settlments of this clan. They are all fine specimen of the Manjha Jat, and frequently take service.

The Dhillons.—The Dhillons are found mostly in the Manjha, in fact along with the Sindhus, Gils, Pannuns, Aulakhs and Sidhus they take up nearly the whole of the Manjha proper. But the Dhillons lie further up the tehsil in the upper half of it, the country in which the Bhangi was once supreme. They hold 28 whole villages, and parts of others, and many of their villages are among the largest in the tehsil such as Kairon, Padri, Gaggobua, Panjwa, Chabal, Dhand, Kasel, Gandiwind and Lijan. All these are typical Manjha villages, and supply many recruits to the Army, especially Dhand and Kairon. Most of them are favoured with canal irrigation, and there are no better cultivated estates in the Tarn Taran tehsil than Kasel and Gandhiwind. In the other tehsils they are more scattered, but they are fairly strong in the Amritsar Bangar, and across the Beas in Kapurthala. The Amritsar Dhillons say they came originally from the Manjha, but this is doubtful. They intermarry with all Gots except with the Bals. The story is that a family bard, or Mirasi, from a Dhillon village was refused help when in difficulties in the Bal country, and in revenge cursed the whole Bal clan. Mirasis in those days were more of a power than they are now, and the Dhillon clan took up the feud which survives to this day in the refusal to intermarry. The

Dhillons of Amritsar, who live alongside the Bals of the Sathiala "ilaqa" do not carry the feud further than this, but those of the Manjha will not eat or drink in a Bal village, or from the same dish as a Bal. Mirasis also keep up the feud.

The Randhawas.—Randhawas come next in order. They are hardly met with in Tarn Taran, but are very strong all along the Batala border, and down the sand ridge in the Amritsar tehsil especially near Mahta, and as far as Kathnangal. They are the strongest "Got" in the Amritsar tehsil and hold 39 villages. Many of them are Mohamedans, and until the first decade of the present century very many of them were Sultanis. They rank high as cultivators. Several leading men in the time of the Sikh rule belonged to this "Got".

The Aulakhs.—The Aulakh Jats, are most numerous in the Ajnala tehsil but there is also a cluster of 9 villages round Shabazpur in Tarn Taran held by this clan. Though quite a small village, Shabazpur is well known, and the corner of the Manjha in which it lies takes its name from the village, and is known generally as "Shabazpur-ki-taraf". But it is round Kohala in Ajnala that the Aulakhs are met with in strength, and their chief villages are Kohala, Koheli, Lopoki, Chandwinda Khurd and Kalan, Madoki, Baran and Chogawan. Their leading men are not above the yeoman class. The larger portion of their country is profusely irrigated by the Bari Doab canal, and they are a prosperous and well-to-do clan, though with small holdings.

The Chahils.—The Chahils own 16 villages near Sheron Bagha in Amritsar, but are mostly found in the Malwa.

The Sidhus.—The Sidhus hold round Atari and Bhakna 14 villages in all. They have few representatives in other parts of the district their country being mostly in the Ferozepore district, where they hold the entire south and west of Moga, the Mahraj villages, the greater part of Mukhtsar, and numerous villages in the sandy tracts of the Ferozepore and Zira tehsils. They trace their descent from Raja Jaisal, a Manj Rajput, from one of whose descendants, Barar, have sprung the ruling families of Patiala, Nabha and Jind. Other details of this well-known clan will be found at page 494 of Vol. I of Griffin's Punjab Chiefs, and in the Gazetteer of the Ferozepore district. The Sidhus of Amritsar are almost entirely Sikhs and live in the Tarn Taran tehsil, where they number about 10,000.

Other Gots of Jats.—The same remark applies to the Bal Jats, who hold the large villages of Bal Khurd and Kalan near the city, besides, Sathiala, Butala, Jodhe and Bal Serai in the Bangar of Amritsar, or 23 villages in all, and to the Pannun Jats who have spread from the Doaba, and who number about 5,000. They own 7 large estates in the Manjha, including Naushera and Chaudriwala. The principal village of the China Jats is Her Seh China near Raja Sansi in Ajnala.

The Sadal Jats.—The Sadal Jats inhabit the Amritsar tehsil.

The Bhullars.—Are a fairly numerous clan, and with the Mans and part of the Hers have the honour of being known as "asli" or original Jats, all others having enrolled themselves in the great tribe of Jats at a later date. These two latter clans exist in great numbers in the Malwa which is their real home.

The Bhangus.—Hold the large village of Khiala (Khurd and Kalan) in the Amritsar tehsil. They and the Sohals, inhabiting the village of that name in Tarn Taran, enjoy the reputation of being among the most lawless in the district.

The Kangs.—Hold a compact cluster of villages near Tarn Taran chief among which are Kang, Kalla and Mal Chak. The Jhawara Jats of Mattewal and the neighbourhood, and the Mahil Jats of Ajnala are classed together.

The remaining Jat Sikh sub-divisions which are to be found in the Amritsar District are as follows :—

Amritsar.

Jat Sub-division.	District total in 1911 Persons.	Distribution by Tehsils.		
		Amritsar.	Tarn Taran.	Ajnala.
Jat Aulakh	5,947	546	1,874	3,527
Athwal	689	221	382	86
Bajwa	958	279	457	222
Bal	5,978	5,066	765	147
Bandar	772	465	273	34
Batha	551	467	84	..
Bhat	1,566	367	1,045	154
Bhangu	1,326	56	277	993
Bhatti	503	184	319	..
Bhoj	639	638	1	..
Boparse	1,217	650	131	436
Bhullar	2,371	1,375	174	822
Chahils	4,509	3,103	1,388	18

Jat Sub-division.	District total in 1911 Persons.	Distribution by Tehsils.		
		Amritsar.	Tarn Taran.	Ajnala.
Jat China	1,946	156	474	1,316
Chima	1,069	456	326	287
Dadwal	515	514	1	..
Des	413	80	198	135
Dhaun	7,570	3,270	4,174	126
Dhanoa	1,120	..	1,111	9
Dhariwal	880	150	464	265
Dhillon	4,734	..	4,030	698
Ghumman	124	..	99	25
Gil	16,070	6,158	6,671	3,241
Garaia	401	279	67	55
Her	1,147	963	169	15
Hinjra	1,563	1,252	160	151
Hindal	321	72	184	65
Jawara	651	651	..	..
Johal	1,531	173	1,233	125
Kang	2,053	312	1,729	12
Kaler	1,544	719	453	372
Kamboh	541	463	77	1
Kara	1,785	89	1,663	33
Khara	675	183	468	24
Khera	566	455	111	..

Jat Sub-division.	District total in 1911 Persons.	Distribution by Tehsils.		
		Amritsar.	Tarn Taran.	Ajnala.
Jat Mahil	2,340	1,600	261	479
Man	1,859	1,136	390	333
Najjar	741	4	..	737
Ojla	861	686	174	1
Opal	1,522	891	535	96
Pannun	4,732	110	4,279	343
Randhawa	14,160	8,308	3,252	2,600
Rai	788	17	771	..
Sadal	2,505	2,505	..	..
Sagwan	501	497	4	..
Sakuni	1,272	1,039	144	89
Sansi	682	175	501	6
Sarai	1,858	542	1,057	259
Sidhu	8,913	2	8,911	..
Sindhu	22,382	6,288	1,861	2,233
Sohal	1,288	20	766	502
Soi	899	867	..	32
Sumra	346	65	243	38
Valia	956	..	956	..
Varaich	690	296	90	304
Virk	679	344	237	98

Lahore District.

The district takes its name from that of the headquarters. "Lohawar" means the fort of Loh, the son of Rama. The district is one of 5 of the Lahore division; it comprises the whole of the plain country lying between the Ravi River on the north, and the Sutlej River on the south, and from the Amritsar district boundary on the east to that of Montgomery on the west. The total area is 2,738 square miles, and consists of 3 tehsils, *viz.*, Lahore, Kasur and Chunian.

The Jats are not only numerically the strongest tribe, but in many respects the most important. In 1931 the Sikh Jats, numbered 122,871.

The lowlands which lie to the south of the Manjha are known as the "Hithar", derived from the vernacular term "het" (below); they were the valley of the Beas river when it flowed through this district separately from the Sutlej. In this portion nearly all the Jats are Sidhu. They occupy principally the western half of the Hithar, which forms the southern portion of the Chunian tehsil. They came here probably from the Ferozepore district on the opposite side of the river. The Sidhu is a far more peaceable, well behaved and industrious member of society than the Sandhu brother. Having lived for many generations on the meagre profits derived from cultivation dependent on a precarious rain-fall, and a slow and expensive process of well-irrigation by the Persian wheel, the Sidhu Jat has gradually become accustomed to regard the cultivation of his land, and constant attendance at his well, as the chief reason for his existence.

The Jats along the Ravi are principally Sandhus, who have some large settlements along the lower course of the river, mostly in the Chunian tehsil.

The Bhullar Jats occupy a few large estates in the centre of the Kasur Manjha. They, in common with the Her and Man sections who are also found in a very few scattered villages of Lahore district, call themselves the "asl" or original Jats, and are said to have sprung from the Jat or matted hair of Mahadeo. In character the Bhullars resemble the Sandhus, but are inferior in physique.

There are several "Gil" Jat settlements near the Sutlej in Kasur tehsil, a few in the Manjha of Lahore tehsil, and three or four on the Ravi in the Chunian tehsil. They have not got a good reputation in the district as cultivators, and give the impression of being both querulous quarrelsome. In physique they are inferior to the ordinary Manjha Jat.

The "Dhillon" settlements are few, and are scattered over the whole district, chiefly in the Manjha. Their largest village is that of Bhasin, on the Amritsar border near the Ravi.

In addition to the foregoing, there are many other miscellaneous sections of Jats scattered about the district, enumerated as follows :—

Name of sub-division.	Total Number in 1911.	Tehsils.		
		Lahore.	Chunian	Kasur.
Jat Aulakh	1,046	185	278	583
Bhati	880	795	85	..
Bajwa	194	57	3	134
Bhullar	9,688	2,392	306	6,990

Name of sub-division.	Total Number in 1911.	Tehsils.		
		Lahore.	Chunian.	Kasur.
Jat Bhuttor	916	3	2	911
Bath	3,302	1,571	127	1,604
Chauhan	5	4	..	1
Chima	182	78	27	77
China	369	25	210	134
Chahil	75	29	5	41
Dew	707	233	169	305
Dhillon	5,828	1,944	977	2,907
Dhariwal	1,448	611	63	774
Gil	9,071	1,773	1,287	6,011
Ghumman	38	..	..	38
Gondal	78	66	12	..
Her	597	464	29	104
Hinjra	353	60	284	9
Khara	1,909	93	1,637	179
Kharral	4	4	..	..
Khokhar	4	..	4	..
Man	1,023	672	122	229
Malhi	639	326	30	283
Opal	1,426	1,284	28	114
Pannun	497	61	5	431
Randhawa	703	219	126	358
Sidhu	6,724	440	5,617	667
Sindhu	36,316	10,747	10,467	15,102
Sarai	629	216	62	351
Sekhon	629	5	121	503
Sial	2	..	2	..
Sumra	250	130	23	97
Virk	2,126	156	493	1,477
Varaich	1,046	185	278	583

Sialkot District.

The total area of the Sialkot district is 1,553 square miles. It lies in the Lahore division, and is bounded on the north by the Gujarat district and Jammu; on the east by Gurdaspur; on the south by the Amritsar district, and on the west by the Sheikhupura and Gujranwala districts. It lies in what is known as the Rechna Doab between the Chenab River on the north and the Ravi on the south. It consists of 5 tehsils, namely:—Sialkot, Pasrur, Zafarwal, Raya and Daska. The Jat Sikh is found all over the district, and forms the backbone of the agricultural community. The principal clans are the Bajwa, Basra, Chima, Ghuman, Kahlon, Sahi and Sandhu.

The Bajwas.—10,000 in number, are found in all the tehsils except Daska. They claim to be descended from Ram Chandra of the Surajbansi line. Their ancester was one Shalip a man of some position, as he enjoyed a large Jagir, and paid tribute to Delhi. He had several sons, amongst whom, only one, named Kals, need be mentioned. Kals founded a flourishing family, which has now grown into the powerful Bajwa clan, who are as good as any of the Jats in the district. They have 3 divisions. The descendants of Manag inhabit Pasrur; those of Manga cluster round Chawinda, while Narowal is the headquarters of the children of Naru, who own 22 villages. The Bajwa Jats are represented by two distinguished branches of the clan. The respective heads both live in Kalaswala, a large village near Pasrur. The clan is found in particular near Kali, or Gharial Kalan in the Pasrur and Raya tehsil. They claim Phagwara in the Jullundur district as their home, famine having driven them with their herds to the jungles of Sialkot, and they settled at Kali and its neighbourhood.

The Chimas.—These number approximately 4,000, and are found mainly in the Daska tehsil, where they hold many of the rich estates which enjoy irrigation from the Ain stream. They claim relationship with the Chauhan Rajputs, as their ancestor, Chima belonged to that clan.

The Ghumans.—This clan numbers 3,400 and is chiefly settled in the Sialkot tehsil, to the west and south of the city, and around Samprial in the Daska tehsil. They are an off-shoot of the Janjua Rajputs, and so claim descent from Raja Dalip of Delhi. One of his descendants Samprial, married out of caste, took service in Jammu, and founded this clan which has 21 sub-divisions. They intermarry with all the leading Jats, with the exception of the Mans.

The Kahlons.—This clan numbers 2,000; their home is at Batala in the Gurdaspur district. There are 3 divisions of the clan corresponding with the 3 sons of Soli, their founder. The first inhabits Dhamthal, the north of the Raya tehsil, and a small part of Shakargarh; the second, the remaining villages in Zafarwal; the third the rest of Shakargarh. They are reputed a quiet and industrious people, and make good soldiers.

The Malhis. This clan is mostly found around Baddmalhi, in the Raya tehsil. They trace their descent from Ram Chanderji of Surajbhansi family. In loyalty they are reported upon as second to none. The people of this clan are also found in 12 or 13 villages round about Badiana, a village midway between Pasrur and Sialkot. One of the rising families in this tract is that of Risaldar Pal Singh of Bathe, of the late 25th Cavalry.

The Sandhus.—This clan (2,400), is found round Satrah in the Pasrur tehsil, and Wadhala Sandhuan in Daska. In this district they call themselves Sandhus, not Sindhus. They claim Solar Rajput origin, and believe that they came from Ghazni, but whether Ghazni in Afghanistan, or in the Deccan, or Bikanir, is not certain. The present head of the Sandhu Jat family of Siranwali lives in the Pasrur tehsil. This family rose to position and power under the early Sikh rule.

The Mans.—This clan numbers only 700, and does not properly belong to the Sialkot district, nevertheless with the Bhular and Her clans it claims to be the oldest and best of the Jat clans. The leading representative of the family lives in the Raya tehsil.

In general, although not so plentiful, the Sialkot recruits are quite as good physically and socially as those from the Amritsar and Tarn Taran areas, and make good soldiers.

The following Jat sub-divisions, in addition to the foregoing are also to be found in the District.

Sub-division.	Total.	Tehsils.				
		Sialkot.	Pasrur.	Zafarwal.	Raya.	Daska.
Jat Aulak . .	302	1	160	..	110	31
Bains . .	108	5	18	..	85	..
Bajwa . .	10,038	612	2,908	1,012	5,284	222
Basra . .	1,320	6	629	..	685	..
Chima . .	3,983	291	340	24	371	2,957
Deo . .	1,799	23	96	800	880	..
Dhariwal . .	600	50	71	29	438	12
Dhillon . .	841	97	305	37	84	318
Dhindsa . .	635	6	600	5	21	3

Sub-division.	Total.	Tehsils.				
		Sialkot.	Pasrur.	Zafarwal.	Raya.	Daska.
Jat Ghuman . .	3,314	2,099	353	47	83	732
Gill . .	1,451	219	341	44	813	34
Her . .	139	139	..	..	..	..
Hinjra . .	405	26	30	46	144	159
Kahlon . .	1,852	..	148	888	799	17
Kang . .	358	11	6	110	64	167
Ladhar . .	149	11	2	..	1,136	..
Man . .	694	108	15	..	71	..
Nagre . .	1,208	109	941	38	21	99
Pannu . .	276	7	142	63	64	..
Randhawa .	1,323	51	195	25	1,003	49
Sahi . .	1,107	10	64	7	7	1,019
Sarai . .	174	11	..	..	20	143
Sidhu . .	87	87	..	..	..	..
Sandhu . .	2,328	304	299	97	465	1,163
Varaich . .	831	41	87	175	471	57
Virk . .	757	70	267	21	71	328

Gurdaspur District.

The Gurdaspur district has a large number of Jat Sikh sub-divisions, most of whom have their habitat in the Gurdaspur and Batala tehsils. Those of any importance have already been explained in considerable detail under one or other of the previous districts and it is only proposed to enumerate these sub-divisions in the present instance.

Jats Sikh Sub-Divisions.

Clan.	Numbers.	Tehsils.			
		Gurdaspur	Batala.	Sakargarh.	Pathankot.
Jat Athwal	597	236	255	106	..
Aulak	939	283	626	30	..
Bajwe	1,237	160	380	692	5
Bains	1,063	343	..	684	36
Bal	523	103	441	..	9
Basra	286	..	..	286	..
Bhangu	341	319	22	..	..
Bhullai	743	243	489	..	..
Bhuttar	382	308	74	..	..
Bhattewid	699	248	451	..	..
Both	794	196	598	..	..
Bopa Rai	1,647	649	993	..	..
Chahil	2,215	1,188	1,017	..	10
China	248	108	127	..	13
Chuna	970	427	543	..	..
Dayar	1,698	..	1,698	..	..
Dheriwal	1,538	825	704	..	9
Dhillon	1,287	769	518	..	..
Gharal	1,004	..	1,004	..	..
Ghuman	1,248	1,143	101	..	..
Gil	2,305	867	1,135	224	79
Goraya	2,538	773	1,254	511	..
Hanjira	261	66	195	..	..
Jokal	523	509	14	..	..
Kahlon	6,212	1,465	1,559	3,179	9
Kamon	734	..	734	..	..
Khera	720	371	349	..	..

Clan.	Numbers.	Tehsils.			
		Gurdaspur.	Batala.	Shakargarh	Pathankot.
Jat Mali	1,858	207	241	1,405	5
Man	764	276	481	..	..
Nat	707	160	547	..	..
Padda	674	186	488	..	..
Pandar. . . .	766	..	766	..	..
Pannun . . .	1,001	264	757	..	..
Randhawa . . .	9,455	1,073	8,141	220	21
Rayar	1,567	507	1,060	..	..
Sarai	1,639	405	1,128	106	..
Sidhu	3,725	1,421	1,996	225	83
Sindhu. . . .	565	180	385	..	..
Sobal	559	313	3	243	..
Samra	621	252	302	67	..
Thatale . . .	151	145	6	..	..
Vahla	1,035	643	102	290	
Varaich . . .	500	386	114	..	..
Virk	512	339	172	..	..

Gujranwala District.

The following Jat Sikh sub-divisions are found in the Gujranwala district :—

Clan.	Numbers.	Tehsils. Gujranwala	Wazirabad.	Hafizabad.	Khangah Dogran.	Sharagpur.
Jat Aulak .	511	304	..	14	161	32
Bajwa .	689	58	..	16	615	..
Bhangu .	203	87	..	..	116	..
Bhuttar .	2	2	..	..	..	..
Chahil .	277	169	..	8	79	21
Chattha .	816	26	333	358	99	..
Chima .	2,130	769	765	46	475	75
Deo. .	278	31	..	9	238	..
Dhariwal .	319	131	44	5	139	..
Dhillon .	904	343	47	19	171	324
Dhotar .	1,175	819	36	253	60	7
Ghuman .	498	180	46	18	254	..
Gill . .	1,116	158	153	54	660	91
Goraya .	1,472	1,080	..	36	345	11
Hinjra .	1,424	638	60	466	256	4
Kahlon .	324	58	..	..	266	..
Man .	163	51	10	..	102	..
Mangat .	114	9	..	..	105	..
Pannun .	255	31	..	..	224	..
Randhawa .	552	55	40	..	420	37
Sahi . .	84	6	..	8	70	..
Sarai . .	61	..	..	..	27	34
Sindhu .	2,456	649	48	61	1,010	..
Sipra .	17	13	4	..	..	..
Tarar .	113	82	27	..	4	54
Varaich .	2,396	1,542	41	22	737	1,550
Virk . .	17,278	5,277	79	539	9,833	..

The Doaba.

Jullundur District.

The Jullundur district is known as the Doaba, and lies between the Beas and Sutlej rivers; it has an area of 1,433 square miles, or is somewhat larger than that of the country of Essex. It has 4 tehsils, those of Jullundur, Nawashahr, Phillaur, and Nakodar. Below the hills the whole Doab is an expanse of alluvial soil, considered with reason by the Sikhs to be the garden of the Punjab. The principal tribe of the Jullundur district is the Jat, who is by far the most important section of the population, forming 1/5th of the inhabitants of the district. Here, as in many other places, a man of this tribe does not call himself a Jat, but a "Zamindar", or agriculturist, if he does not give the name of his clan. Jat Sikh villages are found all over the district. There are a very large number of sub-divisions, or "Gots", though as in Ambala there are few clusters of villages belonging to any one clan.

The following is a list of "Gots" with their numerical strength, which will be found in the district :—

Jat Athwal	2,100
,, Bains	2,150
,, Bajwa	600
,, Bal	500
,, Basi	1,900
,, Bhullar	250
,, Chahil	900
,, Chattha	350
,, Chima	975
,, Dhariwal	2,300
,, Dhillon	3,000
,, Dhindsa	550
,, Dosajh	2,150
,, Jhumma	75
,, Gil	3,500
,, Her	1,500
,, Johal	3,500
,, Kahlon	600
,, Kang	1,800
,, Mahil	1,450
,, Man	2,000
,, Pawania	1,050
,, Randhawa	1,100
,, Sari	265
,, Saholei	2,200
,, Sanger	2,750
,, Sarai	1,000
,, Sidhu	750
,, Sindhu	5,000
,, Sohal	1,400
,, Sumea	2,000
,, Virk	1.050

Kapurthala State.

The following Jat-Sikh sub-divisions are to be found in this State :—

Bal Sikh	1,150
Basi	2,000
Dosanj	2,000
Johal	1,000
Sandere	200
Sahota	75

The total number of Sikhs in this State, according to the 1911 census was 23,000, but the majority are those other than Jat.

Hoshiarpur District.

Hoshiarpur is a district of the Jullundur division, comprising so much of the Siwalik range as lies between the Sutlej and the Beas, together with a broad strip of country at the foot of the range, and the greater portion of the valley of the Sohan which lies between it and the outer Himalayas. Its length is 94 miles and its breadth varies from 20 to 32 miles; it consists of 2,232 square miles. The district was annexed by the British with the rest of the Jullundur Doab at the close of the 1st Sikh War.

The Jats come first numerically, and are found almost entirely in the plains. The principal Jat clans in point of numbers are the Bains, who have a "barah" of 12 villages near Mahilpur; the Gil of the Kuk "Muhin" who have a "baiya" of 22 villages round Khararawal Bassi, Achharwal, Rajpur and Lakhsian; and Man Jats near Dhada. There are many other clans, but they do not own clusters of villages situated close together, as in the case of those mentioned. They are as follows :—

—	Hoshiarpur.			
	Hoshiarpur.	Dasuya.	Garhshankar.	Una.
Jat Athwal	180	20	36	..
Bains	1,000	30	3,400	1,300
Chabil	20	50	130	50
Dhariwal	20	..	20	450
Dhillar	50	150	550	250
Gil	220	500	2,000	300
Her	3,000	150	560	125

	Hoshiarpur.			
——	Hoshiarpur.	Dasuya.	Garhshankar.	Una.
Jangal	650	5	20	50
Kang	30	150	..	350
Mahil	10	..	120	150
Man	70	20	2,600	200
Pat	75	..	1,500	60
Randhawa	150	100	25	100
Rai	10	..	600	..
Sahata	..	50	200	..
Sidhu	200	..	350	150
Sindhu	150	375	450	250
Sohal	30	1	100	60
Tara	500	..	100	..
Thari	520	..	..	..

CHAPTER VII.

Customs.

General Remarks.—It has already been remarked that during the latter half of the last century Sikhism tended to relapse towards Hinduism, with the results that observances regarding birth, death and marriage ceremonies were carried out largely in accordance with Hindu rites and customs. It has also been pointed out how the army played no small part in combating this tendency. In the present century, however, the inauguration of Singh Sabhas, the Sikh Educational Conference, the teaching of the moderate Akali doctrines and various other social bodies have played an important part in the revival of Sikh ceremonies being carried out in accordance with the customs and rituals prescribed in the Granth Sahib. Nevertheless some Hindu customs are still maintained especially amongst the poorer and lower classes of the community.

In this chapter, an endeavour has been made to avoid any description of such customs and to confine the text to those which are in practice amongst orthodox Sikhs.

It must, however, be realised that in no two districts are ceremonies conducted exactly on the same lines and full details for any particular district should be sought for in the customary law and gazetteers of the districts in question from which the majority of the units' recruits are enlisted. For all practical purposes, however, the paragraphs which follow may be held to be generally applicable; at the same time the influences of education and various other factors such as the changing conditions of society will all exert their influence in the future and these should duly be borne in mind.

Marriage Customs.—In general the distribution of males and females in the Punjab is such that more than half the males are unmarried, whilst about 1/12th are widowers.

On the other hand, especially amongst the Sikhs, nearly every female is married; there are few of a marriageable age who remain unmarried, however, infirm they may be. The excess of unmarried males is due partly to their emigration partly to the paucity of females, and partly to the tendency to have a plurality of wives, resulting mainly from marrying "a deceased brother's wife".

The universality of marriage is due to the fact that marriage, according to the Sikhs, is a sacrament and not merely a social function or a matter of convenience. This is clear from the fact that at the ages of 40 and over approximately only 14 females out of every 10,000 of that sex remain unmarried and these are mostly those who are suffering from some infirmity. Conversely approximately 259 male Sikhs out of every 10,000 remain unmarried after 40 for the reasons described above.

In the connection of marriage generally it may be stated without hesitation that marriage is the aim of every Sikh and his status socially on the event taking place is greatly increased in the eyes of his neighbours.

The parents of every family are imbued with the idea that their daughters should marry and if a girl remains unmarried after the age of 25 it is not unusual for this to be considered a disgrace. No girl however, as a rule has any say in the subject of her own marriage arrangements, and parents may prevent her marrying up to as late as 30 years of age for the following reasons :—

(i) That they consider their social status a high one and yet being poor cannot afford to give a large dowry. They therefore prefer to wait hoping that fortune may favour them thus enabling them to marry their daughter to greater advantage.

(ii) That among certain classes of the ordinary Jat Zamindar a bad custom has been prevalent for the last 30 years causing parents virtually to sell their daughters, and failing a suitable sum being forthcoming immediately, they prefer to wait until it is. This is done sometimes because either they cannot find a girl for their sons and by selling their own daughters they are thus enabled to buy a girl for the son, or again the parents may be badly in debt and have no other means of liquidating it.

The process of parting with the daughter is done very secretly through an agent or medium called a "Bachola". At the same time it is not the intention to convey the impression that marriages contracted through a Bachola are always effected by money, for many honorable marriages are also arranged through this same medium, without this adjunct.

Many Sikhs have perforce to remain bachelors because they cannot afford to pay the price demanded by the girl's parents, who, very possibly well-to-do, will not give their daughters to a poor man. Even under the best circumstances the subject is one to which half the indebtedness of the Zamindars is due.

The following comparative table, which is only approximate, shows the ages at which marriages take place amongst the Sikhs, per thousand of the population :—

Age period.	Sikh Males.	Sikh females.
0—5	..	1
5—10	7	20
10—15	100	300
15—20	300	650

Amongst the Sikhs, marriages still take place even when an infant is under 4 years of age; this custom however is rapidly declining and appears to be chiefly confined to the North West dry area and occurs mostly among the Sajdharis.

When the children live under the protection of the father the custom regarding the order in which they are married is that the sons are generally married in the order of seniority; similarly in the case of daughters, the elder must be married before the next younger sister. In the absence of special reasons it is considered a disgrace to marry the younger son or daughter before the elder one. This custom is general among the Sikhs. Exceptions are only made when, owing to some physical object or for other reasons, it is not possible to find a match for the elder son or daughter, while a suitable alliance can be arranged for a younger member to the advantage of one or both parties, if contracted without delay. The younger son or daughter is also sometimes married before the elder, if convenient, provided that the elder son or daughter has been betrothed.

The age of marriage for boys is, however, being raised gradually and consequently the objection to the younger sister being married before the elder brother is losing its force, especially with the Sikhs, where the marriageable age of boys being higher, the marriage of girls is not put off in favour of the elder boys.

Where sons grow up independent of the father, or if the brothers separate at the death of the father, they marry at their own discretion, usually without precedence to birth. In these cases a friend is despatched to go about the country and arrange a suitable match. Amongst the Hindus seasons are either auspicious or inauspicious for the celebration of marriages, thus no marriage is allowed when Jupiter or Venus are invisible. These general observances do not hold good with the Sikhs, though some Zamindars are still under the influence of village Brahmans to whose doctrines however they do not adhere very closely. The Arya Samaj and the other Reform Societies do away with all astronomical observations.

A proportion of the Sikhs still however celebrate marriages according to Hindu rites. The more orthodox go by the "Anand" form of marriage, which has now been recognised as legal and will be described further on.

Formalities before marriage. Preliminary Steps.—No special procedure is followed in the informal arrangements of alliances. Whether the boy's or girl's side will take the initiative depends upon circumstances. Direct communications are not out of the question with Sikhs whereas they are so in the case of Hindus and Mahomedans. Practically all the marriages among well-to-do Sikhs are arranged by direct communication between the parents of the boy and girl and this tendency is on the increase. Messages are usually sent through friends, priests, or Bhats, or through the class of menials to whom this duty is specially relegated, *viz.*, the barbers or mirasis.

After selecting a propitious day, the father sends out his "Lagis" or matrimonial agents to some other village, frequently at considerable distances, to seek for a suitable bridegroom. These "lagis" are generally three in number, one being a Brahman, another a Nai, while the third is a Mirasi. They select a candidate and having satisfied themselves as to his social position, the means of his parents, and his freedom from physical defects, return to their employer and report progress. Whether the match has to be arranged for a boy or girl, the formal communication is not made till after the matter has been practically settled by the exchange of informal messages. Matters connected with dowries and ornaments are usually entrusted to servants in preference to agents of standing. At this stage the boy's people must invariably sue for the hand of the girl and the girl's parents or guardians must take the initiative in confirming the alliance.

The proposal on behalf of the boy's parents, etc., is made in various ways. In castes and families where the correspondence of certain aspects shown in the horoscopes of the boy and girl is an essential condition of marriage, the proposal takes the form of sending an extract from the boy's horoscope to the girl's parents, but where the precaution is not considered necessary, as in the Western Punjab, a number of the boy's relatives, often males, and sometimes females, wait upon the elders of the girl's family to communicate the request. The acceptance of the offer by the girl's parents takes the form of either a verbal or written message to that effect or the "Sagan" (presents for the boy) is sent straight away.

The presents range from one rupee and a few "kuzas of Misri" to a 100 sovereigns together with a maund of "Misri", all being dependant on the circumstances of the financial situation of those of the boy.

All the village lumberdars, relatives and other villagers are collected together with the village menials. The boy concerned is seated on a small wooden "Takht" called a "Chowki", and the Brahman or Nai who has come from the side of the girl puts the money brought by him into the boy's lap, while he places a small piece of misri into his mouth. This finishes the ceremony called "Larki Ke chowki baithna", except that some money is distributed by the "Panchayat" to all the village servants, this having been duly provided by the boy's parents for this object. The procedure is known as "Lag". The Brahman or Nai coming from the girl's side is given some money as his "Pushtna" in addition to that to cover his travelling expenses called "Rahdari". On occasions also robes and ornaments for the girl are sent by the boy's parents by the hand of these Brahmans or Nais. This is known as "Charahwa". It is to be noted that orthdox Sikhs instead of causing the boy to sit on a "chowki" make him sit in front of the Granth Sahib which is opened for this purpose.

The details of the betrothal ceremony however vary a great deal all over the Punjab and are given in the gazetteer and customary law of each district and State; the above is the practice most in vogue.

The ceremony recently described corresponds to our betrothal and is generally alluded to as "Sak", "Sargai" or "Kurmai". In some respectable families, the exchange of messages alluded to is considered sufficient to complete the betrothal, but frequently the foregoing ceremonial is completed in its entirety. In general the betrothal is a contract between the parents or guardians of the boy and the girl. A grown up male sometimes enters into the contract personally, if he has no guardians or parents to act for him. The perpetual tutelage of women is, however, strongly asserted throughout the province, and so at no age can a woman enter into a contract regarding her own marriage.

Amongst the Sikhs the contract is not revocable, except under certain conditions, *viz.*, if the boy turns out to be incapacitated by some incurable disease or infirmity. The idea seems to have originated with the recognition by Manu of the gift of a girl by word of mouth as tantamount to marriage. The modern tendency however is to treat the betrothal as revocable and numerous instances exist of the annulment of the contract without sufficient cause. In any case a breach of betrothal contract makes a party liable to damages, but the recording party is never forced to complete the contract.

Bride-price and Bridegroom price.—The charging of a price for the bride or the bridegroom is not authorised by the Hindu Shastras still less so is this the case with the "Granth Sahib". One of the injunctions of Guru Govind Singh to his followers was that no price should be taken by a Sikh for his daughter. The bride is supposed to be given away with befitting clothes and ornaments, and a dowry, howsoever great, is not considered objectionable; but when a fixed sum or a certain standard of dowry is demanded by the bridegroom's parents, as a condition of the acceptance of the girls' hand, the gift amounts to nothing short of "bridegroom-price". In the better classes, both practices are considered highly objectionable, but amongst the masses they prevail in varying degrees, the payment of a bride-price being much more in vogue than the other custom, owing to the deficiency of females. Nevertheless well-to-do people do want a big dowry for their sons, thus indirectly it is said to be the price of a bridegroom.

The following extracts from two of the district codes of customary law corroborate the prevalence of the custom amongst certain castes throughout the Province :—

> "A girl is looked upon as a valuable piece of property and betrothal is a contract by which the girl's family bind themselves, often for a monetary consideration, or in exchange for another betrothal, to transfer the ownership of the girl to the boy's family on her reaching a marriageable age. If either of the parties die before

the marriage actually takes place the contract is at an end and the boy's family are not, as in Sirsa, considered entitled to claim that the girl should be married to another boy of their family, if her original betrothed should die. The ceremony of marriage actually transfers the ownership of the girl from her agnates to those of the boy"—(Customary Law, Shahpur).

"The Garewals and other high Gots of Jats profess to regard the taking of a consideration for a girl as a sin; but there are not many families in any of the 'Gots' that refrain from doing it now-a-days. Where money is taken the girl is the commodity to be sold; and the boy's people begin. No 'Lagis' are sent by them; but the boy's father or some near relation with one or two others goes to the girl's house and a bargain is struck. The price in former times is said to have been Rs. 40 at the time of the betrothal, and Rs. 80 at the time of marriage, but as much as Rs. 500 is not at all an uncommon price now—half being given before the betrothal and half at marriage. This sum even reaches the figures of one and two thousand. When the bargain has been struck the girl's parents send their 'lagis' or generally one man (Nai), to the boy's house and the necessary ceremonies are performed"—(Customary Law—Ludhiana District).

The Invitation.—The fixing of the date of marriage rests with the bride's father or guardian, and when an auspicious date has been determined, after consulting the astrologer, an invitation is sent by the bride's guardian, by letter two or three months before the date selected. If the boy's side have no objection to urge, preparations begin to be made on both sides. The regular invitation is, however, sent only a few days before the marriage (usually between 9 and 21 days). The priest, accompanied by the barber or some other attendant conveys the note, which mentions the date, hour and minute at which the marriage ceremony is to be performed, and asks the bridegroom's guardian to come and celebrate the wedding at the appointed time. The number of followers expected is also sometimes mentioned. The arrival of the priest with this letter is made the occasion of a regular gathering of friends and relatives at the bridegroom's house. Some ceremonies are gone through after which the priest and barber return with presents, according to the means of the boy's people.

The letter is sometimes accompanied by gifts of clothes and ornaments for the mother of the boy. This is called "Ropna" or "Tika".

Superstitions.—The anxiety to keep off evil influences is not absent from marriage ceremonies even amongst Sikhs. The custom of wearing an iron ring, the tying of an iron ring in the "Kanga" and "Baddhi" (The "Kangna" is a ban made of "Mauli" string in which various articles counteracting evil spiritual influences are tied. It is prepared by seven women and is worn by the bridegroom on his right wrist. A similarly prepared band tied with the same purpose on his right ankle is called "baddhi". "Kangna" and "Badhi" are similarly worn by the bride, but on the left wrist and right ankle respectively), or keeping a knife about the bridegroom's person from the commencement of the marriage procession till his return home, is mainly a precaution against the interference of the evil spirits. The reverence of the Guru comes into prominence even in connection with marriage. The family priest is indispensable, and has to perform certain ceremonies before the bridegroom can be dressed.

Among well-to-do Sikhs a bridegroom keeps a sword in his hand while the ordinary Zamindar keeps an iron stick and wears either a yellow dress or at least a yellow pagri. Superstitions are, however, rapidly dying out, anyhow before the 3 days of marriage ceremony itself; the boy and girl are nevertheless not allowed to go out and always keep the iron stick on hand to ward away the evil spirits. The boy goes by the name of "Sahebaya" and the girl by that of "Manji pai hui hai".

The marriage.—Broadly speaking the following is the usually adopted procedure in a Sikh marriage. The date of the ceremony having been fixed, invitations to the marriage feast are issued by the parents of both parties to their relations and friends, who are expected in their turn to make a collection in aid of expenses. On the morning of the bridegroom's departure for the bride's village, he is dressed in yellow, wreathed with a "sera" or necklace of flowers and crowned with a "Mukat", or headdress, made of mica and tinsel paper faced with a fringe of gold threads as a screen from the evil eye. A Brahman ties the "Kangna" or seven knotted bracelet on the boy's wrist, and marshalled by the Nai, the "Barat" or procession is ready to start. The bridegroom usually rides a mare, whilst the procession is composed entirely of males, as many of them as possible being mounted. The "barat" then goes to the house of the bride. As it approaches the limits of her village, which should not be before sunset, her relatives and other males of the village who have been bidden to the ceremony meet it at a place which is usually an open one just outside, called "khet". This procedure is known as "milni" and the father or other senior relatives of the girl gives something to the father of the bridegroom in the shape of a present which may range from a costly shawl and a horse to a rupee and some khaddar cloth. At the same time the procession is refreshed with either some "sherbat" or "lassi" if the weather is hot, or tea if it is cold. After dark the bridegroom is conducted to the bride's house, surrounded by her friends and relations. He subsequently returns to his party where a feast takes place. Early next morning, even as early as three or four o'clock, the marriage ceremony takes place either by that known as "Phere", "Lawan" or by "Anand". It will be advisable to deviate here in order to briefly describe what these ceremonies are.

Sikh marriages were, in the past, celebrated according to the ordinary Hindu rites, performed by Brahmans, with the difference that hymns of the fourth Guru were sung simultaneously by the females during the ceremony in place of the Hindu songs. Later on a dual ceremony was adopted, whereby the Hindu rites were gone through first, and then the wedded couple circumambulated the Granth Sahib four times, while the Sikh priest read the "lawan" above mentioned. The orthodox Sikhs of modern times have, however, completely given up the Hindu ritual and content themselves with the circumambulation of the "Granth Sahib". and the reading of hymns by the Sikh priest. The "lawan" which are a counterpart of the four "Pheras" (going round the sacrificial fire) but known to the Sikhs as "Parkarma", constitute the binding part of the ceremony, at the conclusion of which, the "Anandbani" is read and "Karahparshad" of Rs. 1-4-0 or more is distributed. This ceremony is known as the "Anand" marriage. Marriages are still celebrated in the old style and regular codes have been printed to regulate both the ancient and the modern (Anand) forms of marriage. Nuptial rites are as a rule celebrated at night but the Anand ceremony may be performed at any time.

A translation of the four "Lawan" composed by Guru Ram Das and contained in the "Granth Sahib" will be found in the Appendices. The first "Laon" (round) is interpreted to represent the launching of the soul on the "Pravritti marga" (path of forthgoing) where it begins to gain experience by taking in knowledge, etc.; adherence to duty is ordained as the safeguard at this stage. The second round is to mark the approach of the disciple to the true Guru, the purification of the mind and the realization of self. In the third round begins the "Nivritti marga" (or turning homewards). The contemplation of God now comes uppermost in the mind. In the fourth round the love of God predominates and the union of the self with the Supreme is attained. Anand is thus a peace-chant, read at the end of every religious ceremony. It is not meant exclusively for marriage ceremonies. Indeed no auspicious ceremony is viewed as complete without its recital.

To resume. After the "Anand" the "Khat" ceremony is next proceeded with. This constitutes the handing over of the dowry to the parents or guardian of the boy whilst other "Baraties" are honoured by the presentation of gifts varying according to the status of the parties. The day is thus generally spent in feasting, rejoicing and observing the ceremonies which precede the departure of the bride. She sets out seated in a dooly and accompanied by her "Lagis" and the Nai's wife, and is conducted to the house of the bridegroom, where on the following day the ceremony of "Got Kumala" is observed.

Marriage should take place in the first, third, or fifth year following betrothal. The even years are considered unlucky. In theory it is considered that a daughter should be married before she is 12 years of age but in most cases, the services of a girl are so valuable to her family that she is detained by her father until she is fifteen, sixteen, or even older.

Miscellaneous Ceremonies.—Certain subsidiary customs which take place before and after the marriage are worth mention.

"*Maiyan*".—Seven or eight days before the date of the marriage, the bride and bridegroom are supposed to be confined to their houses. The latter cannot go out until the marriage procession and the former until the "doli" ceremony. This is called "Maiyan" or "Sahe baithna". This is obviously a precaution against accidents but it is also probably intended to avoid exposure to the sun and to enhance the beauty as far as possible. With this view, both parties have to rub oil all over the body every morning, after which they are sponged with a mixture of flour and ghee called "Batna" before taking their bath. Neither party is supposed to change clothes during the period so that by the time that it is over, they are wearing very dirty clothes, and consequently the sudden change to dazzling costumes has a strikingly marked effect.

"*Vari*" *and* "*Khat*".—"Vari" is the name given to the ornaments and clothes made by the parents of the boy for the bride. All these are shown at the bride's house to relatives of the bride. "Khat" is the ceremony in which the parents of the girl give cash, ornaments, utensils, clothes, to the parents of the boy. This ceremony is performed during the days of the actual marriage itself while the "Barat" (procession) is still in the house of the bride before starting back.

"*Chhand*".—This ceremony is dying down but it still holds good amongst certain classes. The bride's rlations appear to have a right to test the intelligence of the bridegroom, and after the wedding ceremony and before the advent of the procession, the bridegroom is sent for to the bride's house by the women folk of the bride, where all the wives and girls of the village collect, and is required to recite verses to them.

"*Lassi Mundri*" *or* "*Kangna khelna*".—This custom is rapidly declining. It consists of filling a tray with whey or diluted milk and throwing a ring or rupee, or some other articles into it. The tray is placed before the couple and they are required to hunt simultaneously for the object named by those present. Whoever picks it up is considered victorious and is lionised. The procedure takes place at the bridegroom's house.

"*Mutthi kholna*".—The parties have to enter into a trial of physical strength. A rupee is, in turn, placed in the palm of each and the hand closed. The other is asked to take the rupee out of the fist. The custom is dying down but still takes place among ordinary classes. Some of these ceremonies are obviously intended either to test the comparative shrewdness of the bride and bridegroom or to familiarize them to engaging in common pursuits.

Consummation of marriage.—In the case of early marriage, deferred consummation necessitates a separate ceremony to mark the completion of connubial relationship. The ceremony amongst Sikhs is known as "Maklawa". There are thus three stages in a marriage :—

1st stage	betrothal or "Mangna."
2nd stage	marriage or "bea."
3rd stage	consummation or "Muklawa".

Sometimes, however, the 1st and 2nd, and the 2nd and 3rd are performed together. As a rule consummation takes place at the third stage, except in marriages of adults when it may take place at the 2nd stage, though the ceremony of "Muklawa" is also performed afterwards. On this occasion there are rejoicings on both sides, the bridegroom goes with a limited following, if not alone, to the bride's house where a ceremony purporting to unite the two parties further is gone through and the bridegroom subsequently goes off with the bride.

Widow Marriage.—The marriage of widows is not allowed by the Hindu Shastras, nevertheless restricted widow marriage appears to have existed in Vedic times. The custom is prevalent among Sikhs and where possible the widow is married without the imposition of any limitations to the brother of the deceased. The feeling against widow marriage has continued unchecked to this day, in so much that its transgression, perhaps more so among Hindus than Sikhs, has resulted in the degradation of individuals to a lower status. The custom despite this is common amongst Jats and other agricultural classes. and the practice most common is for the widow to marry the deceased husband's brother. In such cases no distinction is made as to whether the husband's brother is older or younger than the deceased, although preferably the widow is married to a younger member of the family. The ceremony is known as "Karewa" or "Chadarandazi". Few formalities are observed. The main point is that the parties should agree to the relationship of husband and wife, or that the parents or guardian of the woman should consent to her being taken in wedlock by the intending husband. The man and woman are seated together and a white sheet is thrown over the pair by some Brahman, Sadhu, or elder of the brotherhood and presents of bracelets, nose-ring ("nath"), ear-rings ("bali") are made to the woman or a rupee is placed in her hand. In some States the ceremony is required to be done before a magistrate. In any case, no "Karewa" is legal until sanction has been obtained in writing on a stamped paper. The occasion is celebrated by a feast.

Very often no formality at all is observed and, if a bride-price has to be paid, as is generally the case, the mere fact of the woman being brought home by the husband after the payment is considered sufficient to mark the commencement of their matrimonial relation.

In the event of there being no deceased husband's brother, a cousin may take the widow, or if he also is non-existent or no one is thought fit by the widow herself or by her parents, she is frequently given by them into another village.

Restrictions on marriage.—Amongst the Sikhs the prohibited degrees for marriage are simple. A man must marry within his own caste, and the collaterals of the father and the mother's father should ordinarily be avoided.

Every Jat clan is exogamous, *i.e.*, while every man "must" marry into his own tribe, no man "can" marry into his own clan, as such a union would be regarded as incest. Besides the above prohibitions, it is unusual for a man to marry into a family of whatever clan it may be that is settled in his own village, or in any village immediately adjoining his own. Unions between persons of different religion are forbidden, but for this purpose no difference is made between Jats who are Hindus and Jats who are Sikhs.

Functions performed by certain kin in ceremonials.—Special functions are assigned to certain relations in certain ceremonials. The maternal uncle takes an important part in the marriage of both a boy and a girl and all other sacramental ceremonies concerning the boy. The maternal grandfather of a boy or a girl is treated as the elder "Samdhi" (Sambandhi) or "Kuram" at a marriage and has to contribute gifts at a girl's marriage. While he partakes of the gifts received at a boy's marriage. The younger brother of a boy has to officiate as his junior ("Sarbahla") at his marriage, and the bride's younger sisters act as her bridesmaids.

Polyandry.—Polyandry, or the custom of a woman having more husbands than one at a time is peculiar to the Himalayas. In rare cases it does exist amongst certain classes of Sikhs, but is not openly practised. It is however, so rare as to be almost considered negligible.

Polygamy.—Among the Hindus there is no limit to the number of wives which a man may marry. Manu himself appears to have allowed more wives than one. The custom is prevalent amongst Sikhs and is permitted in certain cases. The reasons therefore would appear to be chiefly economic. In order to keep the family property a deceased brother's wife has to be remarried by "Karewa" to her husband's surviving brother. The usual practice, however, is that a man may have but one wife and does not marry a second during the life-time of the first unless the latter fails to bear a son, suffers from some infirmity, is false to her husband, or there is some disagreement between her and her husband.

Marriage by Service.—This is rare amongst the Sikhs, and as a rule only happens when the girl's father has no son. The familiar form of this marriage is that in which a daughter is married to a "ghar-jawai" (resident son-in-law) who has to live permanently with the girl's parents and work for them at their profession, agriculture, trade or whatever it may be. The work done by the son-in-law may be taken as a bride-price, but he gets a return for it in so far that he either inherits the property of his father-in-law, retaining his own "got" (family name), or more generally his eldest son is adopted by his father-in-law who is thus able to continue his lineal descent, while the son-in-law gains by one of his sons inheriting the property of his father-in-law. The younger sons retain the "got" of their own family.

Hypergamy.—In India where the selection of husbands for their daughters is entirely a parental concern, uninfluenced by the feelings of the chief contracting party, it is only natural that they should wish to provide the best possible home for their female children who are to depend for the happiness on the earnings and social status of their would-be husbands. Hygergamy, therefore is regarded as the ideal choice so far as the female is concerned; while the practice seems to have begun in attempts of individuals to give their daughters into families of higher social status, it crystallised into a rigid rule the disregard of which came to be penalised. The bonds of the whole social fabric being now in a state of relaxation, owing partly to the spread of education and chiefly to mercenary considerations, radical changes in social status are taking place, and instances are becoming more and more frequent of men of high social standing giving their daughters into a family of much lower status, who possess wealth or prospects, or to promising young men of education but of low birth, who belong to the same caste or sub-caste, *i.e.*, to the same endogamous group. Amongst the Sikhs this is very true.

Divorce.—Divorce is a recognised institution among Mohamedans, but with Hindus and Sikhs no such custom is authorised. Marriage, according to the Hindu Shastras, is a sacred union intended not merely for the procreation of species and of mutual happiness, but also for the performance of religious duties, and is irrevocable. Mutual fidelity terminating alone with death is inculcated. By being assimilated to the husband's family ("gota"), the wife is supposed to become incapable of disclaiming her connection with that "gotra" and uniting hereself to another, for "once only a girl is given in marriage, once only one says, Let me give", (Manu).

Among the lower caste (especially menials) of Hindus and Sikhs, a wife is sometimes given up on account of infidelity without any ceremony, but usually on payment of a sum of money. This only happens when she carries on a liaison with some other man and the husband is powerless to stop it. The husband then accepts a price for the wife, more or less than that paid by him, and the man who pays the money marries the woman by "karewa". A custom which may be considered equivalent to divorce exists in the Western Punjab among those people who have, on account of paucity of females in their brotherhood, to buy females brought in from other parts of the province and marry them with only a nominal ceremony and sometimes with none. In such cases the husband, if he disapproves, of the wife, usually passes her on to somebody else at a smaller price than that which he paid for her.

Freedom after marriage.—As a matter of principle, a wife is expected by all religions and castes to be perfectly chaste and true to her husband. But it is an open secret that laxity of morals prevails amongst all grades of society to a larger or smaller extent. The menial classes do not, as a rule, take serious notice of the looseness of their women's characters, and there are certain castes such as the Pernas and Mirasis, whose women make a profession of prostitution. But even among some castes who do not connive at such liberty, a son born to a wife during her elopement is not disowned by her husband if she eventually comes back to his protection. The idea underlying this seems to be that the woman is considered to be the property of the husband and consequently the husband is supposed to have the right to own the child born in the wedlock; if he disowns the child he has also to discard the wife. On the other hand, the desire to have a male off-spring seems to have gone a long way to popularise the acceptance of illegitimate sons. The poorer Jat classes of the Sikhs are no exception to the foregoing, but statistics would appear to show that the subject is comparatively rare. The reason underlying the acceptance by the husband of the wife appears to be largely forced by circumstances, where a man cannot get a second wife and the first is a necessity to him for the running of his house, cooking of his food, etc., which he can only do himself at the expense of his agricultural pursuits.

The Purdah system.—The social reforms of the day generally condemn the Purdah system (seclusion of women) as a foreign institution dating from the Mohamedan invasions. This view is apparently erroneous. Traces of the system are found in the Code of Manu, who advocated the perpetual tutelage of women "the father protects her in childhood, the husband in youth, the son in old age, hence a woman is never fit for independence". He also laid down that women should be preserved even from very ordinary social intercourse with males.

Amongst the Sikh peasantry this system is not observed, but the wives of the villagers do not come out of their houses unveiled when going to their fields, or to draw water at the village well, and as a rule they remain veiled, especially in the sight of a stranger, until they remain old. Daughters go everywhere in the village when it is necessary to do so, as a rule unveiled: even when they return as married women to their parents' village, but generally speaking until a girl is married she does not go about and is kept to the house where her household duties fully occupy her time.

In high families, however, the Purdah system is observed, though not to the same extent as with the "Sayads". With the educated Sikhs the custom is dying out and cultured wives are beginning to go about with their husbands. The tendency will probably increase in the future and will become very much more common.

Restrictions on the use of the name of certain kin.—There are certain relations whose names may not be mentioned, *e.g.*, a husband may not mention his wife's name, nor the wife the husband's. The usual way to get over the difficulty is by saying so and so's father or mother.

Nor again may the daughter-in-law mention the name of her father-in-law or that of any elder relation of her husband, she can only mention them by the term of relationship, the form of address being generally the same as that used by the husband.

Birth customs and ceremonies.—During pregnancy no rites are observed amongst Sikh women except that great precautions are taken during the Solar and Lunar eclipses. A woman is thus not supposed to work during an eclipse and is often not allowed even to move, as it is believed that any movement of the mother is likely to affect the appearance of the child. This idea especially holds good among elderly women. Before child birth purgatives and laxative food are generally avoided, especially in the advanced stages. In the first few days after delivery the parents of the girl send some "Panjiri" for the girl and ornaments and clothes for the child. "Panjiris" is a confection of Ghi, sugar, almonds, flour, raisins, dates, cocoanut, etc., fried in a pan, and is a very favourite dish. Amongst the Sikhs the mother is confined to the room for a period of 13 days, after which there is no restriction to leaving the house. For the first five days strict seclusion is observed. Only a few selected persons, usually one or two elderly women in the family who are present at the time of confinement are allowed in the room besides the mid-wife. No stranger, even of the female sex, may go in, and the other male and female members of the family may not step inside the door of the room. A cat must on no account be allowed to enter the room. All these precautions are taken to prevent the evil influence of malevolent spirits, although they may have been based originally on hygienic principles. The room must never be in utter darkness and so a lamp is kept burning throughout the night. A little fire is kept smouldering in the room for the burning of incense from time to time, which, though believed to drive off evil spirits, really serves to disinfect the air. Midwives nearly always come from the lower classes and frequently include Mohamedans. These are known as "dhais". The birth of a son is the occasion of great rejoicing in contradistinction to that of a daughter. In the case of the former, village menials welcome the parents and offer green grass called "Dub" a symbol of happiness; they are duly tipped by the father. In the case of a daughter no "dub" is presented. The only relic of the old custom still prevailing is the hanging up over the doorpost of a branch of "Siris" tree. The suckling of the new-born is usually delayed for 10 or 12 hours. The first thing given to the baby is a potion ("ghutti") of the nature of a purgative and to prepare the digestive organs for food. It is usually administered by some elderly female of the family. The baby is supposed to absorb the nature and habits of this first feeder. The prescription varies with different localities, castes and even families, but in all cases contains a considerable number of ingredients. It is administered by means of cloth wick which the baby learns to suck. The warrior castes and tribes used to stir the "ghutti" with a sword in order to instil courage and the love of arms in the child, but the Arms Act has practically put a stop to the custom. No solid food is given to the baby until he has cut some of his first teeth, *i.e.*, till about the sixth month.

On the eve of the 13th day the females of the family "leep" the whole of the house, clothes are washed, all earth vessels which have been used are broken, and all metal utensils are cleaned and scoured. On the day itself the "parohit" visits the household, lights the "hom" or a sacred fire, and by way of purification sprinkles its members with Ganges water. The Brahman, Nai, and relatives of the family are then feasted, and the father gives presents of clothing to his female kinsfolk; on the same day the various village menials bring the new-born infant toys, typical of their various callings, and receive gifts from the parents in return. In the case, however, of the birth of a girl the feasting and almsgiving, if not altogether omitted, are on a very much smaller scale.

On the 13th or on any odd day after his birth, a name is given to the child. The "Granthi" or any elder member of the family opens the "Granth Sahib" at random. The first letter of the first line on the left hand page at which the book opens, must be the initial letter of the name bestowed on the infant. Thus if "G" ("Gagga") is the first letter above described, any of the names Govind, Ganga, Gajan, Gurbux, etc., may be given. The suffix Singh is usually added at the "Pahul".

Superstitions regarding illnesses of infants.—Among the masses most diseases of children are ascribed primarily to the effects of the evil eye or the influence of some evil spirit. Spiritual remedies are sought therefore before resorting to medical treatment. Matters are however, changing under modern conditions and the use of medicines is being substituted more and more for charms and incantations.

Thus infantile pneumonia was widely believed to be due to the child being possessed by some evil spirit of the crematorium which could only be driven away by a spell (known chiefly to sweepers, chamars, fakirs, or sadhus).

As however already stated superstitions are dying out now, especially in the houses of cultured Sikhs, it is not proposed to go further into details which can be ascertained from various district gazetteers.

Ceremonies reltaing to death.—The death ceremonies prevalent amongst Sikhs are simple compared with those carried out under Hindu auspices.

When death is approaching the patient is laid on the floor, though amongst the educated community he is allowed to remain on his charpoy until death overtakes him. The principle adhered to is that he should be cremated before sunset. If, however, death occurs in the night, the corpse is kept and watched until morning. In the meanwhile wood is collect on the burial ground. The corpse is then lifted on to a bier and carried on the shoulders of four men, near relatives of the deceased, to the place of cremation. A procession follows the bier reading "Shabads". The body is put on the funeral pyre and set on fire. When the body is nearly burnt the procession returns, halting at some well or tank, where they bathe or sometimes only wash face, hands, and feet.

"Karaparshad" is either prepared on the spot or at the house of the deceased of which all members of the procession partake. They then disperse. A male member of the family remains outside and a female member inside to receive the sympathies of relatives and other villagers who come there for the purpose. The reading of the "Granth Sahib" commences and is terminated on the 10th day after death.

Relatives are informed and they usually come on the 10th day, the day of "Bhog", meaning completion of the reading of the "Granth Sahib", to give their sympathies, returning to their homes next day.

On the third day after death the bones of the deceased are collected and are sometimes sent to the Ganges, but by more orthodox Sikhs they are taken to Amritsar where they are thrown stealthily in the tank of the Golden Temple or else are ground to powder and are scattered in the pathway known as the "Parkannia". The object of this latter custom is that the dust of the deceased touching the feet of Holy Sikhs will cause peace to his soul in the next world.

No "Sharadhas" are performed by the Sikhs.

A child of under five years of age is usually buried, if over, is usually cremated. Children of under one year of age are invariably buried.

Terms of Relationships.

A list of the terms of relationship which are common to all the dialects in the Punjab is given below :—

Terms of relationship.	Terms commonly used.
Father	Bap, Bapu.
Father's father	Dada.
Father's Younger Brother	Chacha.
Father's Sister	Phuphi.
Father's Sister's husband	Phuphar.

Terms of relationship.	Terms commonly used.
Mother	Man or Ma.
Mother's sister	Masi.
Mother's brother	Mama.
Mother's brother's wife	Mami.
Mother's father	Nana.
Mother's mother	Nani.
Mother's father's father	Parnana.
Mother's father's mother	Parnani.
Wife's or husband's father	Saohra.
Wife's or husband's mother	Sass.
Wife's brother	Sala.
Wife's sister	Sali.
Wife's Sister's husband	Sandhu.
Daughter	Beti or Dhi.
Son	Beta or Putr.

CHAPTER VIII.

CHARACTERISTICS AND MATTERS PERTAINING TO VILLAGE LIFE.

Influence of the Jats in forming the national character of the Sikhs.—Sikhism, as has already been explained, originated in a religious movement which drew its adherents from all classes, each of which possessed distinctive manners and customs; the social and numerical preponderance of the Jats, however, carried such weight in the formation of the national character, that the customs of the Sikh, whatever his origin, may now be considered as practically identical with those of the Punjab Jat.

The Jat of the Punjab.—The Jats of the Punjab, whether Sikh or Hindu, are in every respect the most important of the Punjab races. In point of numbers, the Jat surpasses the Rajput, who comes next to him in the proportion of one to three. Politically he ruled the Punjab till the Khalsa yielded to the British arms; "ethnologically he is the peculiar and most prominent product of the plains of the five rivers; while, from an economical and administrative point of view, he is, par excellence, the husbandman, the peasant, and the revenue payer of the province. His manners indeed do not bear that impress of generations of wild freedom which marks the races of Afghan hills, but he is more honest, more industrious, and at least their equal in couarge and manliness, if he does not actually surpass them in steadfastness and doggedness in sticking to his post in the hour of danger. In bravery and courage Sikhs and Pathans may be coequal, but the former excel over the latter in this, that the Pathan in his own element will rarely stand a determined attack whereas the Sikh will".

General characteristics.—Sturdy independence and patient vigorous labour are perhaps the strongest characteristics of the Jat Sikhs. In certain tracts, where the Jats have the field to themselves, and are compelled, in default of rivals of other castes, to fall back upon each other for somebody to quarrel with, tribal ties are strong. "But as a rule the Jat is a man who does what seems good in his own eyes and sometimes what is wrong also, and will not be said nay by any man. He is far from turbulent, but is independent and selfwilled. He is usually content to cultivate his fields in quietness if people will leave him alone, though when he does go wrong he takes to anything from gambling to murder, with perhaps a preference for abducting his neighbours' wives and carrying off their cattle.". Although ready to fight on occasion, he is not of a cruel or vindictive disposition, but always asserts personal freedom, as against communal or tribal control, more strongly than any other class. He has neither prudence nor is he gifted with foresight; rarely can he foresee, nor does he care what the results of his action may be. Amongst his own kith and kin he is of haughty disposition and he humbles himself to no man.

The Jat as an agriculturist.—In agriculture the Jat Sikh is pre-eminent. No one can rival him as a landowner and yeoman cultivator. He calls himself a "Zamindar" or husbandman as often as a Jat, and his women and children work with him in the fields. Indeed, it is a common saying in the Punjab that "the Jat's baby has a plough-handle for a plaything.". Among the higher classes of Jat Sikhs, the women do not perform the harder descriptions of fieldwork as is the custom among their Hindu brethren; nevertheless they assist their husbands in various ways, and thus form a marked contrast to Rajput and Mohamedan females, who, being secluded, are lost to agricultural labour.

Condition of the people.—Taken as a whole, the Jat Sikhs are comfortably off. Almost all their villages have a prosperous air, and give evidence of the owners having a very fair standard of comfort. Well-kept Dharmsalas (village rest-house and place of prayer) and well-built drinking wells are seen in almost every district; the peasants are well clothed, and judging from their physique, well and sufficiently fed. Canal irrigation and the export of wheat have done much to enrich the people, but they are apt to squander much of their wealth in costly litigation, and in the extravagant observance of marriages and religious festivals.

Disposition of the Jat Sikh.—It has been truly said of the Jat Sikhs that "they are manly without false pride, undemonstrative, independent without insolence, reserved in manner, but good-natured and industrious. No one could be associated with them for any time without conceiving both respect and liking for them.". These qualities, however, are differently impressed upon different races and localities. Thus "the Jat of the Manjha is conspicuously genial and good-tempered, joining heartily in games and recreations, while the Malwai, if less genial, is more stubborn, and works quite as conscientiously but less cheerfully; this very stolidity renders him perhaps less liable to panic, and though the Manjha Sikh was preferred by Ranjit Singh to his confrére from the Malwa, there is really very little to choose between them".

Thus the District Gazetteer of Amritsar gives the following description :—"The Sikh Jats of whom the Manjha are the pick, are the finest of the Amritsar peasantry. In physique they are inferior to no race of peasantry in the Province, and among them are men, who, in any country in the world, would be deemed fine specimens of the human race.

The Sikh Jat is generally tall and muscular, with well shaped limbs, erect carriage, and strongly marked and handsome features. They are frugal and industrious; though not intellectual, they have considerable shrewdness in the ordinary affairs of life, and are outspoken and possessed of unusual independence of character. They are certainly litigious, their natural stubbornness leading them to persevere in a case long after all chance of success is gone, but at the same time they are perhaps as honest and simple a face as is to be found in India, for the false speaking, common in the law courts, is conventional, and hardly indicative of moral depravity. They make admirable soldiers, when well led, inferior to no native race in India, with more dogged courage than dash, steady in the field, and trustworthy in difficult circumstances, and without the fanaticism that makes the Pathan always dangerous. In private life they are not remarkable for chastity, and they are largely addicted to the use of intoxicating drugs or spirits, but on the whole their faults are less conspicuous than their virtues. The women are inferior in physique to the men, and age sooner, probably from the effects of early marriages, and are not remarkable for beauty. But they have the same industrious habits as the men and make excellent house wives frugal and careful in management, and exercise a very considerable amount of influence in the family."

On the other hand the district customary law of the Ludhiana district states :—

> "The Jat of this district deserves all the good things that have been written of the tribe. If the Jats are the best peasantry in India, I think we may say that the Malwa Jat possesses in a greater degree than any other branch of the tribe the qualities which have earned for them this distinction. In physique he is not surpassed by any race in India, if indeed he is not to be put at the top of the tree in this respect. The Malwa Jat surpasses his brother of the Manjha in prudence and thrift, and he is a better cultivator, more capable of managing his farm, etc..........................".

Both are undeniably excellent fighting material and the fact remains that there is little to choose between them. Preference for one or the other must largely be a matter of opinion, for each has decided characteristics.

Some of the proverbs* of the Punjab would lead one to suppose that the Jat is not very popular with his neighbours, but this disfavour may be attributed to the jealousy of weaker and less industrious races, envious of the prosperity of their Jat rivals, such for instance as the following conceived by other than a Jat Sikh, *viz.* :—"Jat mewa achcha hai parharde jote nal hai" (literally, Jat is a good fruit but can be knocked down with a shoe), in other words, the Jat shows his stubbornness, gives nothing of his own free will, but when pressed will give more. And again :—"Jat ganna na de Bheli de", meaning that a Jat will not give one stick of sugarcane but will give a "Bheli",

---

*** The following sayings of the Punjab peasants are typical of their jealousy of the Jats :—**

> **" The Jat, the Bhat, the caterpillar, and a widow woman, these four are best hungry ; if they eat their full they do harm."**
>
> **" The soil, fodder, hemp, clothes, munj grass and silk, these six are best when beaten, and the seventh is the Jat."**

that is, eight seers of gur made of a hundred such sugarcanes when required to do so. The typical Jat Sikh is faithful and true to his employer, seldom shows insubordination, and with a good deal of self-esteem has a higher standard of honour than is common amongst most Orientals. His disposition is such that he cannot stand sarcasm or nagging. He requires a strong hand, and punishment, when it is meted out, should not err on the side of leniency, but should savour rather of the principle of full weight, if seldom, as opposed to that of lightly and often; this latter method approximates too closely to pin pricks thus causing a feeling of discontent in his mind.

Social position of the Jat in relation to other classes.—Among races of purely Hindu origin, the Jat stands next after the Brahman, the Rajput, and the Khatri. He is of course, below the Rajput, for the simple reason that he practises karao, or widow-marriage, but he stands first among the classes in which this custom is permissible. "The Baniya with his sacred thread, his strict Hinduism and his twice-born standing, looks down on the Jat as a Sudra, but the Jat looks down on the Baniya as a cowardly spiritless money-grabber, and society in general agrees with the judgment of the Jat.". The position of the Jat Sikh, however, is considerably higher than that of his Hindu confrére. This may be attributed partly to the fact that he is a soldier as well as an agriculturist, and partly to the freedom and boldness which he has inherited from the traditions of the Khalsa. The haughty Rajputs, who, according to Hindu ideas, are the natural leaders of society, were offended by the democratic ideas of Guru Govind, and declined to join his standard. They soon paid the penalty of their pride. The Jats who composed the great mass of the Khalsa rose to absolute power, and the Rajputs, who had formerly despised them, became the peculiar objects of their hatred and oppression. As the Sikhs became the dominant landowning and military class of the Punjab, they gradually acquired the social position usually accorded to Rajputs, a position which they have been able to maintain as much through the impulse given to Sikhism by the constant demand for soldiers of this class, as by the high esteem with which they have been regarded by the British authorities since the Mutiny.

Education.—Education amongst the Sikhs has in recent years shown an extraordinary development. Schools have been opened up all over the Punjab and are either assisted by Government or are privately subscribed to and run by a committee of villagers. The old epithet of the Sikh as slow and thickheaded is fast dying down. The Khatri Sikh, as opposed to the Jat, is admittedly quick and well-educated; the nature of his profession demands that he should be so, his intelligence similarly compares favourably with that of the Zamindar, but in his case it is hereditary. The traditional hatred of the Sikh for the Mohamedan went so far as to cause them to object occasionally to the use of the Persian character but the old antipathy to learning Urdu is now a dead letter and great strides are being made in the matter of education all over the Province. The old village dharmsala which constituted the seat of learning for the village is now being discarded and its place is being taken by local schools at which there are frequently large attendances. The standard, however, varies greatly according to districts; the further to the south the lower is the standard, whilst in the extreme southern limits of the Sikh recruiting area, especially in the outdistricts at considerable distances from the railway, the progress of education is very slow, and little difference can be traced to conditions existing at the commencement of the century. In the central Punjab, however, education is rapidly progressing and there are in existence several girls' schools which are turning out a good number of educated girls in the Province.

The Sikh Educational Conference, established for some years in the Punjab has been greatly responsible for this improvement. The standard of education in the units of the Indian Army has recently changed out of all recognition owing to the introduction of the new system, and thus whereas at the commencement of the century approximately 80 per cent. could be said to be almost illiterate, conditions now are such that there are few sepoys who at the end of three years' service cannot write an intelligent letter to their homes.

Progress in future will even be more rapid than it has been in recent years, and concurrently the problem of recruiting may become even more acute than it is now, for it cannot be gainsaid that the educated youth shows considerable reluctance to enlisting as a sepoy, one reason being, having spent a considerable amount on his education the pay appears unattractive, and furthermore his teaching has been to the effect that "the pen is mightier than the sword"; the tendency is thus towards taking up a profession connected with the law courts, medical and political activities, rather than to the hereditary one of arms.

Military qualities.—As has already been explained, the virtues of the Jats are identical with those of the Sikhs, but the latter possess in a higher degree the ardent military spirit which had its origin in the warlike precepts of Govind Singh. After the defeat of the Khalsa army and the annexation of the Punjab Sikhism declined, and the soldier laid aside his sword and musket and returned to the plough. The outbreak of the Mutiny, however, caused an immediate revival of the faith; hundreds of young Jats became Sikhs, and those who but a few years before had proved our stoutest opponents, now joined our ranks and fought for us with a valour and loyalty that is beyond all praise. Since that time service in the army has been eagerly sought after, both in the cavalry and infantry. The Sikh is essentially a fighting man, and his fine qualities are best shown in the army, which is admittedly his natural profession. "Hardy, brave, and of intelligence too slow to understand when he is beaten, obedient to discipline, devoted to his officers, and careless of the caste prohibitions which render so many Hindu races difficult to control and feed in the field, he is unsurpassed as a soldier in the East." There are many warlike races in India whose military qualities are of a high order, but of these the Sikh indisputably takes the leading place as a thoroughly useful and reliable soldier. Wherever fighting is going on, there the Sikh is to be found. Offer him but good pay, and there is no service, however difficult or dangerous, for which he will not gladly come forward.

Value of Sikhism in imbuing the lowest castes with a military spirit.—One of the highest qualities of Sikhism is its power to improve the social condition of its adherents by removing the trammels of caste. As a Mazbhi Sikh, the despised Chuhra or sweeper at once becomes a valiant and valued soldier, and, imbued with the spirit of his martial faith, loses all memory of his former degraded calling.

The Sikh is at his best in the infantry. He no doubt becomes an excellent cavalry soldier with training, but he has not the same aptitude for horsemanship as some of the races which are admittedly his inferiors on foot. In the infantry he is the bravest and steadiest of soldiers. It is part of his creed never to turn his back to his enemy; he has a high opinion of his own military worth, he is stubborn and earnest in action; and while lacking the clan and dash of the Pathan, is more faithful, more trustworthy, and far less liable to panic.

Physique and sports.—The Jat Sikhs have always been famous for their fine physique and are surpassed by no race in India for high-bred looks, smartness, and soldierly bearing. Their length of limb makes them excellent marches, and their physical activity is developed by active habits. They are fond of running, jumping, wielding enormous wooden clubs called mugdars, and lifting and tossing heavy weights. The younger men are fond of wrestling, and quoit-throwing, the latter a pastime which had fallen into desuetude, but is now again encouraged in the army. The steel "chakri" or quoit, which was invariably worn round the turban, is generally from six to eight inches in diameter, with a razor edge, and properly thrown makes a formidable missile. The Jat Sikh is usually too much occupied with agricultural labour to spare much time for games, and the latter are consequently seldom played, except by the boys of the village, or occasionally at melas or fairs. The most common are "Saunchi" and "Kabbadi". In "Saunchi" the spectators form a large ring, inside which are two smaller ones. A man from one of these inner rings advances and is chased by two or three men from the other, to elude whom he may trip up, or strike in the chest with the open hand. "Kabbadi" is very much the same as "Prisoner's Base". Among the wealthier classes hawking and coursing are still favourite pastimes.

Personal habits and customs.—The Sikh is clean in his personal habits, but does not pay as much attention to his ablutions as a Brahman or Hindu Rajput. Before praying he considers it necessary to bathe in cold water, so as to render his devotions more acceptable. If prevented by sickness or other causes, he must at least wash his face and hands, and swallow water in view to purification. Twice a day he should comb his locks and rinse his mouth. Nudity is held in special abhorence and is strictly prohibited. The head should always be covered by a turban, never by a cap, and no food should be taken until after the repetition of the name of the Guru and the Jap, or morning prayer.

When two Sikhs meet, the younger will address the other with the salutation of "Wah guru ji ka Khalsa, sri wah guru ji ki fateh". In its abbreviated form some times only "Wah guru ji ki fateh", or even "Sat Siri Akal" are used.

The Sikh, generally speaking, is not a frugal liver, although the idea used to be prevalent until recently that this was so.

Seeing his Hindu brethren living rather more comfortably than he does himself, he has of recent years been very enterprising and goes far afield in order to earn money and live as comfortably as possible. This love of money, however, has not been without its advantages; combined with a spirit of adventure and a taste for fighting, it has tempted him to distant countries and thus enables us to get an ample supply of recruits for the Burma Battalions of Police and those of Hong Kong. The profits derived from their military service add greatly to their prosperity and enables them to tide over the difficulties of bad harvests, and goes far to provide comforts and luxuries which would otherwise be beyond their means. The Sikh is of course a lover of land above all else, thus when he has made a little money he often proceeds to invest it on land, or lends it on mortgage, not so much with the view of making profit by taking interest, but for the sake of getting more land into his possession and eking out the profits of his own small holdings.

He is rather expensively inclined in his food, and likes rum, meat, and sugar; his fondness for the first of these three sometimes outruns his discretion, so much so that occasions have been known where he has parted with the whole of his land and his personal belongings piece by piece in order to be able to satisfy his indulgence.

Dress.—The dress of the Sikh cultivator is simple in the extreme. The material is almost always unbleached cotton called "ghat" made up by the village weaver from home-grown materials, spun by the women of the family. His clothes consist in the simplest form of three articles—a large pagri of coarse cloth, a dhoti, or waistcloth, worn round the loins kilt-fashion, and a chadar or wrap thrown over the shoulders. To this might be added a kurta or loose blouse with wide sleeves. Rough shoes of the usual pattern are worn.

In winter the jacket is either of woollen cloth or quilted like a razai and it is usual to wear a thick cotton wrap or blanket folded round the body like a plaid. This is coloured and made of superior quality if the wearer is well-to-do. The kachh or short drawers are usually worn. Pyjamas or trousers are a hindrance to those who have to labour in the fields, and the wearing of these garments is usually a sign that the man is either in military service or of superior social position, the loincloth however, is seldom thrown off.

The turban or safa may be white, pink, yellow, red, or blue, and among better classes of Sikhs there is generally an inner pagri of a different colour, of which a small triangular portion, called the "pag" (this is a survival of the old "Sidha pag" or true Sikh turban which consisted of twelve yards of cloth, and completely protected the head from sword-cuts. It is now only worn by old men, and Kukas) is generally left showing on the forehead. The well-to-do Jat has his clothes made of better materials, and will generally indulge in a well-fitting waistcoat and a black or coloured coat made of broad cloth or alpaca according to the season.

The dress of the women is brighter and there is always some colour in it. A wrap is always worn over the head and it is considered indecent to appear in public without it. With this are worn a loose jacket, coloured red or blue, or of some printed cotton stuff, and either an ample pair of blue-triped pyjamas tight at the feet, or a petticoat. The chadar or head wrap may take the form of a "phulkari", a cotton cloth of black or red ground with a flowered pattern embroidered in floss-silk.

Ornaments.—Women, unless widowed, are usually loaded with silver ornaments, worn on the ears, neck, arms, and ankles, and much of the wealth of the family is invested in this manner. At a marriage no bride's outfit is complete unless she wears and is provided with the ornaments usually worn by her class. Among the men ornaments are rare, as their use is considered a mark of effeminacy, but pensioners who have saved money often invest in a string of gold mohurs worn round the neck, a tighter necklace of gold and coral heads called a "mahla," or even a pair of gold bangles called "kangan", which they love to display at marriages and festivals.

Morality and crime.—The mass of Jat Sikh population may fairly be said to be contented and law-abiding. Crimes of violence are not numerous. The prevailing crime among them is cattle-lifting and the abduction of married women. Murders, when they occur, usually arise as a consequence of conjugal infidelity, or of quarrels regarding land, crops, and cattle-tresspass. The relations of the sexes permit of a good deal of freedom. Immorality is discountenanced by the elders of the villages and the strong feeling which exists against inter-marriage in the same "got" is also no doubt a deterrent to debauchery; nevertheless the number of criminal prosecutions arising out of illicit amours and guilty intrigues appear to be steadily increasing. The paucity of women among Jats and Sikhs makes marriage difficult and expensive. The birth of a daughter, indeed, has come to be regarded as a piece of good-luck, and female infanticide, which is still so common among Rajputs, has entirely disappeared among the Jats.

Love of litigation.—A love of litigation appears to be increasing throughout all classes of the agricultural population. Jats and Sikhs are by nature persistent, and never drop a claim however trivial, which they believe to be based on equity. Law is a matter for which they have no regard and of which they know very little, except that it will get them all they want if they can get it on their side.

Food.—The ordinary food of the Sikh peasants consists of "chapatis", made either with wheat, or barley meal, or with jowar, *i.e.*, millet. (In poorer households the staple food is berra, *i.e.*, wheat and grain mixed.) These cakes are eaten with "dal" or with a kind of porridge, called "daliya," prepared from wheat, jowar, and makai, the grain being bruised rather than ground, and then thrown into a cauldron and boiled with salt and dal. Salt is always used, and mirch or red pepper is generally added as a seasoning. The whole is washed down by copious draughts of lassi or buttermilk. Carrots, turnips, onions and pumpkins may be eaten, but the favourite substitute for vegetables is sarson, *i.e.*, green gram. Raw milk is seldom drunk, and rice is only used during sickness, at festivals, or by the richer families. Sugar or gur makes its appearance in various forms at marriages and other festive occasions, but like ghi is generally regarded as a luxury. Before starting for his daily work, the Sikh will partake of a light meal. If he is well-to-do, he may treat himself to a sweetmeat ball, called "laddu", made of gur, til, and wheatmeal. This is followed by a substantial repast of cakes and lassi, which is brought to him in the fields by the women or children when the sun begins to get powerful, and the oxen have their midday rest. The heaviest meal is taken in the house at sundown, when the toil of the day is over. The cooking is mostly done by women, but some villages have a langar-khana or cook-house where chapatis are baked by the Jhinwars during the hot weather.

Although the eating of flesh was one of Guru Govind's injunctions to his followers, meat is but rarely eaten, and when it is indulged in the animals must be killed by "jhatka", *i.e.*, decapitation by a blow at the back of the head. Beef is of course unholy, for the Sikh has an intense veneration for the cow, but there is no objection to mutton, kid, and goat's flesh, or to that of the wild boar, which, when killed in sport, need not be treated to the "jhatka".

A Sikh will take food cooked by any orthodox Hindu, or by any other Sikh except a Mazbhi, Chuhra, or Chamar. In theory Sikhism acknowledges no distinctions of caste, but in practice they are more or less admitted. In times of necessity, however, all such restrictions disappear, and food may be eaten even at the hand of Mohamedans. Sikhs of every grade take water without any objection from the mashaks and pakhals of Musalman bhistis, and in regiments feed altogether in messes, their food being prepared by the langris or cooks assisted by the men themselves.

One of the principal objects of Guru Govind Singh in instituting the Sikh communion was to remove the restriction in the matter of food imposed by differences of caste. The "kara parshad" or sacramental food consists of equal portions of flour, sugar, and ghi, with a double proportion of water. Any Sikh will eat this at the hand of any other Sikh, except a Mazbhi or a Chamar. "Kara parshad" is much given in charity, and is a standing dish at all religious ceremonies, such as the administering of the "pahul", when all present, including those initiated, eat out of the same dish. Those who take the "pahul" together are called Gurbhais.

Indulgence in drugs and liquor.—The prohibitions against the use of tobacco, which is one of the most important of the rules drawn up by Govind Singh for the guidance of his followers, originated in a desire to preserve them from the gossiping and idle habits engendered by the use of the huqah. With Mohamedans and Hindus (except the most high caste Brahmans) the pipe is always within reach, whatever work they are doing, and this, no doubt, is a serious check on their industry, and places them at a considerable disadvantage with the Sikhs. The Guru's injunctions against tobacco, however, have had the effect of encouraging indulgence in narcotics and liquor. The Malwa Sikhs are consumers of opium, while those of the Manjha have a great partiality for bhang, a powerful stimulant extracted from wild hemp. A fondness for liquor and opium is the cause of a good deal of the indebtedness of the Sikh agricultural classes, and illicit distillation give rise to many prosecutions on the part of the Revenue authorities.

Cooking pots.—Sikh cooking utensils are generally made either of brass or "kansi," *i.e.*, bell-metal, so as to be readily purified by scouring. The only earthen vessels used are the "garha" or water jug, and the "taori" or cooking pot for vegetables. In a regiment the duty of cleaning cooking pits is generally performed by a special class of company servants, called bhisties. The names of the different cooking utensils and their respective uses are as follows :—

"*Parat*," a brass platter in which atta is kneaded into chapatis.

"*Gadwa*" or "*Lota*," a brass vessel, to contain water.

"*Dolni*" a large vessel of the same kind in which water or milk is kept for use.

"*Batlohi*" and "*Gagar*," large brass or iron vessels for water.

"*Thali*," the brass plate on which food is eaten after it has been cooked.

"*Tawa*," an iron plate on which chapatis are baked on the chula or hearth.

"*Kaul*" and "*Katora*" or "*Belua*," a small brass cup used for drinking milk and lassi, and water.

"*Karchi*" and "*Chamcha*," spoons made of brass, wood, or copper, used to stir food while it is being cooked.

"*Chimta*," iron tongs used for arranging a fire.

"*Sandasi*," an instrument used for lifting a lota off the fire.

"*Karahi*," a large iron vessel used for cooking vegetables and puris, *i.e.*, chapatis made with ghi instead of water, and making kara parshad.

Sikh women.—Among Sikhs, as among Jats and other classes of Hindus, the women do not join in the society of the men, and are not admitted to an equality with them. Even when walking together, the woman always follows the man, although there may be no obstacle to their walking abreast. Nevertheless, the position of the Sikh women is undoubtedly higher than that of her Rajput and Brahman sisters, for, instead of being secluded and lost for field labour like the latter, she is of great assistance to her husband, and performs a good deal of the lighter kind of agricultural work. In some villages, however, women do not go to work in the fields at all; for instance there are 36 Sikh villages in the Ludhiana district called "Chhatri Thakamas" in which the women never go out except for purposes of nature and even this is limited to between the hours of sunset and sunrise. People of other villages consider it a great honour to marry their daughters in these villages.

The industry of the Jat women is referred to in the proverb of the people: "Of good kind is the Jatni who hoe in hand, weeds the fields in company with her husband." Their household duties do not differ from those of females of other classes. Their chief occupation is to grind the corn and cook the food required by their husbands and brothers, to take it out to them in the fields, and to spin cotton. They also milk the cows, gather maize and millet heads, collect fire-wood, pick cotton, boil the milk to be made into ghi, sweep out the houses and yards every morning, and make the cattle dung into cakes for fuel. To the women is also assigned the duty of drawing water from the wells, as the performance of this office by a man is considered to be very "infradig." On the whole, women are treated by their husbands more as servants than as companions. In addition to the occupations already described, they have to play the part of a professional mourner on the death of a relative, by beating their breasts, and wailing for the prescribed period. (Sikh women were expressly forbidden by Guru Govind Singh from making offerings at Hindu or Musalman shrines, and from taking part in this mourning ceremony. The rules are however more honoured in the breach than in the observance.) The Sikh or Jat women may not eat in her husband's presence. If he ill-treats her, she cannot get a divorce, and her only chance of happiness is to bear him a son, and thus keep out other rivals for his affection.

The village community.—Next to caste, there is no institution in India more permanent than the village community, which dates back to the time of the early Aryan commonwealths. In the Punjab the headmen of every village are called lumbardars. They are recognised officials, and are directly responsible to the zaildar or tehsildar for the collection of the revenue due from the village and its lands, being assisted by the patwari or village accountant who is responsible for the maintenance and preservation of the records. The typical village is almost always divided into wards, called, "pattis," "pannas," or "thulas," each "thula" embracing a branch of the clan descended from some common ancestor, and perhaps a few strangers settled by that branch. Each ward is in charge of elders who form the panchayat or village council. Grazing grounds are held in common (and are called Birs); the income derived from grazing-dues, hearth-fees, and the rent paid by persons cultivating the common lands, are credited to a general fund; and certain charges. such as cost of entertaining subordinate officials, travellers, and beggars, are debited to it, forming a primitive system of self-government. The "panchayat" settle all questions relating to the general well-being of the village; they audit the accounts of the local fund, and all matters affecting the community as a body, such as breaking up jungle land and cutting down trees, must invariably be submitted to their decision. The zamindars or landowners consider themselves infinitely superior to the traders and kamins or village menials, the distinctive sign of whose inferiority is their liability to pay hearth-fees. Such are the Jat villages. They are communities of clansmen linked sometimes by descent from a common ancestor, sometimes by marriage, sometimes by the fact of a joint foundation of the village. Though often of heterogeneous composition they are united by close ties, self-supporting, vigorous, and admirably adapted to resist the evil effects of bad seasons, epidemics, and other evils incidental to this country.

The Sikh village.—The Punjab village is almost always composed of houses built of sun-dried bricks or of large clods of caked mud taken from the bottom of a pond. But there are few villages which do not contain one or more masonry houses, the home of a well-to-do headman, or the village money-lender or perhaps of a pensioned native officer. These "pucka" buildings are increasing enormously and frequently consist of three stories. They are also being built on hygienic principles. Villages have undergone a complete change in the present century, but their state of sanitation lags sadly in arrears. To the European mind it may practically be said to be non-existent. The houses, crowded as closely as they can be, are separated by narrow winding lanes, only a few feet wide. The houses of a "patti," or ward, often lie together and have a separate entrance with a gateway. The gateways in the best Sikh villages are commodious structures, with a roofed shed to the right and left of the entrance, the roof extending over the entrance itself, the foundations of which are raised two or three feet above the level of the pathway. In these travellers are housed, and the owners of the patti assemble when the work of the day is over, sitting on the matting spread on the floor, or on the large wooden "takht" or bedstead with which they are generally provided. Between the actual buildings and the cultivated fields is an open space running right round the village, sometimes shaded by pipal trees, and almost always in a very insanitary condition. Carts which would take up too much room in the village stand there, and there it is that the cane press will be seen at work in the winter. At one or more sides of the village there are ponds from which earth is excavated for repair of houses, and where cattle are bathed and watered. The backs of the houses are usually blank walls forming an outer boundary to the settlement. In the space running round the village are found the manure heaps, and stacks of crowding fuel, belonging to each of the households. The space used for storing these is as a rule limited, and disputes as to the right to occupy a particular site for a dump heap are keenly fought out.

Entering the village we find the doorways of the houses opening on the main streets, or on side lanes running off them. Ordinarily the front door leads straight into an open courtyard, with cattle troughs along one or more of its sides. The dwelling houses will be generally found along the side of the courtyards which fronts the doorway. These are long and narrow, with or without a small verandah in front called a dalan, and are generally provided with a flight of steps or a wooden ladder giving access to the roof. Light and air are admitted by the door, and smoke finds its way out by the same way, or perhaps by a hole in the roof; though under modern conditions windows are being more generally substituted. Cooking is carried out for the most part in a partly roofed shelter in a corner of the yard, for the people live as much as they can in the open air, and are only driven indoors by cold or rain. A noticeable object in every house is the larger jar-shaped receptacle for grain, called a "bharola," made of plastered mud, with a stoppered hole low down in the side by which the grain may run out. Each family living within the enclosure has a separate dwelling house and cooking place, while in the yard, outside the doors, much of the available space is taken up by the charpoys and water pots of the household, and the spinning wheels and grindstones of the women. The roof is used for storing heaps of jowar, fodder, and bundles of cotton twigs for roofing purposes, also for drying chillies, seed grains, etc., in the sun. Occasionally there is a small upper chamber in the roof, but this is rare. Sometimes the front door, instead of leading directly into the court, leads into a lodge or deorhi out of which a smaller door, placed so that the interior of the yard cannot be seen from the street, leads into the yard itself. The "deorhi" serves as a cart lodge, tool-shed, and stable, and also as a lodging for such guests as are not sufficiently intimate to be taken into the interior of the house. "Deorhis" are only found in the houses of well-to-do zamindars, and occasionally have their outer gates ornamented by cornices of carved wood.

Almost every village, and in large communities every patti or thula has its guest house and meeting place, known as a "dharamsala". The dharamsalas are always kept scrupulously clean, and in most of them a copy of the granth is placed in a window, whence the Sadhu or Granthi in charge, who is also the village schoolmaster, reads aloud to himself, or to those who have leisure to listen. Fire is kept for the use of such non-Sikh visitors as may wish to smoke, and there is generally a well hard by. Food and beds are provided for guests by the village headmen, who are supposed to recoup themselves at the expense of the other owners, by levying a small contribution on the land-revenue, or debiting the cost to the Malba or village fund.

Family life.—It is a general custom among Jats, subject of course to exceptions, for brothers to live together so long as their father is alive, and to separate at his death. We may thus find four or five brothers, with their families, living in separate houses, ranged around a common courtyard, the whole forming but one household. The usual practice among the yeoman classes, which furnish the majority of our sowars and sepoys, is for the elder brothers to remain at home, cultivating the ancestral lands, while the younger ones take service in the army and police, and contribute to the family purse by savings from their pay and the pensions granted to them on retirement. The death of a brother often compels a sepoy to ask for his discharge, not from any dissatisfaction of the service, but simply to enable him to look after his land. The establishment of an active reserve has done much to lessen this difficulty, and has on many occasions enabled the soldier to retain his connection with the army without sacrificing his agricultural interests.

The village money-lender.—Almost every village has its money-lender or "Sahukar" who is generally a Khatri or Bania. He is usually well-treated by the villagers; even those not dependent on him for advances, are civil to him. The money-lenders never bank their money, but keep it circulating in loans as much as possible, or failing this, bury it in the ground. The rate of interest varies from 18¾ per cent per annum "paisa rupaya" per month, *i.e.*, 3 pies per month) to 8 annas per hundred per month. It depends on the nature of the security and on the social position of the borrower. Interest is low when it is taken on the security of land, and high when the lender has no security for the return of his money. If disputes arise between the money-lender and his debtors, panchayats or committees of arbitration are sometimes appointed from among the land-owners or others of the debtor's class to settle the dispute. But arbitration is now not nearly so freely resorted to as it was in former days. At present the richer Jat proprietors of the Manjha, who have accumulated wealth from their irrigated land, appear likely to supersede the ordinary money-lending classes in their trade; but they are said to be no easier than the latter in the terms on which they make their loans.

The village menials.—The population of a Sikh village always produces a number of persons of the menial and artizan classes, called sepis or kamins, who, in return for performing certain customary services, called sep, receive from the landlords a certain share of the produce of each harvest. Those whose trade or habits are unobjectionable, such as Tarkhan (carpenter) or the Nai (barber) live in small houses within the gates; but Chuhras (sweepers) and Chamars (leather-dressers) being considered unclean, generally have an abadi or quarter to themselves situated on the outskirts of the village. An account of most of these classes and their respective functions has already been given.

Laws of inheritance.—The Jats of the Punjab have two customs, one known as "chadar band", the other as "bhaiband," by which they regulate succession to property. By the first, which is generally practised by Manjha Sikhs, the property is divided among the mothers; by the second, which is generally in vogue among the Sikhs of the Malwa, the estate is divided in equal shares among the sons. For example, if a man left two widows, one of whom had one son and the other three; by "chadarband" the single son of the first wodow would take half the estate, and his three half-brothers would each take a sixth. By "bhai-band," or "pagband" as it is sometimes called, the four sons would each receive a quarter. This, howeever, does not apply to Brahman, Khatri, and Rajput Sikhs who generally adhere to the laws of inheritance customary in their own castes. In the absence of sons, the widow takes a life-interest in the deceased's estate, but where sons succeed, she can only claim a suitable provision. Daughters and their issue cannot inherit, but the former are entitled to maintenance and to be suitably betrothed and married. A widow who remarries loses her rights, even if she marries her husband's brother. A sonless man, or a man whose only son has changed his religion can adopt an heir. A boy so adopted counts as a real son even if children are born subsequent to his adoption. The boy to be adopted must be a brother's son, or if there are none available, a cousin in the male line, and no relation in an elder degree than adopter can be adopted. The ceremony of "Godlina," or adoption, is as follows. The man seats the boy in his lap (god), feeds him with sweetmeats in the presence of the brotherhood, and publicly declares that he has adopted him.

Panchayats.—Panchayats now play a less important part in the social regulations of the people than they did in former times. A panchayat may be described as a court of arbitration for the settlement of disputes, which are also cognisable by law, without having recourse to the courts of justice. It generally consists of from three to five persons, one of whom acts as "sirpanch," or chairman, decisions being arrived at by the opinion of the majority. A panchayat deals generally with caste matters, and though it has no legal authority, is a powerful tribunal, whose decisions are seldom appealed against. It passes sentence of various degrees of severity. Sometimes the offender is ordered to give a feast to his brotherhood, sometimes to pay a fine, and if refractory, he may be excluded from social intercourse with his caste fellows. In grave cases he may incur the most terrible penalty of all—total excommunication. (A Sikh who breaks one of the Rahits or Sikh commandments is required to take the pahul a second time. He must in addition pay a fine which varies in amount from Rs. 5 if the infraction was committed wilfully, to a few annas if it arose through thoughtlessness or ignorance.)

Amusements generally speaking are few. After the day's work is done the younger men may occasionally be seen wrestling or competing with heavy wooden weights close by the village. Marriage festivals and fairs come round, which are eagerly attended, and visits of condolences have to be paid, but the breaks in the round of labour are few for the men and still fewer for the women.

The European games of hockey and cricket have become very popular in the towns in recent years and all schools have a regular programme of fixtures over which great keeness is evinced; in the villages, however, there is little time and as a rule no space for such amusements, and the zemindar when his day's work is done is early abed on the principle of early to bed and early to raise which, in the case of the Oriental, is an outstanding feature of his daily curriculum.

CHAPTER IX.

AGRICULTURAL.

The Punjab has been described repeatedly as the province of peasant proprietors, and statistics show that agriculture is the means of subsistence of 580 persons out of every 1,000. Looking into the figures in individual districts and States, it appears that fewer persons belong to this profession in districts which have large trading or industrial centres. Thus in Amritsar the proportion is only 374 per thousand, and in Lahore 450, while in the southern portions of the Malwa area the proportion is considerably above these figures.

As agriculture therefore forms such an important part of the life amongst the sepoys that are enlisted in the Indian Army, it is considered that no account of the Sikhs can be complete without further reference to this subject.

Classification of land.—Land under cultivation is generally classed into two main groups, *viz.*, "Seju" or ground artificially watered by means of canals or wells, or "Maru", *i.e.*, that which is dependent on the annual rainfall.

The former term may again be reclassified into the following subdivisions :——

"*Chahi*".—Land regularly irrigated from a well.

"*Nahri*".—Land regularly irrigated by means of canals.

"*Abi*".—Land watered from tanks, jhils, ponds, or drainage channels.

"*Sailab*".—Land usually flooded in the rains by rivers or their branches, or land near these rivers which is always moist.

The terms given to these classifications vary in districts, those above quoted are current in the Amritsar district.

The irrigated land tends ever to increase except in the southern portions of the Ferozepore district, the Sirsa tehsil, and certain dry sandy tracts, which, rising above the general level of the surrounding country, cannot be brought under irrigation.

Rainfall.—The rainfall varies annually and its advent and quantity looms very large in the prospects of the cultivator who is beyond the radius of our irrigation system. The average annual rainfall is about 24 inches of which about 75 per cent falls in the monsoon (1st July to 30th September) ; the remainder may fall at any time in the cold weather between the 15th December and the end of February. These winter rains are of vital importance to the agriculture of the whole of the Punjab, as the spring cropped area is generally double that of the autumn, and wheat, especially in the Manjha districts, is the main staple. Hence a failure of the winter rains would have more disastrous effects and cause more suffering than a failure of the monsoon. The best harvests occur after moderate, and above all, timely, winter rains.

Soil distinctions.—The natural distinctions of soil known to the people are briefly as follows :—

"*Rohi*".—Land lying in or near a depression, which by reason of surface water collecting has become hard and clayey.

"*Maira*".—A firm level loam, easily worked, and often reddish in colour.

"*Tibba*".—Soil much mixed with sand, which will not form into clods, found in undulating ground and liable to be blown into ridges.

"*Doshahi*".—A somewhat indefinite term, used to describe a soil which is none of the above three, usually mingled clay and sand.

Of all the above the "Rohi" soil gives the heaviest yield but requires moisture, steadily and constantly applied. It is the soil most valued by the people and is the best for valuable irrigated crops.

"Maira" is the next in value, being a clear soil, easily worked and weeded. Excess or failure of moisture works less harm to crops grown in it than those raised in "Rohi", and it is especially suited to maize and wheat.

"Tibba" is looked on as an inferior soil and on this the yield is never heavy. It is not suited for irrigation as water travels slowly on it. But it succeeds with less rainfall than either "Rohi" or "Maira" and the more sandy it is the less it suffers from drought. Evaporation takes place slowly, so long as the sand is fine and not coarse, and it is therefore classified as a cool or "thandi" soil.

"Doshahi" is not easy to recognise. The cultivators will describe their own "Rohi" as "Doshahi" when they wish for any reason to depreciate it.

System of cultivation.—The agricultural year begins with the "kharif" harvest, or, say from the 15th June. Before this, while the "Rabi" harvest is ripening, or in the month of March, arrangements for the next year are usually made, and men who have not enough land of their own for their needs enter into agreements for the lease of lands belonging to others for the coming year. But whether the cultivator be owner or tenant, he has to take advantage of what rain falls during the months of May and June to plough what lands he intends to sow in the "kharif". When the first heavy fall of rain occurs in July the land is ploughed again, and when ready, is sown with great millet ("jowar") mixed with pulses, such as "moth" or "mung", or both. From this the cultivator expects to get some grain for himself and his family, but chiefly fodder for his cattle. The crop is reaped in November and the fodder is stacked for use in the winter months. The amount of grain obtained from the jowar depends on the season and on whether it is sown thick or thin. A good head of grain will only be obtained if it is grown sparsely. "Moth" leaves make excellent fodder but cannot the place of millets. After the "kharif" crop has been reaped, the land lies fallow as a rule for two harvests or a whole twelve months, but is ploughed whenever rain allows this to be done in July and August. Then in October or November it is sown with mixed wheat and gram ("channa") the proportion of wheat being 5/8ths and 3/8ths or it may be two-thirds of the whole. The proportion, however, depends a good deal on whether good rain has fallen just before sowing time. If it has, the proportion of wheat is increased. According to the character of the winter season the wheat or the gram succeeds best. If the winter rains are short or untimely, the gram comes up better than the wheat; if plentiful, the wheat is far the better crop. Very often "Saron" is sown in drills, wide apart, among the wheat and gram. This crop is reaped about April, being cut separately, unless it has been pulled up green for fodder before. The wheat and gram are cut together; if intended for home consumption they are threshed together; if the wheat is to be sold, it is winnowed out. Harvest operations last up till the beginning of June, if all goes well, after which the land is ploughed as above stated for the "kharif" crop of "jowar". This is the ordinary rotation on unirrigated lands and is rarely departed from. No cultivator will put all his land down with either a "kharif" or a "rabi" crop, but the unirrigated land is cropped in alternate blocks, that on one side of the village being under wheat or gram (known as "berrera") and the other being in its second season of fallow.

Superior cultivation on "well" lands.—On "well" lands the staple crops are maize, cotton, sugar cane, and wheat. The three first will generally be found occupying fields lying close to the well, so as to admit of their being watched and for economy of water in the hot season. Rotations are not very strictly observed, but it may be taken as a rule that cane is put in, either in land which has been especially kept fallow for a year, or in land which has borne maize and cotton in the previous "kharif". After the cane comes wheat. Much land however is kept for wheat alone, with a fallow between each crop, the succession being broken by a "kharif" crop to prevent exhaustion. The cultivation of "well" lands is neat and careful, the limits of the fields are seldom changed except they are sub-divided and the land is economised to the utmost. Usually the cane crop is the only one which is fenced with thorn branches stuck into the ground all round it, but the paths by which the cattle pass to and from the well are nearly always edged or protected by barks of earth, topped with thorn or cactus.

Cultivation of canal irrigated land.—Canal cultivation is less tidy. Cane, wheat and maize are again the chief crops grown, and to a less extent, cotton. There is even less adherence to rotation on "nahri" than on "chahi" lands. More double cropping, less manuring, and on the whole less careful and more varied cultivation. The charges on account of canal water are usually too heavy to admit of the land being given up wholly to the growing of inferior crops. This form of irrigation brings in large return with a smaller expenditure of labour than well irrigation, but the cos is considerable. The average payment for canal water supplied being nearly Rs. 4 for every acre of crops raised in the "kharif" and about Rs. 3-8-0 in the "rabi" season. The people like it on account of the saving of labour and the certainty of the crop, though there is the disadvantage of not always getting water when most required and of having to submit to more official interference.

Sailab lands.—"Sailab" crops are not of very great importance. Much depends on how the village has been treated by the river and on the nature of the silt deposited. Manure is rarely applied, for the silt itself is fertilizing and it is not often that more than one crop is taken off the same land in a year.

Manure.—A considerable part of the cattle dung is used for fuel, being preferred for cooking purposes to wood, which also is too valuable to be used for burning. The burning of wood is confined to the funeral pyre and sometimes to brick kilns, but the rest of it, excluding shade trees, is only sufficient for the making and repair of agricultural implements, roofing, well-tackle, hedging, and so on. The manure used consists of the remainder of the cattle dung mixed with ordinary farmyard and house sweepings and refuse fodder and litter. The "goira" or land near the village site naturally receives a fertilizing supply of night soil, the habits of the people being still, in this respect, very primitive, but it is not always that this is deposited on the cultivated land. The lanes and waste land within easy reach of the village are usually foul with night soil, which it is no ones' business to remove. From the manure heaps round the village the stuff is carted on to the fields and such well-lands, as there are, receive the most of it. Maize, sugar cane, and cotton, are always manured, and sometimes wheat also, but this crop more often follows other manured crops and so is benefitted indirectly.

Agricultural implements.—The plough used is a very simple instrument, made entirely of wood, with the exception of the coulter which is supplied by the village blacksmith as part of the work for which he receives a harvest wage in kind. Both the "hal" and "hallar" are used, the latter always in the Manjha. The "hallar" is of the same nature as the "munna" which is used in the Doaba, but is not quite so heavy. The whole is so light that it can easily be carried on a man's shoulder. Practically the whole apparatus consists of only 4 parts, (1) the wooden yoke ("panjali") which lies across the necks of the bullocks behind the shoulder hump, and which is kept in place by four vertical bars (the outer ones or "arlies" moveable, and the inner ones or "mattias" immoveable) fitting on to the lower cross bar under the neck : (2) the pole fastened to the yoke with a piece of leather termed "nara" and fitting into (3) the iron shod sole which does the work, and (4) an upright handle with which the ploughman does the guiding.

Land is often ploughed ten or twelve times for valuable crops; the field may be ploughed in sections up and down or in narrowing circles, beginning round the edge of the field, but the turn is invariably to the left (the course followed in the track round the well wheel) and the bullocks are so used to this that they could hardly be made to turn to the right, even if so wished. Three or four ploughs may often be seen at work in one field, each following the other (but in a different furrow), when it is wished to take immediate advantage of the state of the ground and to get the seal in at the right time. The people often do a day's work for a neighbour, the obligation being returned some other time, just as they do in the building of each others houses in the off seasons.

The "Sohaga".—Ploughing is succeeded on most soils by working over the ground with the flat levelling beam, or "Sohaga", which crushes the clods and flattens the surface to keep the moisture in. If the seed has been sown the "Sohaga" covers it in the furrow. Two yoke of oxen are harnessed to the "Sohaga" all four abreast and a man is required to each yoke. They ride standing on the "Sohaga" to weight it down, steadying themselves and encouraging the cattle to further efforts by holding on to the tail.

Other agricultural implements.—Other agricultural implements are the "kohari", or common axe for cutting wood and the "toka" an axe or chopper with a long handle fitted with an iron blade about 6 inches in length; it is used for cutting up "jowar" stalks for fodder. When fitted with a lighter blade and a longer handle, it is known as a "gandasa" or "chhawi" and was used for cutting branches for hedging. Its possession has now been made illegal under the Arms Act, and the "kohari" very generally takes its place instead. Reaping is done with a small toothedge sickle called a "datiri" which requires frequent sharpening of the teeth. For weeding, a short-handled tool called "ramba" is used, the cultivator going through the field in a sitting position and digging out the weeds between each plant. The "kahi" or mattock is an indispensible implement, and at some times of the year is the one most often in the Zamindar's hands. It is used for all kinds of shovelling or digging earth. The "sapang" is a wooden fork with two prongs, rather like a pitchfork with which the Jat Sikh gathers heaps of the prickly "malha" or thorny dwarf "ber" for hedging for cattle enclosures round wells. "Chhar", a long stick with a hooked blade at the edge of it is used for cutting branches from high trees.

Threshing is done on the hard beaten ground, on which the crop is spread; the thresher ("phalla") is then dragged round by two bullocks, in some cases even more, till the grain is extracted from the husk. The grain is finally separated from the husk by being tossed in the air, where the breeze carries the lighter husk away, or winnowing baskets (called "chaj") are filled with the broken straw, husks and grain, and emptied in the air when the action of wind separates the grain from the bhoosa or chaff in a similar manner.

Hired labourers.—Owing to many land owners being away on military service the employment of hired labourers is frequently necessary for the reaping of the spring harvest. The precise extent to which hired labour is employed is difficult to estimate for it varies greatly from year to year. A severe outbreak of plague, which disease usually coincides with the ripening of the wheat harvest, means that labour must be imported from elsewhere and liberally paid.

Crops. Wheat or Kanak.—The chief among the "Rabi" crops is wheat. On irrigated land it is grown unmixed, but on irrigated (or "Barrani" lands it is usually grown mixed with gram, the mixture being known as "Berrera". Both wheat and "Berrera" are sown in October or November, the latter generally before the most of the wheat on irrigated lands. The "Barrani" crops do well enough without rain up to Christmas, if there has been the proper amount of moisture in the soil at sowing time. But about Christmas rain is expected, if only to keep down the ravages of white ants which in many districts do the crop much harm. After good rain in January and February, not much more is required in March, and the crop is ready for harvesting by the beginning of April. Reaping, according to custom, begins immediately after "Baisakhi" (the Punjabi new year). Threshing and winnowing take a long time, and it is often the beginning of June before the whole crop has been cut, carried, threshed, and taken home.

The grain is separated from the straw and chaff in the well known primitive way which has been followed by the people for centuries. The sheaves are heaped up, near a well for choice, and close to the smooth bit of hard ground selected for a threshing floor. A sheaf is about as much as a man can carry as a head load and will yield from 12 to 16 seers of grain. A number of sheaves are then loosed and spread out round a stake driven into the ground. To this stake the muzzled oxen, three or four abreast are fastened and round it they tramp, beating out the grain with their feet, or to hasten the process, dragging after them a rough arrangement of wood and brushwood, shaped like a raft, and weighted with anything handy. The grain thus becomes gradually separated and is then winnowed from the chaff as previously mentioned. The bhoosa is carefully stored in a sheltered place in conical stacks and forms the main supply of dry fodder for the working cattle during the next winter. The grain is taken away to the village where it is stored, for subsequent use, or is taken to the nearest "mandi" where it is disposed of to grain dealers at market rates, in which the latter it may be mentioned rarely get the worst of the bargain.

Cotton or kapah.—Cotton is grown both on well and canal lands and has increased enormously in recent years in popularity. It is now the most important of the kharif crops. Its popularity is due to the continuous advance in price and to the fact that it involves comparatively little labour, as four waterings and two ploughings produce a very fair yield. As a rule it is only weeded twice and does not receive much, if any, manure. Picking begins in November and lasts till January. This is done by the women and children of the family. When the leaves drop and the last picking (which is by custom allowed to the chuhras) has taken place, the sticks are cut down close to the roots and used for roofing purposes, or are wattled to form the enclosing sides of dung carts and shelters for chopping fodder. The yield of good irrigated cotton may be taken as about 240 seers to the acre, but this of course is in an uncleaned condition with the seed still adhering to the fibre.

Sugarcane or ikh.—The cultivation of this commodity would appear to be decreasing owing to its being supplanted by cotton, and also on account of the vast amount of labour it requires and the long period for which it occupies the ground. After repeated ploughings the soil is ready for the reception of the seed in March or April, when the seed canes, for which about one-twentieth of last year's crop is required, are unearthed from the pit (in which they have lain buried for three or four months), cut into lengths of about nine inches, and placed in the highly pulverised soil. The young crop needs constant watching, watering, and weeding during the months of extreme heat which follows until the rains break, and until the crop is ready for cutting, watering has to be given steadily. The canes it will be noticed when touring, are always carefully fenced. Cutting begins about January, though in a wet season they may stand uncut till March or even April. The canes are stripped of leaves, and when cut, are from three to five feet long; they are then passed through an iron sugar mill which has practically everywhere superseded the old cumbrous arrangements of cogged wooden wheels and rollers. The juice is boiled in shallow iron pans in the "gurial", or boiling house, and is generally sold by the Zamindar in the form of "gur" in lumps, or "roris", weighing about a pound and a half each.

The canes grown on an acre will fetch from Rs. 300 to Rs. 350 but the cost of cultivation is very large indeed. The chief centres of cultivation are Hoshiarpur, Jullundur and Gurdaspur, whilst Amritsar, Ludhiana, and certain parts of the Phulkian States grow it in smaller quantities. The gross value of the out-turn is large but the plant occupies the ground for at least a twelve month and the labour and cost of cultivating it and extracting the juice are great. It is purely a revenue crop and very little of the produce finds its way to the cultivator's family.

Great millet or jowar.—This crop is universally grown and covers a large area. The Zamindar of the Manjha rarely hopes to obtain any grain therefrom and the almost universal custom is to cut it all as fodder, in opposition to the Malwai who often depends on the jowar grain for food throughout the winter. As a rule it is not manured. and where allowed to ripen, is not irrigated. It is sown at the beginning of July after the first heavy fall of monsoon rain. When cut the stalks are stacked in the field for a time to dry and then piled on the roof and other dry places to be used as fodder during the early winter. The crop is known either as "jowar" or "Chari", sometimes by the double name "chari-jowar", but "chari" is the name by which the fodder part of the plant is known. Speaking generally the cattle are so dependent on "jowar" for food, at the time of the year when the bullocks are hardest worked, that a failure of the crop is looked upon as a calamity. Fortunately it does not often occur. Rain in the first week of July, and steady rain at intervals throughout the month and the next six weeks is quite enough to ensure the success of the "jowar" crop.

Kharif pulses, "Moth", "Mung", "Mash".—"Moth", "Mung", and "Mash" are the three principal pulses grown in the "Kharif" harvest, but have greatly declined in popularity in the present century. "Moth" is chiefly raised on light sandy soil and does not require so much rain as the other "Kharif" crops. The grain enters largely into the food of the people, and the dark green bhoosa, formed of the leaves after the grain is beaten out is a valuable fodder for cattle. "Mung" can be, and usually is, grown on firmer land. The times of sowing and reaping are the same as for "jowar"; "Mash", is perhaps the most valuable pulse and gives a larger yield than the other two. For this a fairly stiff soil with a good deal of moisture is required.

"Sesanum" or "Til", and "Kangni", "China", "Swank" and "Bajra" are little grown, being looked upon as inferior grains only to be resorted to as food when all else fails.

Chillies or Mirch.—The only other "Kharif" crop that may be mentioned is "Mirch" or Chillies. The crop is a popular one and forms one of the staple ingredients of the limited diet of the Jats. The raising of the crop requires much manure and careful tillage and gives a large money return. The seed pods are picked by the women (the process causing much irritation to the hands) and are then dried in the sun.

Rape or Saron.—"Rape" is well known by sight from the show which it makes with its yellow blossoms. It is however, a risky plant to grow as so much depends on nothing untoward happening while it is in blossom. Much of it is plucked up unripe for fodder and for use as "Sag", or greens, when the wheat is about a foot high. The harvest is an early one if the frost has not injured it.

Toria or oil-seed.—"Toria" which is a late "Kharif" or early "Rabi" crop has come largely into favour of recent years, owing to the high price of oil-seed, and has to a great extent supplanted rape. It is grown on both irrigated and unirrigated lands.

Lentil or Massar or Dal.—"Massar" furnishes the pulse best known to Europeans as "dal". It is a hardy plant and may be grown with success on the most unpromising soils, it is however especially liable to damage by frost in late February, a single night of which may ruin the whole crop.

Trefoil or Senji.—"Senji" is a luxuriant trefoil grown exclusively for fodder for cattle. It is cut green and chopped up with bhoosa, jower maize stalks of cane tops. Once cut it does not give a second cutting like "lucerne". It is an indispensible crop for stall fed cattle and is grown in every village where there is cultivation.

Hemp.—Hemp is grown in two varieties, "San" and "San Bokra". The latter is generally planted as a fencing round sugarcane or maize. "San" is only grown in sufficient quantities to provide the ropes necessary for agricultural purposes. It ripens in October when it is cut and steeped in water, after which it is dried in the sun and worked by hand into ropes.

Vegetables.—The cultivation of vegetables is confined mostly to the neighbourhood of large towns and well irrigated lands. The favourite are "Bangans" or egg plant, "Bhindies" or ladies' fingers. "Piaz" or onions, "Kharbuza" or water melons, although all sorts are becoming increasingly popular and enter into the daily diet wherever they can be made obtainable.

Agricultural stock.—Owing to the scarcity of grazing generally speaking throughout the Sikh area both Malwa and Manjha, cattle are not bred to any great extent, and consequently the majority have to be imported from districts further to the south. The grazing area is in fact so limited that the bulk of the working and milch cattle have to be stall-fed. Twice a year the people have the opportunity of buying and selling at the "Baisakh" and "Diwali" fairs but they also purchase largely from itinerant cattle dealers called "Hers", who travel up from the Delhi and Hissar Districts with picked animals suitable for cart and well work. In the Malwa male bullocks are used on the wells, but in the Manjha both these and male water buffaloes are extensively used. In the Malwa the Sikh has a prejudice against the use of this latter type. The price of cattle has increased threefold in the present century. As a rule, a landholder does not keep more cattle than are necessary to work his well and plough, and to keep him and his family in milk and butter. In the Malwa area, especially in the dry sandy districts to the south, camels are extensively employed and can be seen harnessed to the plough or the well in addition to their duties as a means of transport. The village cattle during the rainy and hot weather months are driven out every day in the early morning on to the village "Bir" usually in charge of the children, but if they depended on what they could find outside they could not be kept in condition. It is for them that the large areas of fodder and "Senji" are grown; the upkeep of his cattle in time of scarcity is a source of constant anxiety to the cultivator.

Horses and ponies are not numerous. The Jat Sikh, exclusive of those who have entered the Army, looks on a horse or pony simply as an animal which enables him to get from place to place with comfort, and little pride is taken in their animals; every well-to-do Jat keeps a pony of some sort, however, and pensioned Indian officers on an average are not often found without.

Sheep and goats are kept by village menials. Donkeys are kept by Kumhars for carrier work and are in general use among the villages for goods which are easily divided up into loads like grain. A good donkey will carry two maunds.

Camels vary greatly in numbers according to the nature of the districts. In the Manjha tract they are comparatively rare in comparison to that of the Malwa, especially in the extreme south, where owing to the absence of any roads and the sandly nature of the country every family has one or more. In contradistinction to the horses or ponies they are extremely well looked after and are rarely seen to be suffering from mange or other skin diseases which are so common in the districts neighbouring on the Indus.

Wells.—The well-apparatus is always of the familiar Persian wheel type which may be roughly described as a string of earthen pots (frequently, and increasingly, tin buckets) placed, one above the other, on a rope ladder hung over the water on a broad vertical wheel. The pots reach a short way below the level of the water and as the wheel, worked by oxen, revolves, the pots on one side come up full, and empty themselves into a trough whence it flows out into the surface irrigation channel, while those on the other side go down empty. From three to four pairs of bullocks are required to work a well continuously for 24 hours, and atleast two men one of whom sits in the "Ghari" to drive the bullocks and the other remains out in the fields directing the flow of the water where required.

In the Malwa area the camel is frequently preferred to the pair of bullocks owing to the fact that it does not require the same attention and can be frequently left to itself, as opposed to the bullocks which soon stop work unless constantly driven. About two "bighas" can be watered in this way in 24 hours. The apparatus, apart from the well itself, cost about Rs. 50 and will last many years if well-built, of sound well-joined wood at the start.

Canal irrigation in certain districts has taken the place of wells, but despite this new wells are constantly being sunk; the cost varies with the depth and may be anything from Rs. 150, where the water level is high to Rs. 500, where it has to be sought at great depth. In the Sirsa tehsil the level is as low as 250 feet and frequently water is brackish at that; and owing to the complete absence of canal irrigation not only has water frequently to be fetched from distances of five miles or more, but can even then only be obtained on payment. The water question in this tehsil is the burning problem of the day.

Tenancies.—Outside the limits of the native States there are generally speaking very few large "Zamindari" estates in the whole of the Sikh populated area. The whole district is essentially a tract of small peasant proprietors. Ordinarily the tenant is himself a small proprietor, whose holding is insufficient for the maintenance of his family. Rents are determined by the relative strength or weakness of the owner's position in regard to his tenant, wherever a smaller rate of "batai", or smaller cash rent than usual on similar lands in the neighbourhood is paid, it is generally found that the owner is an absentee, having emigrated either to one of the canal colonies or is on military service, and that he has let his holding to a relative on favourable terms.

Rents in kind are of two descriptions. The tenant either contracts to pay a fixed weight of grain, or else to allow the landlord to take a certain share of the produce, usually one half. Fixed rents in kind are paid, as a rule, only on secure irrigated land are supposed to be roughly equivalent to half the produce. The commonest rate is five maunds per "bigha", or roughly five maunds per acre on irrigated land, though in exceptionally fine villages rents of six, seven and even eight maunds per "bigha" are not uncommon. The whole amount paid, less the land revenue demand, is clear profit to the landlord, as the tenant is responsible for all expenses of irrigation, and for all menial dues. On unirrigated land the rate is generally from two to four "kacha" maunds per "bigha", but considerable variations occur not only in different districts, but even from village to village in any one district.

Village menials.—In all villages members of the menial and artizan classes are found who perform certain services for the landowners, and secure in return a certain share of the produce of each harvest. It is impossible to state with accuracy what each of these receives, for the usage varies from village to village, and depends much on the generosity of the individual landlord, or the willingness of the individual menial, and to some extent on the character of the harvest. The menials are known as "Ramons" or "Sepis", the customary duty performed being called "Sep". The principal "Sep" is the "Chuhra" who is quite indispensible to the cultivator. Agricultural occupations could hardly be carried on without his help, on whom falls a large share of the irksome part of field labour. The minimum of work which he performs is that of removing the refuse from the dwelling-house and the dung from the byre to the owner's dung hill outside the site. But this is work which Chuhra women can perform, and but a small wage would be given in return for this. To earn his full wage as a "Sep" the Chuhra has to help in removing the manure to the fields and scattering it. He is expected to help in all kinds of ordinary field work, such as cutting and bringing in fodder, feeding the cattle, ploughing and irrigating the land. He is expected also to provide baskets for manure and for winnowing. He is also employed as a farm labourer pure and simple. If so he does no house-work, but does whatever field work his one employer requires of him, he rarely can serve more than one family as a regularly entertained ploughman.

The other "Sepis" are the potter, the carpenter, and the blacksmith. The potter thrives best in a village with many wells. He supplies several families with pots for the well and earthen pots for the house. The carpenter is better off than the potter in that he has always services to perform. His work is to make and repair ploughs and other implements, besides wooden furniture used in the house, such as beds, spinning wheels, churns and stools. He repairs the well wheels and carts when required. The wood is either found for him or else he is paid extra for providing it.

The tendency at present is to make a cash payment to all servants employed in addition to the customary dues of grain owing to the increasing disposition of all menials to desert their hereditary calling and to seek an independent livelihood in a new field of activity, thus causing a reduction in their numbers and making it more difficult for the Zamindar to obtain the necessary labour. Like elsewhere it is a question of supply and demand and costs vary accordingly.

Weights and measures.—The unit of cloth measure is the "girah", the width of the first three fingers, 16 girahs going to the "gaz" or yard. In the "gaz" used for "pashmina" there are said to be only 14¾ "girahs". The "gaz" is two cubits ("hath") *i.e.*, twice the length from the elbows to the tip of the middle finger.

The scale for weight is as follows :—

37 "paisa mansuri" = 1 "ser kachcha".
40 "sers kacha" = 1 maund kachcha.

The "mansuri paisa" is the old copper coinage of the country. The "kachcha" scale is used everywhere and the whole of the grain trade is done in it. Weighing is usually done with a 10 seer (kacha) weight, called "Dasera", which has a Government stamp on it. Almost every agriculturist has a weighing balance ("takri") of his own. A "Map", or earthenware vessel is used in the field for finding out roughly the amount of grain, but in selling, the balance and weights are always used. Milk is sold by the "ser", but it is generally measured in a "gadwa" or brass vessel of known quantity.

The measure of area is interesting for it has been the subject of much inquiry. Mr. Gordon Walker thus discusses the subject :— "The Emperor Akbar fixed one standard "bigha" for the whole empire, *viz.*, a square of which each side was a chain. The chain was 20 "ghattas", each "ghatta" being three "Ilahi Gaz". Thus 3 "Ilahi Gaz" was Akbar's standard of linear measurement, and is somewhat less than ours, so that the "ghatta" is 2¾ of our yard. The Sikns introduced their own land measures, of which mention will be made hereafter. The Imperial "bigha" was restored as the official standard in our settlement of the villages acquired in 1835, and in the whole of the Ludhiana District in 1870, but the people have not adopted it. They know it very well, but they say that it bears a certain relation to the local measure. There is no connection between "Gaz" or "Ghatta" on which it is built and the pace on which the people always fall back. The ancient measures of the country are the "ghumao" and the "kachcha bigha". The latter is the standard of Hindustan or the Cis-Sutlej country; and the former appears to be in use all over the Punjab proper, and it has also partly spread in the Malwa. In the uplands of this district the "ghumao" is used in the greater part of Jagraon, and the "bigha" in the rest. The scale of the "ghumao" is as follows :—

3 karams, double paces each way = 1 mandla.

7 mandlas = 1 kanal.

8 kanals = 1 ghumao.

But generally the "ghumao" is said to be 4 "kachcha bighas". A "kachcha bigha" is 20 "karams" each way. The "karam" however is a very varying quantity, and it was here that the difference came in. The rulers had constant necessity for using a measure either for the land on which cash rates were charged ("zabti") or for "kankut" appraisement of the crop. The "karam" would be fixed by the ruler at so many "chappas" or hand breadths 16 to 18 and the pacing was done to suit this.

The scale of the "kachcha bigha" is :—

20 "karams" by 1 "karam" = 1 kachcha biswah.

20 "karams" by 20 "karams" = 1 kachcha bigah.

I may say here that we have finally adopted for the district for future use a "kachcha bigha", one third of the old "pakka bigha" measured by a chain of 29 "karams", the "karam" being 57 inches and the chain 95 feet.

CHAPTER X

Recruiting.

This Chapter on recruiting has been divided into two parts, namely :—

1. Recruiting measures during the Great War.
2. Peace time recruiting.

Part 1 has been included, as apart from being of interest, there are several lessons to learn therefrom which it is as well to remember should we, as a nation, ever be required to put forth the same efforts again.

Part 1.

Recruiting during the Great War.

General.—At the outset it must be remembered that under pre-war conditions many parts of the Province had no military connections or traditions. Even in the most martial districts, many castes and classes knew nothing of the Army.

The long drawn out years of the war were to call for more and yet more men. The problem of the supply of man-power was thus no less real than it was at home in spite of India's teeming millions; it was organisation that was required and this the Army could not effect by itself without the assistance of the Civil authorities.

The Punjab as has already been described in Chapter I, is far from uniform. In the hills, cultivated holdings are very small, and there are plenty of men to spare, when all the claims of cultivation have been met. In the foot hills and Indo-Gangetic plain, holdings, albeit not in all districts, are larger, but there is much less land available for grazing and other pastoral pursuits, and the standard of comfort is much higher than in the hills. So, there have long been many men of these parts willing to add to the family income by seeking employment away from home.

In the recruiting campaign which was commenced in 1917, by far the most important factor in every district was the existence, or non-existence, of a healthy public opinion. Those officers who achieved good results in areas not spontaneously eager, did so invariably by infusing the right spirit into the people, such as the Sirsa tehsil of the Hissar district.

The importance of public opinion cannot be sufficiently emphasised. The great increase in the number of soldiers and the steady improvement in the rates of army pay and enlistment bonus brought large sums of extra money into the Punjab. The best of the fighting districts received more than enough money in the form of money order remittances to pay the land revenue for the year—a factor which greatly facilitated recruiting. At the same time it is not easy in a province like the Punjab to gauge public opinion accurately, owing, to its varied composition and great distances. To arrive at a generalised impression of what the war meant to the 'man in the village' something of the general mind could be ascertained by the writings of the press; the many fantastic rumours which sprang up and died down like weeds, merely gave an indication of the infinite credulity of the masses, which had no abiding effect.

The war brought Government into very close touch with the people in all sorts of ways. The numerous associations which had sprung up had often to turn to officials for assistance and advice and this lead to much cordial co-operation. The relations induced by the recruiting campaign, however, were not so uniform. On the one hand, in districts like Ludhiana, it led to the closest intimacy—district officials took lively interest in the home-life and welfare of the people who were showing so much public spirit, and the people appreciated the desire to help. On the other hand there were certain districts in which the news that a Government officer was coming sufficed to empty the village within a five mile radius! In these there was undeniable estrangement.

In most districts there were certain classes or tribes which fought shy of the army; enthusiastic officers were apt, after appealing in vain to their better feelings to fall back upon the sense of shame; sometimes —rarely it must be admitted—this was effective, but much more often it evoked resentment.

The supply of recruits 1914-16.—For the first twenty nine months of the war there was no attempt on the part of the army itself to change the system of recruiting which had previously been in vogue. This system consisted partly of "direct enlistments" and partly of "class recruiting". Under the former units in peace time made their own arrangements for the supply of required recruits either by calling up lads according to a "waiting list" who wished to serve in the particular unit, or by sending out recruiting parties under a British or Indian Officer, when these were found to be necessary, to enlist the number required. These were enrolled by the Commanding Officer and medically examined by the unit Medical Officer, who was an integral part of the unit establishment in the pre-war era.

Under "class recruiting", recruiting officers were posted at various Cantonments with a view to enrolling recruits of a "particular class" —thus the R. O. for Sikhs was at Jullundur. He was given a small clerical staff and one or more assistants. His duties were to enlist any recruits brought in to him by recruiting parties sent out for the purpose.

These two systems had worked excellently under peace conditions, but the chief objection was that it naturally tended to restrict activity to certain well-recognised areas.

In India, recruiting for military service, like many other things, is largely a matter of custom, and in point of fact there were whole districts which were, relatively unknown to the army. The reason was not far to seek, because under pre-war conditions, the supply generally greatly exceeded the demand and the necessity for going outside recognised unit recruiting areas, did not exist. There was also considerable conservatism maintained in adhering to the enlistment of certain definite tribes, in definite areas. Another feature of the old system, which, during the early part of the war, made it difficult of extension in fresh fields, was the fact that a would-be recruit had to find his way at his own expense, to the recruiting office in a distant Cantonment, and even then might find that the particular office did not cater for his particular class.

Recruiting, however, went on steadily in the early part of the war and there were no serious complaints of shortage of man-power until about March of 1916.

About this time, however, units were instructed by Army Headquarters that their efforts should aim at the enlistment of 100 recruits per month. The magnitude of the measures rendered necessary for enlisting these numbers and the organisation required in units for their housing, training, and administration generally, at a time when trained personnel, owing to casualties and various other factors, were seriously depleted, can best be realised when a comparison is made with the pre-war demand for an average supply of 75 annually.

The immediate effects of the additional efforts then made to obtain recruits, were that the demand for man-power in the recognised recruiting areas rapidly exceeded the supply. The problem then arose as to where to obtain the necessary numbers. Efforts made in outlying districts hitherto unrecruited, on the part of certain units, demonstrated that there was latent man-power in abundance, but that it could not be got to come forward owing to reasons already explained in the earlier part of this chapter.

In October 1916, Army Headquarters invoked the assistance of the Civil authorities with a view to raising 10,000 drivers for the transport; the whole number was made good in 18 days.

This clearly showed that a valuable means of man-supply had hitherto been ignored, and, as units reported increasing difficulty in obtaining their requirements, while it was clear that the end of the war was still a long way off, a new system was introduced in 1917.

New system introduced in 1917.—With the opening of the new year, therefore, the "class" system of enlistment was discarded and the "territorial" took its place, which, it may be remarked, is the system in vogue at the present time and will be referred to again in Part 2 of this Chapter in greater detail.

In the meanwhile it may be explained that each division (civil) was given a Divisional Recruiting Officer, and to each suitable district, a District Assistant Recruiting Officer (taken in most cases from the ranks of the civil officials) was appointed. It was their duty to enrol all recruits of all classes within their jurisdiction. This system was most beneficial, and, in the first six months of 1917, a total of 30,000 of all classes were enrolled. Even this, however, was not sufficient and it was decided in the middle of the year to hand over the control of recruiting definitely to the civil authorities. A provincial Recruiting Board, with the Lieutenant Governor as president, was then formed, and at once set itself the task of popularising the army amongst those who had taken no part in it before. In addition it assessed the amount of man-power which each district might reasonably be expected to contribute, these were then given "quota" up to which they were exhorted to work.

The improvement in the results obtained are worthy of notice. for during the last six months of 1917, a total of 61,000 recruits were enrolled, that is, double the number during the first half of the year. In the first five months of 1918 even better results were obtained with a total of 67,000.

The Punjab thus maintained a steady stream of recruits throughout the war, which increased in volume in the latter part in response to efforts on the part of the civil authorities.

During this period, however, there existed the evil of competition between "private" regimental recruiters and the civil authorities under Divisional Recruiting Officers. This competition took the form of "who was to gain the credit for enlisting the recruit". The regimental recruiter sent out from his unit had no illusions as to what would be said to him if he did not obtain recruits for his unit. Similarly the village lumbardar was determined that if any man left his village to enlist he would do so in his name, and in his name alone. Thus it befell that regimental recruiters were frequently debarred from entering a village and, in the writer's own experience, frequent reports were received of fracas in the villages. The Board, however, did their best to minimise the evil.

It has always been a maxim that the best recruiter is the newly enlisted recruit. This was just as true during the war as it was before or since, in fact it was even more so. It was a common experience to find a lad who had but a short time before been hardly prevailed upon to leave his village, coming back full of an enthusiasm and self-esteem, and persuading his friends to follow his example. One of the most successful innovations tried by one or two units, was the opening of local depots in places where there were large numbers of men with no previous military connections. These depots were completely self-contained and recruits remained there for the first two months of their service. This enabled the district to see for the themselves what military service was like, and also enabled recruits to pay frequent visits to their homes, thus exhibiting to their relations what regular exercise, good pay, free rations and clothing did for them.

These depots did a great deal not only towards increasing the supply of recruits, but also towards establishing cordial relations between the army and the local population. Needless to say that the best instructors alone were selected for them.

Even before the introduction of these depots, local patriotism had in various places taken steps to smooth the path of the recruit. Some districts, such as Ludhiana, placed their "zail ghar" at the disposal of batches of recruits on their way to their regiments, and even made arrangements for free medical treatment of those who were prevented from enlistment by some temporary complaint.

Results by Divisions, Districts and Tribes.—In practically every part of the Province the Sikhs came forward in strength; statistics show that they provided nearly double their fair share of recruits. and established an all-round record which left little room for criticism. At the same time it must be remembered that the pre-war standard and the standard obtaining during the war were very different things. Units whose standard pre-war were 5′ 9″ with proportionate chest development, were through force of circumstances obliged to take men at 5′ 3″, and moreover, instead of maintaing a Jat Sikh standard were required to open their ranks to every kind of castes such as Jhinwars, Chhimbas, Nais, Brahmans, etc.

Among the country-folk who made up the bulk of the Punjab's population, there was keen competition to show the best results, and the majority of districts displayed fine enthusiasm in trying to win a good place in the monthly lists.

Among the divisions enlisting Sikhs, Jullundur, Ambala and Lahore, in this order, showed the best results of percentage of men enlisted. Of the Jullundur division the Ludhiana district was easily first, doing especially well for its size whilst Hoshiarpur and Ferozepore showed fine aggregates. In the Ambala division Hissar did well; Malerkotla showed the highest percentage and could challenge comparison with the best British districts. Jind, Nabha, Patiala, Kapurthala and Faridkot all did well; Patiala produced four times as large an aggregate as any other State, and slightly more men than the best British district.

In practically every district in which they occur in any quantity, the Jat Sikhs sent a very high percentage of their eligible men to the army. The Labana Sikhs did even better in Hoshiarpur, Gurdaspur, Lahore, Sialkot, Gujranwala and Gujrat. The Mazbhi Sikhs everywhere reached a very high standard. Of the humbler tribes it may generally be said that they were willing to follow their "betters". In fact they would have enlisted in far greater numbers if they had been allowed to do so in the same units as their agricultural neighbours.

The following items extracted from District Histories will help to show some of the tribal percentages.

1. 30 per cent. or upwards Jat Sikhs of Ludhiana, Amritsar and Shahpur.
2. 70 per cent. or upwards Labana Sikhs of Gurdaspur and Gujrat.

As a few instances of villages which gave practically every able-bodied man and boy, are mentioned below :—

Ludhiana District.—Brahmans Majra—Maima Singhwala—Isewal—Bhattian—Ghalib Ram Singh—Dotar—Naurangwal—Akal-i-garh—Majara and Assi Khurd.

Gurdaspur.—The Labana villages of Gohot Pokhar—Chak Sharif—Jhanda Labana.

Hoshiarpur.—Badsali—Chalola and Dulchar.

Where whole villages enlisted "en masse" it naturally follows that whole families in those villages did the same. From the war histories of Ludhiana and Amritsar can be seen the readiness with which families would send "only" sons, or all their sons to the Army. Still more commonly, in families of three, four or more, all the sons would enlist except one left behind to keep the house together. But enough on this subject has been said.

To those who are interested in recruiting, and all should be so interested, a perusal of these war histories will well repay the study. But theory and experience, where possible, should go hand in hand and the recommendation cannot be too strongly emphasized that every officer once, if not more, in his service, and preferably within a short period of his joining his Indian unit, should make a point of touring in the district, when it may confidently be asserted that not only will a stronger liaison with the civil authorities be maintained, but he will receive a warm welcome in the villages and will derive much benefit from his tour.

PART II.

Peace time Recruiting.

For recruting purposes the Punjab has been divided into three recruiting areas, *viz.*, Rawalpindi, Lahore and Jullundur. In peace time the staff of each of these areas consists of a Recruiting Officer and one or more Assistant Recruiting Officers, under whom work a permanent staff.

Each recruiting area is organised so as to be capable of expansion on mobilization by the formation of branch offices and increased staffs.

The Recruiting Officer of each area is responsible for obtaining any recruits of any class or religion who live in his area and are wanted for the Army.

Their areas of responsibility are as follows :—

Recruiting Officer, Rawalpindi.—Hazara civil district (N. W. F. P.). Rawalpindi civil division (less Gujrat civil district). Kashmir (North and South) and Poonch States.

Recruiting Officer, Lahore.—Lahore civil division. Multan civil division. Gujrat civil district. Jammu and Bahawalpur States.

Recruiting Officer, Jullundur.—Jullundur civil division. Simla district. Sikhs from the Ambala civil division (less Simla district).

The Recruiting Officers who are chiefly concerned with the enlistment of Sikhs are therefore those of Jullundur and Lahore, the former being responsible for the Malwa country and the Doaba, and the latter for the Manjha. In the Rawalpindi recruiting area the Sikhs are mostly confined to the Khatri class.

Firstly a word with regard to the Recruiting Officer and his staff. His is no light task nor is it an enviable appointment; in plain words he receives as a rule more kicks than "hapence" for it is in human nature to complain and units frequently do so concerning the quality of their recruits. He should not be considered, as he so often is, in the light of an unsympathetic bureaucrat who unreasonably rejects good recruits, and deals harshly with good men who are working as recruiters under his supervision. In reality his one aim in life is to supply the best recruits he can put his hands on and to see that if possible recruiters keep the same object in view. Therefore, if a word of counsel may prevail remember the old adage of "don't shoot the pianist, he is doing his best". Apart from the question of the supply of recruits, his appointment carries with it many duties which are not immediately apparent. His visitors are legion, being largely those who have some demand to make; it may be in connection with grants of land, non-receipt of pensions or medals, and requests for employment or assistance in some way or others. Amongst his duties those of peace preparations for the supply of personnel on mobilization are a most important and far-reaching one. Briefly, therefore, it may be stated that the appointment of a Recruiting Officer is no sinecure or bed of roses and it is held for any period up to 4 years.

The tenure of appointment of Assistant Recruiting Officers is ordinarily two years. It is a difficult appointment to fill as units are frequently averse to sparing one of their small establishment of British Officers for this purpose. Nevertheless the officers so appointed will derive much practical experience and knowledge from his tour of duty and can benefit his own Regiment as well as the Army generally by maintaining a close liaison with the civil authorities and the old pensioners.

Forming part of the staff at each Headquarters remains the medical officer. His appointment is perhaps the most difficult to fulfil of any and usually speaking he is the recipient of much abuse. Formerly recruits on joining their training battalions used to be subjected to a second medical examination at which they were frequently rejected, the anomaly has now however been eliminated and the decision of the specialist Medical Officer at the Recruiting Headquarters is now final, and rightly so.

The ordinary procedure for procuring recruits is for the Officer Commanding the training battalion, or of other formations who are responsible for the training of recruits, to submit to Recruiting Officers concerned a monthly statement showing the number of recruits of various classes required and any special instructions which they may wish to give.. This statement is considered cancelled at the end of the month and a new demand is submitted which includes all previous requirements.

Recruiting parties are sent out from active units or from the recruit training formation, or from both. The usual time that a recruiting party remains on this duty under the Recruiting Officer is from 6 weeks to two months. During this period they are given dates at intervals of about a fortnight to bring in recruits for approval.

A party sent out should whenever opportunity offers be sent out under a British Officer, or at least under a Sikh officer and should be carefully chosen and composed of the men of the districts from which the recruits are required. They report prior to setting out at the office of the Recruiting Officer under whom they have been detailed to work.

Generally speaking the duty is a popular one and eagerly sought after. The reason is not far to seek for each recruiter is as a rule on his own, to come and go as he likes in his search for recruits, or, it must be admitted, to place his duties as secondary in importance to matters of a more urgent and domestic nature. The remedy can however always be applied that in the event of his failing to bring any possible candidates before the Recruiting Officer he is not employed on this duty again. At the same time, however, considerable discretion must be exercised, for in many districts recruits do not readily come forward, and the recruiter may have been doing most conscientious work. Thus several units have a system by means of which large parties are sent out under a British Officer twice or three times a year during the best recruiting seasons, which has the additional advantage from the point of view of training that suitable squads can be formed. The matter is really one which must be decided by each unit's requirements and special circumstances. If large numbers are required.

special steps must be taken and no hard and fast line can be laid down as to what procedure should be adopted. The point to remember is that the recruit of to-day is the Non-Commissioned Officer or Sikh Officer of the future, and that as such it is worth while making really strenuous efforts to obtain the best that the market has to offer. This market is an extensive one but the difficulty of bringing the goods to the market is a no mean one, thanks to the system of education and modern developments the former of which causes large numbers of likely lads to turn their noses up at military service and seek more lucrative employment in the higher paid professions, while the latter causes them to leave their villages and similarly seek employment elsewhere, frequently *ex*-India.

The best seasons for recruiting are in July and August and again in January and February. During these periods work on the fields is at a minimum and the men will be found in their villages; at these seasons also the villagers have more leisure and lads frequently can be induced to come in which at other seasons of the year would be impossible. Touring in July and August is a most exhausting duty on all alike, but the hottest parts of the day can be avoided if use is made of the canal bungalows which cover a complete network in most of the districts of the Punjab. Permission to use them should previously be applied for from the canal authorities.

One word on the subject of touring. If this form of recruiting for the British Office has been decided upon it should be carried out on horse or on camel from village to village in a definite area, and not by rail to certain previously selected rendezvous. The mere fact of a British Officer touring from village to village, especially if accompanied by a gun, will ensure four times as many recruits being forthcoming as by the latter method, especially under present day conditions where pressure of office and routine work and the introduction of Indianisation rarely admits of a British civil administrator making extensive tours. The value of military officers touring cannot be over-estimated, for apart from the main object of obtaining recruits, liaison is maintained with old pensioners, whose grievances, fancied or otherwise, receive a sympathetic hearing, and they realise that though they have left the active ranks of the battalion, they are not forgotten.

As soon as a recruit is passed fit at the Recruiting office by both the Recruiting Officer as regards his general standard, suitability and correct class for the unit for which he wishes to enlist, and by the Medical Officer as regards his general health and physical fitness, he is immediately enrolled for service in the unit of his choice. He is then given a railway warrant to the station of the unit which is responsible for the training of recruits for the corps for which he has been enrolled. Each recruit on enrolment is authorized an advance of pay to cover subsistance and other expenses incidental to his journey to join his unit, who recover this advance when drawing his first pay. His pay starts from the day of enrolment.

The rules for payment of travelling expenses incurred by him, or by his recruiter on his behalf when travelling to the recruiting office, or to meet the Recruiting Officer at any other place which may be fixed are laid down in Recruiting Regulations, India, Part I, Peace.

In regimental recruiting without the agency of the Recruiting Office care should be taken that judgment of a recruit's fitness should not be swayed by such considerations as the recruit's family connections with the unit, or sympathy with his evident desire to be enlisted. A recruit who is under the minimum standard should not ordinarily be accepted except for some very special reason, in the pious hope that he will fill out later.

When men on leave are given permission to bring recruits before the Recruiting Officer they should be instructed as to the necessary physical standard; none should be below the standard of height and chest measurement, nor should they have obvious physical defects such as knock-knee, flat-feet, bad varicose veins or bad teeth. Should this happen a disallowance of the money spent on subsistence of such recruits will be pretty sure to prevent a recurrence. Recruiters will sometimes spend the greater part of the time in their villages and when only a few days remain, pick up any material that offers and bring it in for inspection. A knowledge, therefore, that this procedure is likely to result in pecuniary loss to themselves generally acts as a deterrent. Men, however cannot usually be held responsible for bringing in recruits who have previously been rejected on medical grounds, as there are men who will offer themselves for enlistment, well knowing that they will not be passed, merely in order to get the subsistence money.

Recruiters should be made absolutely responsible that the men they bring in are of the right class, and what they represent themselves to be. It cannot be too strongly impressed on recruiters, that a few really good recruits of the right sort are better than a number who only just come up to the required standard.

A really good recruiter is invaluable and well worthy of being rewarded, as the duty is by no means an easy one. Every encouragement should be shown to men who do well in this duty. An entry to that effect may be made in their sheet rolls, or such other recognition accorded as the Commanding Officer may consider most suitable. On the other hand, as previously mentioned, it is perhaps not good policy to punish men who do not give satisfaction, unless they have shown great negligence, for if they are liable to punishment, they may not volunteer readily for the duty through fear of failure to do well. The best plan is not to employ such men again.

Much assistance can be obtained by notifying the presence of a recruiting party to the civil authorities through the Recruiting Officer. "Tehsildars" and "Thanadars" can send out messages and give notice in the villages of the date when the party will probably arrive, and collect "Lambardars" and intending recruits.

The verification of a recruit's caste and character, unless he happens to be personally known to the recruiter, depends almost entirely on the village "Lambardar". Though his honesty can as a rule be depended upon, it is not absolutely reliable. There are many wheels within wheels in these matters and frequently personal bias or other reasons not apparent on the surface may cause a deliberate mis-statement to appear on the verification roll. It is as well, therefore, to be on one's guard.

A method of recruiting which is frequently resorted to is to send parties to the various "melas" or fairs, which are held at many places in all parts of the country and at almost all seasons of the year. Good recruits may sometimes be picked up in this way, but as a rule lads only go to these fairs to enjoy themselves and the results in the writer's experience have in every instance been most disappointing. Lads however do go, either because no parties have been to their districts lately or because their parents will not allow them to enlist at their homes. The method has its disadvantages, however, the chief among which are that the recruits offering themselves are certain to be unknown to the men, having come from all over the country, and it is impossible to verify the description they give of themselves; frequently they give the party the slip having been fed for several days and cannot then be traced.

A list of the principal places where fairs are held is given at the end of this chapter.

Generally speaking it is very noticeable that the proportion of recruits forthcoming from the different districts vary in inverse ratio to the prosperity of the land. Thus in the Lahore area, Jhang, Lyallpur and Montgomery produce few recruits compared to the comparative by non-irrigated districts of Amritsar, Lahore, and Sialkot, which produce, in addition to numbers, a very good type of recruit. At the same time the number of recruits who come forward for enrolment cannot be entirely estimated by the prosperity of the country. Certain districts or tehsils have always supplied numbers out of all proportion to their strengths even in highly cultivated tracts, such as Ludhiana. The reason for this is partly due to the small size of individual holdings which necessitate younger sons seeking their livehood elsewhere, and also to a highly developed sense of military service which is inherent in the population. On the other hand can be quoted the instance of the Sirsa tehsil of the Hissar district, which although perhaps one of the most sparsely cultivated and waterless tracts of the Punjab has never regarded military service in a very favourable light. Much can be done in such districts by patient endeavour to develop a spirit for military service, but it is a long process and the natural tendency is to go to the easiest market. The inevitable result is that this market is apt to be over-recruited and the type of lad enlisted rather under standard.

From the point of view of recruiting remains little more to add. Success is largely a matter of experience combined with a thorough knowledge of the country and the customs and characteristics of the people, and last but not least, where touring is concerned, a good knowledge of the language, tact, sympathy, and perhaps above all, patience in listening to and dealing with the many problems which will confront the British Officer when visiting his recruiting area.

Name of fair.	Where held.	Date on which held.
	FEROZEPORE DISTRICT.	
Abohar Cattle Fair ..	Abohar	February each year.
Bathing Mela	Haripur, *alias*, Barah Tirath, Tehsil Fazilka.	Midddle of March, early November.
Moga Cattle Fair	Moga	Each year August early.
Muktesar Maghi Fair ..	Muktesar	10th to 17th January.
Mela Mian Gharaya ..	Village Rupana, Tehsil Muktesar.	28th February to 3rd March.
Mela Pothi Mala	Gauransahib	13th April.
Jalalabad Cattle and Horse Fair	Jalalabad	1st week of January.
Ferozepore Cattle Fair ..	Ferozepore	October each year.
	LUDHIANA DISTRICT.	
Bhai Bala Mela	Village Dad	11th February.
Chhappar (Mari) Mela ..	Village Chhappar	10th September.
Dusera Festival	Ludhiana	6th October.
Roshni Fair	Ludhiana	10th October.
Roshni Fair	Jagraon	24th February.
Chet Chaudas Fair ..	Ludhiana	1st April.
Dusera Festival	Samrala	6th October.
	HOSHIARPUR DISTRICT.	
Holi	Anandpur and Mari Tehsil Una.	15th to 19th March.
Baisakhi	Bubbhor, Tehsil Una ..	13th April.
Baisakhi	Bahadurpur, Tehsil Hoshiarpur.	13th April.
Baisakhi	Badal, Tehsil Dasuya ..	13th April.

Name of fair.	Where held.	Date on which held.
Moharram	Hoshiarpur, Tanda, Dasuya, Mukerian.	10th July.
Mela Devi Chimat Purni ..	Chintpurni	6th August.
Dusera	Hoshiarpur, Tanda Dasuya, Mukerian, Kot Fatuhi, Una, Mahilpur.	2nd to 5th October.
Mela Shah Nur Jamal ..	Salairen	In month of March.
	JULLUNDUR DISTRICT.	
	Jullundur Tehsil.	
Ghug Baisakhi	Bhudian	13th April.
Holi	Jamsher	18th March.
Desar	Hardo Pharala	13th April.
Baisakhi	Daroli Kalan	13th April.
Guga Naumi	Daroli Kalan	31st August.
Baisakhi	Kartarpur	13th April.
Baisakhi	Jullundur City	13th April.
Moharram	Jullundur City	16th to 21st July.
Dusera	Jullundur City	16th October.
Harballab	Jullundur City	26th to 29th December.
Imam Nasir Uddin Sahib ..	Jullundur City	24th June.
Janab Pir Usaf Ali Sahib ..	Landra	3rd June.
	NAKODAR TEHSIL.	
Chaukian	Khanpur Dhadda.. ..	27th February.
Chaukian	Heran	26th February.
Chaukian	Boparai	25th February.
Wrestling	Shamkar..	17th October.
Wrestling	Saireh	25th October.

Name of fair.	Where held.	Date on which held.
	NAKODAR TEHSIL—*contd.*	
Baisakhi	Mahatpur	13th April.
Mohavram	Mahatpur	20th July.
Dosehra	Maharpur	15th October.
Moharram	Uggi	20th July.
Saidrana	Saidpur	20th September.
Punjab Kaur Fair ..	Nangal Umbian	18th August.
Moharram	Nakodar	20 h July.
Moharram	Lohian	20th July.
	TEHSIL NAWANSHEHAR.	
Sain Abdulla Shah ..	Kultham	28th June to 5th July.
Jhanda Ji	Khatkar Kalan	14th June.
Dosehra	Khatkar Kalan	16tn October.
Dosehra	Banga	16th October.
Dosehra	Mukandpur	16th October.
Dosehra	Mahal Ghela	16th October.
	TEHSIL PHILLOUR.	
Sain Soda Shah Sahib ..	Phillour	23rd June.
Shah Fateh Ali Shah ..	Nur Mahal	17th June.
Khoja Roshan Shah Wali ..	Man	22nd Jnne.
Moharram	Phillour	21st July.
Chaukian	Barapind	21st February.
Chaukian	Boparai	22nd February.
Chaukian	Rurki Kalan	24th February.
Chaukian	Bundala	24th February.
Chaukian	Jandiala	25th February.

Name of fair.	Where held.	Date on which held.
	DISTRICT AMRITSAR.	
Baisakhi	Amritsar	13th April.
Dewali	Do.	5-6th November.
Dusehra	Do.	16th October.
Moharram	Do.	21st July.
Taru Idulfitr	Do.	16th April
Taru Idul Zuha	Do.	21/22nd June.
Ram Naumi	Do.	21st April.
Sangrana Sahib	Do.	17th May.
Basant Panchmi	Wadala Guru	6th February.
Guru Teg Bahadur ..	Baba Bakala	13th August.
Kotah	Wallah	16th February.
Dewali	Amritsar	25th October.
Baisakhi ..	Do.	13th April.
	TEHSIL TARN TARAN.	
Chet Choudas	Tarn Taran	2nd April.
Bhadon Amawas ..	Do.	26/27th September.
Jag Guru Amar Dass ..	Goindwal	10-11th September.

NOTE.—Amawas fair held every month.

	TEHSIL AJNALA.	
Ram Tirath	Ram Tirath	October.

Name of fair.	Where held.	Date on which held.
	Lyallpur District.	
Horse and Cattle Fair ..	Lyallpur	October and March.
Do.	Jaranwala	October and March just after Lyallpur fair.
Do.	Tandlianwala	26th and 27th of every month.
Do.	Gojra	1st and 2nd and 3rd every month.
	Lahore District.	
Chathianwala	Chathianwala, Kasur ..	16th and 17th February.
Pattoki Horse and Cattle Fair	Pattoki	21st to 24th February.
Kasur Horse and Cattle Fair	Kasur	1st to 5th March.
Panne Shah	Bhila, Kasur	30th October.
Ghariayala Sher Shah ..	Ghariayala Kasur	22nd to 27th March.
Chirigan	Shalimar Garden, Lahore ..	6th to 19th April.
Baisakhi	Ram Thuman, Kasur ..	13th April.
Bhadarkali	Nizabeg, Lahore	27th May.
Kahna Nau Horse and Cattle Fair.	Kahna Nau Khana Kacha ..	2nd week of October.
Basant Panchmi ..	Samadh Haqiqat Rai, Lahore	6th February.
Jor	Samadh Guru Arjan Dev, Lahore	3rd June.
	Gujranwala District.	
Horse Show and Cattle Fair	Gujranwala	12th to 16th March.
Diwali Cattle Fair ..	Gujranwala	22nd to 28th October.
Baisakhi	Eminabad	11th to 17th April.
Baisakhi	Wazirabad	13th to 14th April.
Cattle Fair	Wazirabad	1st February to 5th March.

Name of fair.	Where held.	Date on which held.
	GUJRANWALA DISTRICT—contd	
Jag Badokki	Badokki Gosain	16th to 17th May.
Sakhi Sarwar Fair ..	Dhaunkal	14th June to 15th July.
Urs	Jalalpur Tehsil Hafizabad..	26th to 28th February.
Kadman	Pindi Bhattian, Tehsil Hafizabad.	3rd to 5th March.
Cattle Fair	Hafizabad	15th to 19th February.
Urs Mian Ghulam Rasul ..	Ramnagar	30th to 31st March.
Urs Sain Gulab Shah ..	Ramnagar	9th to 10th June.
Tappsi Cattle Fair ..	Ramnagar	27th to 29th March.
Urs Sain Natha Shah ..	Ramnagar	24th September.
Bhirri Fair	Bhirri Shah Rahman ..	21st May to 23rd May.
	GURDASPUR DISTRICT.	
Moharram	Gurdaspur	8th to 10th July.
Dusehra	Gurdaspur .. .. Dinanagar.	5th October.
Baisakhi	Village Talabpur Pandori. Village Lil.	13th April.
	BATALA TEHSIL.	
Nanwin Daswin	Achchal	3rd November.
Baisakhi	Achchal .. .. .. Dera Baba Nanak ..	13th April.
Chola Sahib	Dera Baba Nanak ..	5th and 6th March.
Ghi	Chuman	13th January.
Shah Badar Diwan ..	Massanian	9th September.
Kastiwal	Kastiwal	15th and 16th June.

Name of fair.	Where held.	Date on which held.
	PATHANKOTE TEHSIL.	
Lakh Data	Sultanpur	29th and 30th June.
Baisakhi..	Barth, Warkuah, Taragarh (new) Gaza Gadri.	13th April.
Holi	Hara	19th March.
Sair	Shahpur Kandi	16th September.
	SHAKARGARH TEHSIL.	
Khangah, Bhai Badda ..	Masrur	2nd June.
Chaunki	Shakargarh	29th June.
Baisakhi..	Tahli Sahib	13th April.
	Kot Naina	
Parewi	Gorala	4th and 5th October.
	MUZAFFARGARH DISTRICT.	
	Muzaffargarh Tehsil.	
Pir Kamala	Kiri Ali Mardan	21st Jeth.
Hazrat Musan Lal ..	Jalwala	15th to 23rd Asuj.
Dedha Lal Fair	Harpallo	May to November on every Wednesday.
Pir Jahanian	Rampur	22nd Chet to 22nd Sawan.
Piran Pak	Walwat	Date not fixed.
Mahbub Jahanian ..	Haji Metla	14th Bhadon.
Bagga Sher	Khanpur	In Sawan.
	LEIAH TEHSIL.	
Lal Isan Cattle Fair ..	Karor	In August.
Hasan Sher Fair	Aulak	Last Thursday of Magh.
Pir Anayat Shah	Aulak	14th to 20th Chet.

Name of fair.	Where held.	Date on which held.
	KOT ADU TEHSIL.	
Nur Shah	Talai Nur Shah	15th Poh.
Sheikh Mohd. Jhander ..	Dureja Shaki	26th Sawan.
Bawa Kashigir	Kot Adu	Phagan or Chet.
	ALIPUR TEHSIL.	
Alampir	Shahr Sultan	In Chet on every Thursday.
Sadiq Shah	Damarwala Shumali ..	18th to 20th Moharram.
Nur Shah	Qadirpur	In Chet on every Friday.
Kohar Piran	Kohar Piran	20th and 28th Chet.
Bodalwala	Jatoi Shumal	1st Phagan.
Sammat Jhuggi Wala ..	Jaguggiwala	28th Chet.
	SIALKOT DISTRICT.	
Baryar Cattle Fair ..	Narowal	3rd to 9th March.
Sialkot Spring Cattle Fair ..	Sialkot	18th to 25th March.
Throh Cattle Fair ..	Throh Tehsil Pasra ..	16th to 22nd August.
Gullau Shah Cattle Fair ..	Koreke, Tehsil Daska ..	2nd to 9th October.
Sialkot Autumn Cattle Fair	Sialkot	20th to 24th October.
Baisakhi Cattle Fair ..	Sambrial	27th March to 1st April.
Sankhatra Market ..	Pr.vi (Shankhatra) ..	3rd to 9th November.
	SHEIKHUPURA DISTRICT.	
Horse and Cattle Fair ..	Sheikhupura	1st to 5th March.
Cattle Fair	Shahkot	24th to 26th March.
Cattle Fair with Shah Massa Diwan.	Bhuchch Tehsil Shahdara.	11th to 16th June.
Cattle Fair	Kanqah Dogran	16th to 18th July.
Cattle Fair with Sain Bahar Shah.	Sheikupura	19th to 21st May.

Name of fair.	Where held.	Date on which held.
	SHEIKHUPURA DISTRICT —*contd.*	
Horse and Cattle Fair ..	Chuhar Khana	10th to 13th November.
	JHANG DISTRICT.	
Atheran Hazari Fair ..	Atheran Hazari .. .. Tehsil Jhang.	30th March to 1st April.
Shah Jiwana Fair ..	Shah Jiwana	9th May to 10th July.
Massan Fair	Massan	5th to 7th October.

APPENDICES.

Pages.

APPENDIX I.

List of districts, States and tehsils with their relative value as Sikh recruiting grounds, and the names of the Jat Sikh sub-divisions found therein as shown in the Census Reports for 1911.

District.	Tehsils.		Value.	Jat Sikh sub-divisions.
Ludhiana	Ludhiana	74,819	Very good	Aulak, Bains, Bal, Bhangu, Bhular, Bopa Rai, Chahil, Chima, Main, Dagar Deo, Dhariwal, Dhillon. Dhindsa. Garewal, Gil, Her, Kang, Man. Mangat. Saroi, Sidhu; sindhu (also Brahmans; Kalals; Khatris; Tarkhans; Jhinwars; Ramdasias; and Chuhras).
Jat Sikh population. 149,725	Jagraon	48,098	Very good	
	Samrala	26,808	Good	
Ferozepore.	Ferozepore	12,333	Very good	*Jats, viz.*, Aulak. Bahar, Bath, Bhular. Bhuttar, Chahil, Chima, Dhaliwal, Dhillon, Garund, Gil, Her, Jakhar Johal, Kaler, Kang, Kangra, Khera, Khosa. Korutana. Mahi. Mahil. Man. Pa nun. Rai, Randhawa, Sang, Sangi, Sarai Shekhun, Sohal. Sumra. Sandhu, Sidhu, Virk, Wandar; (also Brahmans; Rajputs; Aroras; Kalals; Tarkhans; Jhinwars; Chhimbas; Mazbhis; Ramdasias; and Chuhras).
Jat Sikh population. 191,415	Moga	97,451	Do.	
	Zira	23.607	Do.	
	Mukhtesar	37,943	Fair	
	Fazilka	20,081	Bad	
Ambala.	Ambala	..	Fair	*Jats. viz.*, Baidwan, Badwal, Bains, Bansil. Bal, Barang, Bath, Basati. Chhalli, Chahil. Dehia, Dehmi Dhariwal, Dharial, Dhillon, Dhindsa. Ghandu. Gil, Her, Kang, Katari, Mahil, Mangat. Man, Pawania, Sarai. Sarawan, Sidhu. Sindhu; Tarkha. Urtal. Varaich, (also Brahmans; Sainis; Kalals; Tarkhans; Jhinwars; Chhimbas; Ramdasias; Mazbhis; and Chuhras).
	Rupar	..	Fair	
	Kharar	..	Fair	
Jat Sikh population. 57,006	Naramgarh	..	Indifferent	
	Pipli	..	Bad	
	Jagadhri	..	Bad	

APPENDIX II—*contd.*

List of districts, States and tehsils with their relative value as Sikh recruiting grounds, and the names of the Jat Sikh sub-divisions found therein as shown in the Census Reports for 1911—contd.

District		Tehsils.		Value.	Jat Sikh sub-divisions.
Hissar.		Hissar . .	136	Nix . . .	*Jats, viz.*, Bal, Bara, Bhainiwal, Bola. Chahil, Channan. Dedwal, Dhillon, hariwal, dhundwal, Dodi, Gil, Godara. Kaswan. Lonba, Man, Nain, Pangal, Puniya. Sahag, Sadu, Saharan, Sara. Sidhu Sindhu ; (also Chamar ; Chhimbe ; Chuhra ; Julaha ; Kalal ; Khatri ; Lohar ; and Nai Sikhs etc).
Jat Sikh population.	26,125	Hansi . .	113	Nix . . .	
		Biwani . .	18	Nix . . .	
		Sirsa . . .	17,387	Fair . . .	
		Fatehabad . .	8,471	Fair . . .	*Jats, viz.*, Athwal, Aulakh, Auntal, Awjle. Bachhal. Bachti. Bagar. Bajwa, Bains. Baidwan. Bandechhe, Bandhel, Banse. Bante, Bandar, Banwaria. Basati, Batthal. Batoe. Beri. Bhainiwal, Bhangu, Bhatti, Bhullar, Bhu'tar, Biling. Birk, Bole, Chahil, Chattha. Chande, Chima, Chohan, Chopare, Dallu. Dangi. Dehia. Deo. Dhaliwal. Dhallan, Dhanoe, Dhanor, Dhandian. Dhandhe, Dhandiwal, Dhawe, Dhillon, Dhindsa, Dholu. Dhota, Dullat, Gadra, Gandhu, Ganghas, Gangore, Garewal, Ghuman, Gil, Godara, Goraya, Gosal. Gurne. Hari. Her, Hinjra, Hundal. Jakhar, Janjh, Janjhar, Jaria, Jatana, Jawinda, Jhalli. Jhund, Kahlon. Kali, Rauni, Kandoe. Kang, Kankar, Kharand. Kharral. Khatre Khera, Khire, Koraria, Lahar, Lamba, Lochap, Mal Mahvi, Maindal; Man, Mandahar, Mander, Mangi. Mangat, Marral Maur, Nadi, Nagre. Nain, Nalla. Naraini, Narwan. Nat, Papre, Pawania, Punder, Punia. Randhawa, Ranwan, Raparia Rathaul, Rathi, Rattiwal, Salu. Sandhu, Sangwan, Sanghare, Sahrawat, Samrao. Sarah. Sarai, Sari, Sarwara. Sekhon, Sidhu, Sihumar, Siri. Sohal, Suhi, Suraj. Tarka, Tawana, Thind, Uppal, Varaich : (also Brahmans ; Kalals ; Tarkhans ; Ramdasias ; Mazbhis ; Chuhras ; Chhimbas ; and Jhinwars).
Patiala.		*Nizamat totals.*			
		Karmgarh .	74,137	Very good . .	
		Amargarh .	86,138	Very good . .	
Jat Sikh population.	323,869	Anahadgarh .	150,038	Very good . .	
		Pinjour . .	13,535	Indifferent . .	
		Mohindargarh .	21	No value . .	

Nabha. Jat Sikh population	56,427	Phul	39,920	Good	Aulakh, Bains, Bhangu, Bhullar, Bhuttar, Chahil, Dhariwal, Dhillon, Dhindsa, Gil Man. Randhawa, Sarai, Sidhu, Sindhu.
		Amloh	16,480	Very fair	
		Bawal	21	Bad	
Jind. Jat Sikh population.	18,205	Jind	368	Nix	*Jats viz.*, Bhullar. Bora. Chahil, Dhaliwal. Dhillon, Ghangar, Gil, Kali Rawan, Mahil, Man, Mandhar, Pawania, Redhu, Sahrawat, Sarao, Shidhu, Sindhu. Sohi.
		Sangrur	17,830	Good	
		Badri	7	Nix	
Fridkot. Jat Sikh population.	43,072	Faridkot	22 287	Very good	*Jats. viz.*, Aulakh, Chahil, Dandiwal, Dewala. Dhunna. Dhariwal. Dhilon, Gil. Man, Sarai Santhu, Sindhu, Vandar, Virk.
		Kotkapura	20,785	Very good	
Maler Kotla. Jat Sikh population.	15,724	Maler Kotla	5,872	Fair	*Jats, viz.*, Baddechha, Bagri, Bandher. Bath, Bopa Rai, Chahil, Chima. Dhariwal. Dhillon, Garewal. Jhalli, Mandahar, Opal, Sindhu, Varaich.
		Punjgrain	9,852	Fair	
Amritsar. Jat Sikh population.	166,889	Amritsar	65,250	Very good	*Jats, viz.*, Athwal. Aulakh Bajwa. Bal Bandar, Bat, Batha Bhangu, Bhatti, Bhoi, Bhullar, Boparar, Chahil. Chima, Chinna, Dadwal, Deo, Dhanoa, Dhariwal Dhaun. Dhillon, Garaya, Ghuman. Gil, Handal, Her, Hinjra. Jawana, Johal, Kaler, Kamboh, Kara, Khang, Khaire, Khara, Mahil, Man, Najjar. Ojla, Opal, Pannum. Rai, Randhawa, Sadal. Sagwan, Sakuni, Sandhu. Sansi, Sarai, Sidhu. Sohal, Soi, Sumra, Uthwal, Valia Varaich, Virk ; (also Brahmans ; Khatris ; Kalals ; Aroras ; Tarkhans ; Jhinwars ; Chhimbas ; Mazbhis, Ramdasias ; and Chuhras).
		Tarn Taran	74,938	Very good	
		Ajnala	26,701	Very good	

APPENDIX I—*contd.*

List of districts, States and tehsils with their relative value as Sikh recruiting grounds, and the names of the Jat Sikh Sub-divisions found therein as shown in the Census Reports for 1911—contd.

District.		Tehils.		Value.	Jat Sikh Sub-divisions.
Lahore. Jat Sikh Population.	98,241	Lahore	29,173	Very good	*Jats, viz.* Aulakh, Bajwa, Bat, Bhati, Bhullar, Bhuttor, Chahil, Chauhan, Chima, Chhina, Deo, Dhaliwal, Dhillon, Ghuman, Gil, Gondal, Her, Hinjra, Khara, Kharral, Malhi, Man, Opal, Pannun, Randhawa, Sarai, Sekhon, Sidhu, Sindhu, Surma, Varaich, Virk ; (also Brahmans ; Khatris ; Aroras ; Kalals ; Kambohs ; Mahtams ; Labanas ; Tarkhans ; Chhimbas ; Jhinwars ; Mazbhis ; Ramdasias ; and Chuhras).
		Kasur	45,339	Very good	
		Chunian	23,729	Good	
Gurdaspur. Jat Sikh population.	78,500	Gurdaspur	24,105	Good	*Jats, viz.*, Athwal, Aulakh, Bains, Bajwa, Bal, Basra, Bhangu, Bhattewid, Bhullai, Bhuttar, Bopa Rai, Both, Chahil, Chima, Chunna, Dayar, Dhariwal, Dhillon, Gharal, Ghuman, Gil, Goraya, Hinjra, Johal, Kahlon, Kamon, Khang, Khera, Mali, Man, Nat, Padda, Pandar, Pannun, Randhawa, Rayar, Samra, Sarai, Sidhu, Sindhu, Sobal, Vahla, Varaich, Virk ; (also Rajputs ; Brahmans ; Khatris ; Aroras ; Kalals ; Sainis ; Kambohs ; Labanas ; Tarkhans ; Chhimbas, and Ramdasias).
		Batala	45,091	Very good	
		Shakargarh	8,616	Fair	
		Pathankot	688	Bad	
Sialkot. Jat Sikh population.	50,475	Sialkot	6,639	Fair	*Jats, viz.*, Aulakh, Bains, Bajwa, Basrai, Chima, Deo-Dhillon, Dhindsa, Dhariwal, Ghumman, Gil, Her, Hinjra, Kahlon, Kang, Ladhar, Man, Nagre, Pannun, Randhawa, Sahi, Sarai, Sidhu and Sindhu ; (also, Rajputs, Khatris ; Labanas ; Tarkhans ; Chhimbas ; Jhinwars ; and Ramdasias).
		Raya	19,275	Good	
		Pasrur	10,910	Good	
		Zafarwal	4,506	Fair	
		Daska	9,144	Good	

Gujrat. Jat Sikh population.	1,222	Gujrat	553	Nix	*Jats, viz.*, Varaich, only.
		Kharian	646	Nix	
		Phalia	23	Nix	
Gujranwala. Jat Sikh population.	47,653	Gujranwala	17,235	Good	*Jats, viz.*, Aulakh, Bhangu, Bhuttar, Bajwa, Chahil, Chattha. Chima, China, Deo, Dhariwal, Dhillon, Dhotar, Ghumon Gil, Goraya, Harral, Hinjra, Kahlon, Kang, Man, Man gat, Pannun, Randhawa, Sahi, Sarai, Sidhu, Sekhon, Sindhu, Sipra, Sumra, Tarar, Varaich, Virk ; (also Brahmans ; Khatris ; Aroras ; Labans ; Mahtams ; Tarkhans ; Chhimbas ; Jhinwars ; Ramdasias ; and Mazbhis).
		Hafizabad	2,220	Good	
		Wazirabad	2,436	Fair	
		Khangah Dogran	22,670	Fair	
		Sharaqpur	3,092	Indifferent	
Karnal. Jat Sikh population.	6,994	Karnal.	1,193	Nix	*Jats. viz.*, Badhan, Bhainiwal, Chahio, Dabdal, Dehia, Deswal, Dhariwal, Dhillon, Dhindsa, Dohan, Ghatwal, Gil, Jaglan, Man, Mandhan, Pawania, Sidhu, and Sindhu.
		Panipat	71	Nix	
		Kaithal	3,486	Nix	
		Thanesar	2,244	Nix	
Montgomery. Jat Sikh population.	4,182	Montgomery	239	Nix	*Jats, viz.*, Aulakh, Sindhu, and usual non-Jat Sikh classes.
		Gugera	430	Nix	
		Dipalpur	1,041	Nix	
		Pak Pattan	2,472	Nix	

APPENDIX I—*concld.*

List of districts, States and tehsils with their relative value as Sikh recruiting grounds, and the names of the Jat Sikh Sub-divisions found therein as shown in the Census Reports for 1911—concld.

District.		Tehsils		Value.	Jat Sikh sub-divisions.
Shahpur.		Bhera	269	Nix	
Jat Sikh population.	7,005	Shahpur	136	Nix	*Jats, viz.*, Bajwa, Chima, China, Ghuman, Hinjra, Sindhu, Varaich, Virk; (also Khatris; Aroras; Mazbhis; and Chuhras; etc., etc).
		Khushab	1	Nix	
		Sargodha	6,599	Indifferent	
Jhelum.		Jhelum	1,621	Nix	
Jat Sikh population.	1,654	Chakwal	6	Nix	Usual non-Jat Sikh classes.
		Pind Dadan Khan.	27	Nix	
Rawalpindi		Rawalpindi		Nix	
Jat Sikh population.	404	Kuhuta		Nix	Usual non-Jat Sikh classes, Khatris predominating.
		Murree		Nix	
		Gujar Khan		Nix	
Jullundur.		Jullundur	32,203	Good	*Jats, viz.*, Athwal, Bains, Bajwa, Bal, Basi, Bhullar, Chahil, Chattha, Chima, Dhaliwal, Dhillon, Dhindsa, Dosajh, Gil, Her, Jhumma, Johal, Kahlon, Kang, Mahil, Man, Pawania, Randhawa, Sahi, Saholei, Sanger, Sarai, Sidhu, Sindhu Sohal, Sumea, Virk: (also Brahmans; Khatris; Kambohs; Kalals; Sainis; Mahtams; Jhinwars; Tarkhans; Ramdasias, and Chuhras, etc).
Jat Sikh population.	105,681	Nakodar	18,516	Good	
		Phillour	28,320	Good	
		Nawashahr	25,642	Good	

Hoshiarpur.		Hoshiarpur	17,048	Fair	*Jats, viz.*, Athwal, Bains, Bhat, Chahil, Dhariwal Dhillar, Gil, Her, Jangal, Khang, Mahil, Man, Pat, Rai, Randhawa ; Sahata Sahol, Sidhu, and Sindhu ; (also Brahmans Rajputs ; Khatris ; Mahtams ; Sainis ; Tarkhans ; Chhimbas ; Ramdasias ; and Mazbhis).
Sikh population	58 142	Dasuya	6,864	Indifferent	
		Garhshankar	24,409	Fair	
		Una	9,821	Indifferent	
Kapurthala.		Kapurthala	..	Fair	*Jats, viz.*, Bal Basi, Dosanj, Johal, Sahota, and Sangere ; (also Khatris ; Kambohs ; Kalals ; Mahtams and Ramdasias ; etc.)
Jat Sikh population.	24,795	(Six tehsils)	..	..	

APPENDIX 2.

NOTE.

A description of the Adi Granth, and the "Daswen Padshah ka Granth", or book of the tenth king, is included as an appendix to this volume.

The reasons for its inclusion are primarily, that, although the Granth Sahib is frequently mentioned there are perhaps few British Officers who understand the nature of its contents.

They are frequently asked to attend at their unit Gurdwaras for certain ceremonies, and it has been considered therefore that a short outline of the contents of the Sikh Holy Scriptures will be of interest.

THE ADI GRANTH, OR FIRST BOOK; OR, THE BOOK OF NANAK, THE FIRST GURU, OR TEACHER OF THE SIKHS.

Note.—The first Granth is nowhere narrative or historical. It throws no light, by direct exposition, upon the political state of India during the Sixteenth and Seventeenth Centuries, although it contains many allusions illustrative of the condition of society and the religious feelings of the times. Its teaching is to the general purport that God is to be worshipped in spirit and in truth, with little reference to particular forms, and that salvation is unattainable without grace, faith, and good works.

The Adi Granth comprises, first, the writings attributed to Nanak, and the succeeding teachers of the Sikh faith up to the ninth Guru, Tegh Bahadur, omitting the sixth, seventh and eighth, but with perhaps some additions and mendations by Gobind; secondly, the compositions of certain 'Bhagats' or saints, mostly sectarian Hindus, and who are usually given as sixteen in number; and, thirdly, the verses of certain 'Bhats' or rhapsodists, followers of Nanak and some of his successors. The numbers, and even the names of the 'Bhagats' or saints, are not always the same in copies of the Granth; and thus modern compilers or copyists have assumed to themselves the power of rejecting or sanctioning particular writings. To the sixteen Bhagats are usually added two 'Doms' or chanters, who recited before Arjun, and who caught some of his spirit; and a Rababi, or player upon a stringed instrument, who became similarly inspired.

The Granth sometimes includes an appendix, containing works the authenticity of which is doubtful, or the propriety of admitting which is disputed on other grounds.

The Granth was originally compiled by Arjun, the fifth Guru; but has subsequently received a few additions at the hands of his successors.

The Granth is written wholly in verse; but the forms of versification are numerous. The language used is rather the Hindi of Upper India generally, than the particular dialect of the Punjab; but some portions, specially of the last section, are composed in Sanskrit. The written character is nevertheless throughout in Punjabi, one of the several varieties of alphabets now current in India, and which, from its use by the Sikh Gurus, is sometimes called "Gurmukhi", a term likewise applied to the dialect of the Punjab. The language of the writings of Nanak is thought by modern Sikhs to abound with provincialisms of the country south-west of Lahore, and the dialect of Arjun is held to be most pure.

The Granth usually forms a quarto volume of about 1,232 pages, each page containing 24 lines, and each line containing about 35 letters. The extra books increase the pages to 1,240 only.

Contents of the Adi Granth.

1st.—The 'Japji', or simply the 'Jap', called also Guru Mantr, or the special prayer of initiation of the Guru. It occupies about 7 pages, and consists of 40 sloks, called Pauri, of irregular lengths, some of two, and some of several lines. It means literally, the remembrancer or admonisher, from Jap, to remember. It was written by Nanak, and is believed to have been appointed by him to be repeated each morning, as every pious Sikh now does. The mode of composition implies the presence of a questioner and an answerer, and the Sikhs believe the questioner, to have been the disciple Angad.

2nd.—'Sodhar Rah Ras,' the evening prayer of the Sikhs. It occupies about 3½ pages, and it was composed by Nanak, but has additions by Ram Das and Arjun, and some, it is said, by Guru Gobind. The additions attributed to Gobind are, however, more frequently given when the Rah Ras forms a separate pamphlet or book. Sodhar a particular kind of verse; Rah, admonisher; a Ras the expression used for the play or recitative of Krishna. It is sometimes corruptly called the 'Rowh Ras' from Rowh, the Punjabi for a road.

3rd.—'Kirit Sohila'—A prayer repeated before going to rest. It occupies a page and a line or two more. It was composed by Nanak, but has additions by Ram Das and Arjun, and one verse is attributed to Gobind. Kirit from Sanskrit Kirti, to praise, to celebrate, and "Sohila", a marriage song, a song of rejoicing.

4th.—The next portion of the Granth is divided into thirty-one sections, known by their distinguishing forms of verse, as follows—

1. **Sri Rag.**
2. **Maj.**
3. **Gauri.**
4. **Asa.**
5. **Gujri.**
6. **Dev Gandhari.**
7. **Bihagra.**
8. **Wad Hans.**
9. **Sorath (or Sort)**
10. **Dhanasri.**
11. **Jait Sri.**
12. **Todi.**
13. **Bairari.**
14. **Tailang.**
15. **Sudhi.**
16. **Bilawal.**
17. **Gaund.**
18. **Ram Kali.**
19. **Nat Narayan.**
20. **Mali Gaura.**
21. **Maru.**
22. **Tukhari.**
23. **Kedara.**
24. **Bhairon.**
25. **Basant.**
26. **Sarang.**
27. **Malhar.**
28. **Kanhra.**
29. **Kalian.**
30. **Parbhati.**
31. **Parbhati.**
32. **Jai Jaiwanti.**

The whole occupies about 1,154 pages or by far the greater portion of the entire Granth. Each sub-division is the composition of one or more Gurus, or of one or more Bhagats or holy men, or of a Guru with or without the aid of a Bhagat.

The contributors among the Gurus were as follows—

1. **Nanak.**
2. **Angad.**
3. **Amar Das.**
4. **Ram Das.**
5. **Arjun.**
6. **Tegh Bahadur (with perhaps emendations by Gobind.)**

The Bhagats or saints, and others who contributed agreeably to the ordinary copies of the Granth, are enumerated below—

1. Kabir (the well known reformer).
2. Trilochan, a Brahman.
3. Beni.
4. Rav Das, a Chamar, or leather dresser.
5. Namdev, a Chhippa, or cloth printer.
6. Dhanna, a Jat.
7. Shah Farid, a Mohamedan pir or saint.
8. Jaidev, a Brahman.
9. Bhikan.
10. Sain, a barber.
11. Pipa (a Jogi)
12. Sadhna, a butcher.
13. Ramanand Bairagi (a well known reformer).
14. Parmanand.
15. Sur Das (a blind man).
16. Miran Bai, a Bhagatni, or holy woman.
17. Balwand.
18. Satta 'Doms' or chanters who were before Arjun.
19. Sundar Das, Rababi, or player upon a stringed instrument. He is not properly one of the Bhagats.

5th.—The 'Bhog'. In Sanskrit this word means to enjoy anything, but is commonly used to denote the conclusion of any sacred writing, both by Hindus or Sikhs. The Bhog occupies about 66 pages, and besides the writings of Nanak and Arjun, of Kabir, Shah Farid, and other reformers, it contains the compositions of nine Bhats, or rhapsodists who attached themselves to Amar Das, Ram Das and Arjun.

The Bhog commences with 4 sloks in Sanskrit by Nanak, which are followed by 67 Sanskrit sloks in one metre by Arjun, and then by 24 in another metre by the same Guru. There are also 23 sloks in Punjabi or Hindi by Arjun, which contain praises of Amritsar. These are soon followed by 243 sloks by Kabir, and 130 by Shah Farid, and others, containing some sayings of Arjun, and so on to the end.

The nine Bhats who contributed to the Bhog are named as follows:—

1. Bhikha, a follower of Amar Das.
2. Kall, a follower of Ram Das.
3. Kall Sahar.
4. Jalap, a follower of Arjun.
5. Sall, a follower of Arjun.
6. Nall.
7. Mathra.
8. Ball.
9. Kirit.

The names are evidently fanciful, and perhaps fictitious; in the book called the Guru Bilas eight Bhats only are enumerated, and all the names except Ball are different from those in the Granth.

Supplement to the Granth.

6th.—'Bhog ki Bani', or Epilogue of the Conclusion. It comprises about 7 pages and contains, first, some preliminary sloks, called 'Slok Mahala Pahla', or Hymn of the first woman or slave; secondly, Nanak's admonition to Malhar Raja; thirdly, the 'Ratan Mala' of Nanak. *i.e.*, the Rosary of Jewels, or string of (religious) worthies, which simply shows, however, what should be the true characteristics or qualities of religious devotees; and fourthly, the "Hakikat", or Circumstances of Sivnab, Raja of Ceylon, with reference to a 'Pothi' or sacred writing known as "Pran Sangli". This last is said to have been composed by one Bhai Bhannu in the time of Gobind.

The Ratan Mala is said to have been originally written in Turki, or to have been abstracted from a Turki original.

The Daswen Padshah ka Granth, or Book of the Tenth King, or Sovereign Pontiff, that is, of Guru Gobind Singh.

Note.—Like the Adi Granth, the book of Gobind is metrical throughout, but the versification frequently varies.

It is written in the Hindi dialect, and in the Punjabi character, excepting the concluding portion, the language of which is Persian, while the alphabet continues the Gurmukhi. The Hindi of Gobind is almost such as is spoken in the Gangetic provinces, and has few peculiarities of the Punjabi dialect.

One chapter of the book of the Tenth King may be considered to be narrative and historical, *viz.*, the Vichitr Natak, written by Gobind himself; but the Persian Hikayats, or stories, also partake of that character from the circumstances attending their composition and the nature of some allusions made in them. The other portions of this Granth are more mythological than the first book, and it also partakes more of a worldly character throughout, although it contains many noble allusions to the unity of the Godhead, and to the greatness and goodness of the Ruler of the Universe.

Five chapters, or portions only, and the commencement of the sixth, are attributed to Gobind himself; the remainder, *i.e.*, by far the larger portion, is said to have been composed by four scribes in the service of the Guru; partly,. perhaps, agreeably to his dictation. The names of Sham and Ram occur as two of the writers, but, in truth, little is known of the authorship of the portions in question.

The Daswen Padshah ka Granth forms a quarto volume of 1,066 pages, each page consisting of 23 lines and each line of from 38 to 41 letters.

Contents of the book of the Tenth King.

1st.—The "Japji", or simply the 'Jap' the supplement or complement of the Japji of Nanak—a prayer to be read or repeated in the morning, as it continues to be by pious Sikhs. It comprises 198 distichs, and occupies about 7 pages, the terminaton of a verse and the end of a line not being the same. The Japji was composed by Guru Gobind.

2nd.—'Akal Stut', or Praises of the Almighty a hymn commonly read in the morning. It occupies 23 pages, and the. initiatory verse alone is the composition of Gobind.

3rd.—The 'Vichitr Natak', *i.e.*, the "Wondrous Tale". This was written by Gobind himself, and it gives, first, the mythological history of his family or race; secondly, an account of his mission or reformation; and, thirdly, a description of his warfare with the Himalayan chiefs and the imperial forces. It is divided into fourteen sections; but the first is devoted to the praises of the Almighty, and the last is of a similar tenor, with an addition to the effect that he would hereafter relate his visions of the past and his experience of the present world. The Vichitr Natak occupies about 24 pages of the Granth.

4th.—'Chandi Charitr', or the Wonders of Chandi or the Goddess. There are two portions called Chandi Charitr, of which this is considered the greater. It relates the destruction of eight Titans or Deityas by Chandi, the Goddess. It occupies about 20 pages, and it is understood to be the translation of a Sanskrit legend executed, some are willing to believe, by Gobind himself.

The names of the Deityas destroyed are as follows :—

1. Madhu Kaitab.
2. Mah Khasur.
3. Dhumar Lochan.
4. and 5. Chand and Mund.
6. Rakaj Bij.
7. Nishumbh.
8. Shumbh.

5th.—'Chandi Charitr' the lesser. The same legends as the greater Chandi, narrated in a different metre. It occupies about 14 pages.

6th.—'Chandi ki Var'. A supplement to the legends of Chandi. It occupies about 6 pages.

7th.—'Gyan Prabodh' or the "Excellence of Wisdom". Praises of the Almighty, with allusions to ancient kings taken mostly from Mahabharat. It occupies about 21 pages.

8th.—'Chaupayan Chaubis Avataran kian' or Quatrains relating to the twenty-four manifestations (Avatars). These 'Chaupays' occupy about 348 pages and they are considered to be the work of one by name Sham.

The names of the incarnations are as follows :—

1. The Fish or Machh.
2. The Tortoise.
3. The lion or Nar.
4. Narayan.
5. Mohani.
6. The boar, Varah.
7. The man lion, or Nur-singh.
8. The Dwarf or Barwan.
9. Paras Ram.
10. Brahma.
11. Rudr.
12. Jalandhar.
13. Vishnu.
14. No name specified, but understood to be a manifestation of Vishnu.
15. Arhant Dev (considered to be the founder of the Sect of Saraugis of the Jain persuasion, or indeed. the great Jain prophet himself.
16. Man Raja.
17. The sun or Suraj.
18. Dhanantar (the doctor or physician).
19. The moon or Chandarma.
20. Rama.
21. Krishna.
22. Nar (meaning Arjun).
23. Bodh.
24. Kalki ; to appear at the end of the Kalyug or when the sins of men are at their height.

9th.—No name entered, but known as 'Mihdi Mir'. A supplement to the twenty-four incarnations. Midhi, it is said, will appear when the mission of Kalki is fulfilled. The name and the idea are borrowed from the Shia Mohamedans. It occupies less than a page.

10th.—No name entered but known as the 'Avatars of Brahma.' An account of seven incarnations or Brahma, followed by some account of eight Rajas of bygone times. It occupies about 18 pages.

The names of the incarnations are as follows :—

1. Valkmik.
2. Kashap.
3. Shukar.
4. Batches.
5. Vyasi.
6. Khashat, Rikhi (or the six Sages).
7. Kaul Das.

The kings are enumerated below :—

1. Manu.
2. Prithu.
3. Sagar.
4. Ben.
5. Mandhat.
6. Dalip.
7. Ragh.
8. Aj.

11th.—No name entered but known as the 'Avatars of Rudr or Siva'. It comprises 56 pages; and two incarnations only are mentioned, namely, Dat and Parasnath.

12th.—'Shastr Nam Mala', or the name string of weapons. The names of the various weapons are recapitulated, the weapons are praised, and Gobind terms them collectively his Guru or guide. The composition nevertheless is not attributed to Gobind. It occupies about 68 pages.

13th.—'Sri Mukh Vak, Sawaya Battis' or the voice of Guru (Gobind) himself thirty-two verses. These verses were composed by Gobind as declared, and they are condemnatory of the Vedas, the Purans, and the Kuran. They occupy about 3½ pages.

14.—'Hazara Shabd' or the thousand verses of the Metre called Shabd. There are, however, but ten verses only in most Granths, occupying about two pages. Hazar is not understood in its literal sense of a thousand, but as implying invaluable or excellent. They are laudatory of the creator and creation, and deprecate the adoration of saints and limited divinities. They were written by Guru Gobind.

15th.—'Istri Charitar' or Tales of Women. There are 404 stories, illustrative of the character and disposition of women. A step-mother became enamoured of her step-son, the heir of a monarchy, who, however, would not gratify her desires, whereupon she represented to her husband that his firstborn had made attempts upon her honour. The Raja ordered his son to be put to death, but his ministers interfered and procured a respite. They then enlarge in a series of stories upon the nature of women, and at length the Raja became sensible to the guilt of his wife's mind, and of his own rashness. These stories occupy 446 pages or nearly half of the Granth. The name of Sham also occurs as the writer of one or more of them.

16th.—The 'Hikayats' or Tales. These comprise twelve stories in 866 sloks of two lines each. They are written in the Persian language and Gurmukhi character, and they were composed by Gobind himself, as an admonitory of Aurangzeb, and were sent to the Emperor by the hands of Daya Singh and four other Sikhs. The tales were accompanied by a letter written in a pointed manner, which, however, does not form a portion of the Granth.

These tales occupy about 30 pages, and conclude the Granth of Guru Gobind.

APPENDIX 3.

Rites of initiation into Sikhism.

Sikhs are not ordinarily initiated until they reach the age of discrimination and remembrance, or not before they are seven years of age, or sometimes until they have attained to manhood. But there is no authoritative rule on the subject, nor is there any declaratory ceremonial of detail which can be followed. The essentials are that five Sikhs at least should be assembled, and it is generally arranged that one of the number is of religious repute. Some sugar and water are stirred together in a vessel of any kind, commonly with a two edged dagger, but any iron weapon will answer. The novitiate stands with his hands joined in an attitude of humility or supplication, and he repeats after the elder or minister the main articles of his faith. Some of the water is sprinkled on his face and person; he drinks the remainder, and exclaims, "Hail Guru" and the ceremony concludes with an injunction that he be true to God and to his duty as a Sikh. For details of particular modes followed, see Forster (Travels, 1·307), Malcolm (Sketch, page 182), and Prinsep's edition of Murray's Life of Ranjit Singh (page 217) where an Indian compiler is quoted.

The original practice of using the water in which the feet of a Sikh had been washed was soon abandoned, and the subsequent custom of touching the water with the toe seems now almost forgotten. The first rule was perhaps instituted to denote the humbleness of spirit of the disciples, or both it and the second practice may have originated in that feeling of the Hindus which attaches virtue to water in which the thumb of a Brahman had been dipped. It seems in every way probable that Govind substituted the dagger for the foot or the toe, thus giving pre-eminence to his emblematic iron.

Women are not usually, but they are sometimes, initiated in form as professors of the Sikh faith. In mingling the sugar and water for women, a one edged, and not a two edged, dagger is used.

APPENDIX 4.

The Sikh Gurdwara Act, 1925.

This Act as Punjab Act No. VIII of 1925 (as supplemented by the Sikh Gurdwaras Supplementary Act, 1925, India Act, No. XXIV of 1925), was passed by the Local Legislature of the Punjab, and received the assent of the Acting Governor General on the 28th July 1925.

It was "An Act to provide for the better administration of certain Sikh Gurdwaras and for enquiries into matters connected therewith".

It extended to the Punjab and came into force on the 1st November 1925; it repealed the Sikh Gurdwaras and Shrines Act of 1922.

The Act was divided into three Parts.

Part I.

Chapter 1 . Dealt with the extent and commencement, and gave certain definitions.

Chapter 2 . Dealt with the subject of petitions to Local Government relating to Gurdwaras.

Chapter 3 . Dealt with the appointment of, and proceedings before, a tribunal.

Part II.

Chapter 4 . Dealt with the application of provisions of Part 3 to Gurdwaras found to be Sikh Gurdwaras by courts other than a tribunal under the provisions of the Act.

Part III.

Chapter 5 . Dealt with the control of Sikh Gurdwaras.

Chapter 6 . Dealt with all matters relating to the composition, members, and powers of the "Board."

Chapter 7 . Dealt with all matters relating to the Judicial Commission.

Chapter 8 . Dealt with all matters relating to the Committees of Gurdwaras.

Chapter 9 . Dealt with Finances.

Chapter 10 . Dealt with the powers and duties of the Board.

Chapter 11 . Dealt with the powers and duties of Committees.

Chapter 12 . Dealt with miscellaneous matters.

From the above, it may be gathered that the Act was a very comprehensive and voluminous one. In point of fact it numbered 100 pages. It is not proposed to deal with any more than one or two of the salient features; for full information the Act, obtainable from the Superintendent, Government Printing, Punjab, for Rs. 1-2-0, must itself be consulted.

Part I.

The definition of "Sikh" is of interest, *viz*:—"Sikh" means a person who professes the Sikh religion. If any question arises as to whether any person is, or is not a Sikh, he shall be deemed respectively to be, or not to be a Sikh according as he makes or refuses to make in such manner as the Local Government may describe the following declaration:—

> "I solemnly affirm that I am a Sikh, that I believe in the Guru Granth Sahib, that I believe in the ten Gurus and that I have no other religion".

Tribunals.—The Local Government reserved to itself the constitution of one, or more tribunals for the purpose of deciding claims for Gurdwaras made in accordance with the provisions of the Act. Each tribunal was to consist of a president, who was to be a Judge of the High Court, and two other members who were to be District, or Subordinate Judges of the first class, or barristers of not less than ten years standing.

Part III.

Control of the Gurdwaras.—This portion of the Act legislated for the constitution of a Board of Control, and for every Notified Sikh Gurdwara a Committee of Management.

The Board.—This was to consist of the following:—

(*a*) 120 elected members.

(*b*) The head ministers of the Durbar Sahib, Amritsar, and the four Sikh Takhts of—
The Sri Akal Takht, Amritsar.
The Sri Takht Kesgarh Sahib, Anandpur.
The Sri Takht Patna Sahib, Patna.
The Sri Takht Hazur Sahib, Hyderabad.

(*c*) 12 members nominated by the Indian States.

(*d*) 14 members resident in India, co-opted by the members of the Board.

The members of the Board were to hold office for three years from the date of its constitution, and an annual general meeting was to be held every year; the Board was also to have an office in Amritsar for the transaction of business.

As regards the duties of the Board:—

It was to ensure that every committee dealt with the property and income of the Gurdwara, or Gurdwaras managed by it, whilst the general superintendence over all committees appointed under the provisions of the Act were vested in the Board.

It was within its jurisdiction to hold and administer trust funds for purposes of a religious, charitable or educational nature, irrespective of whether such funds were derived from allotments duly made by a Committee out of the surplus funds or income of a Gurdwara under its management, or from donations or contributions or endowments made direct to the Board for such purposes.

The Board was also accorded sanction to consider and discuss any matter with which it had power under the Act to deal, and any matter directly connected with the Sikh religion, but was *not* to consider, or discuss, or pass any resolution or order upon, any other matter.

The Judicial Commission.—This portion of the Act also legislated for the constitution, appointment of members, jurisdiction and procedure of a Judicial Commission (referred to in Part I as Tribunals).

The proceedings of the Commission were to be connected in accordance with the provisions of the Code of Civil Procedure, 1908, and all its orders were to be final.

Its powers were to be the same as those vested in a court by the same Code of Civil Procedure, and it was to have jurisdiction unlimited as regards value throughout the Punjab.

Any decree or order of the Commission was to be executed by the District Court of the district in which the Gurdwara, in connection with which the order or decree was passed, was situated.

Gurdwara Committees.—This portion of the Act legislated for all matters in connection with Gurdwara Committees, their constitution, election of members, meetings tri-annually, decisions of questions brought before them, powers of control, etc.

In general a Committee was "to have full powers of control over the office holders and dependents of, and of all properties and income of whatever description belonging to, the Gurdwara, or Gurdwaras under its management, and of enforcing the proper observance of all ceremonies and religious observances in connection with such Gurdwara, or Gurdwaras, and of taking all such measures as may be necessary to ensure the proper management of the Gurdwara, or Gurdwaras, and the efficient administration of the property, income and endowments thereof".

APPENDIX 5.

THE CASTE SYSTEM.

The ideas conveyed by the terms "Race," "Caste" and "Tribe," as applied to the conditions existing in the Punjab, and amongst Sikhs, are generally very vague.

The object of this appendix is to endeavour to explain what these are.

In vulgar parlance, the terms "Caste" and "Tribe" are used as synonyms. There is apparently no equivalent for "race" in the Indian vernaculars. The words commonly used are "Zat" (from Jati Sanskrit), which is intended to signify "caste," and "Qaum" (Arabic) which is the equivalent of tribe." The latter word is foreign to India and, so far as the Indian castes are concerned, is used only as a substitute for "Zat". But the essential characteristic of a tribe is common descent, *i.e.*, descent from a common ancestor and residence in a specified tract at one time or another. Now common descent and endogamy which are the universal feature of caste are a contradiction in terms and cannot co-exist. For, people descended from a common ancestor, howsoever distant, cannot intermarry according to the first principles of caste. It, therefore, follows that whenever a caste was formed, it must have included more than one group of families (descended from a common ancestor). It would consequently not be quite correct to say that certain castes were of a tribal nature.

It is a patent fact that all social groups, which came under the influence of the caste system, were so completely Hindu-ised that they lost all traces of tribal organisation and identity. Consequently, as matters now stand, the term tribe can only be applied to foreign bodies of comparatively recent immigrants.

The impossibility of defining a foreign term applied to a complicated Indian institution, of which the introducers of the term had but a superficial knowledge, and which in its present form is the sum total of most varied and conflicting influences is obvious enough. Various authorities in writing on the subject have given different definitions, and it must suffice to say that about the best yet devised, is that defined by Mr. Gait in the Encyclopedia of Religions as:—"Caste is an endogamous group or collection of such groups bearing a common name, having the same traditional occupation, claiming descent from the same source and commonly regarded as forming a single homogeneous community".

The earliest indication of castes is contained in the well-known 'Purshta Sukta,' which gives a fourfold division of society. This division is regarded by the orthodox Hindus as the basis of what is now known as caste. Others consider the division only to indicate classes. It is, however, impossible to believe that any society could exist without some sort of a division of labour for thousands of years. Whether the basis of caste is racial, or functional, is the burning question of the day.

The racial theory is based upon the Aryan invasion of the Punjab and their conquest of the Dravidians who formerly occupied the country, but were gradually driven to the south or converted, and admitted into the society mainly as "shudras," belonging to the menial class. The fusion of different racial elements, under the hierachy of caste appears to have been so complete, and the mixture of castes by intermarriage and degradation has been so large, that it has become extremely difficult to distinguish between the various castes on an ethnic basis. There is no lack of members of the Brahman, Khatri, Artizan, Chamar, Chuhra and other castes possessing similar features and probably similar measurements.

Sir Denzil Ibbetson held the basis of caste to be functional, but if criticism can be levied then it must be remarked that in judging the conditions of remote antiquity from existing conditions certain important factors and intermediate influences are apt to be overlooked.

The opinion, however, generally seems to be held that tribe was prior to caste, and that whole tribes or clans coming under the influence of the Hindus formed the classes which crystallised into castes.

Space forbids a description of the present condition of the institution of caste, which is partly the result of the counteracting political religious and economic influences. The present Hindu community may be divided into 3 sections, (*i*) the orthodox, who follow the caste system, more or less strictly; (*ii*) those who have ignored the restrictions of inter-dining, but still adhere rigidly to the limitations prescribed for marriage; and (*iii*) those who have given up both. That the restrictions of caste are fast dying out is obvious enough, but it will not be correct to ascribe this to the theory that birth was not originally the essential of caste. It is laid down in the "Smritis" that there will be only 2 castes, *viz*:—the "Brahmans" and the "Shudras". The writers could obviously foresee the effects of the disintegrating processes that were then at work. But they did not reckon upon the influences which would come to bear adversely on the institution in later days, and accelerate the process of disintegration. The changes have been more rapid than anticipated, but it is wonderful that while caste restrictions were said to be disappearing thirty years ago in the same way as they are said to-day, yet the number of persons, who disown allegiance to one caste or another is extremely small, being only 221 Sikhs. The modern classes like Khalsa and Arya, which are being substituted for the old castes will probably, in course of time, become as rigid as any others.

The revolt against caste is due mainly to the inconvenience of restrictions of inter-marriage and inter-dining. The upshot of the modern tendency will, therefore, probably be a complete disappearance of restrictions of both kinds, while the name of the caste, or tribe may be retained in the case of higher castes as a traditional distinction, the lower castes grouping themselves in large democratic classes of uniform status. But how long this process will take is difficult to predict. The general conclusion is that there has been little change during the past 40 years with reference to the basis of caste distinctions, but that the restrictions have become very lax; the rules are being disregarded with impunity in respect of inter-marriage and inter-dining; the traditional occupations are being given up owing to the functional revolution which is in progress, and a general re-action has set in whereby members of lower, or menial castes, are trying to rise to the level of the higher ones, either by connecting themselves with a forefather belonging to one of those castes, or by discovering a new origin for their tribe or caste.

APPENDIX 6.

The Tankha Nama, or letter of Fines or Restrictions on Sikhs. (Abstract of).

Written in reply to the question of Bhai Nand Lal, who asked Guru Gobind what it was proper for a Sikh to do, and what to refrain from.

Nand Lal asked, etc., and the Guru replied that such were to be the acts of the Sikhs. A Sikh should set his heart on God, on charity, and on purity (Nam, Dan, Ishnan). He who in the morning does not repair to some temple or visit some holy man, is greatly to blame. He who does not allow the poor a place (in his heart) is to blame. Without the favour of God nothing can be accomplished. He who bows his head (*i.e.*, humbles himself) after having offered up prayers is a man of holiness. Charity (Karah Prasad, *i.e.*, food) should be distributed in singleness of mind to all comers equally. Prasad should be prepared of equal parts of flour, sugar and butter. The preparer should first bathe, and while cooking it should repeat 'Wah Guru' continually. When ready, the food should be put on a round place.

The Sikh who wears the (written) charms of the Turks, or who touches iron with his feet, is to be condemned. He who wears clothing dyed with safflower (of the colour called suhi), and who takes snuff (naswar) is to be condemned.*

He who looks lustfully upon the mother or sister of one of the brethren —he who does not bestow his daughter becomingly in marriage—he who takes to himself the property of a sister or daughter—he who wears not iron in some shape—he who robs or oppresses the poor, and he who makes obeisance to a Turk, is to be punished.

A Sikh should comb his locks, and fold and unfold his turban twice a day. Twice also should he wash his mouth.

One-tenth of all goods should be given (in charity) in the name of the Guru.

Sikhs should bathe in cold water; they should not break their fast until they have repeated the Jap. In the morning, Jap, in the evening, Rah Ras, and before retiring to rest, Sohila, should always be repeated.

No Sikh should speak false of his neighbour. Promises should be carefully fulfilled.

No Sikh should eat flesh from the hands of the Turks.

No Sikh should delight in women, nor give himself up to them.

The Sikh who calls himself a Sadh (or Holy Man) should act in strict accordance with his profession.

A journey should not be undertaken, nor should business be set about, nor should food be eaten, without first remembering or calling on God.

A Sikh should enjoy the society of his own wife only. He should not desire other women.

He who sees a poor man and gives him not something, shall not behold the presence of God.

He who neglects to pray, or who abuses the Holy, or who gambles, or who listens to those who speak evil of the Gurus, is no Sikh.

Daily, some portion of what is gained is to be set aside in the name of the Lord, but all business must be carried on in sincerity and truth.

---

* This is the only recorded prohibition against tobacco, to refrain from which in every shape is now a rule. The Afghans of Peshawar and Kabul continue to take snuff, a practice but little known to the Indians.

Flame should not be extinguished with the breath, nor should fire be put out with water, a portion of which has been drunk.

Before meals the name of the Guru should be repeated. The society of prostitutes is to be avoided nor is adultery to be committed with the wife of another. The Guru is not to be forsaken, and others followed. No Sikh should expose his person. He should not bathe in a state of nudity, nor when distributing food should he be naked.* His head should always be covered.

*The practices of many Hindu ascetics are mainly aimed at.

GIPD—L554 Army-III—21-2-41—1,000.

INDEX TO HANDBOOK ON SIKHS.

CONTENTS.

CHAPTER I.—INTRODUCTORY.

CHAPTER II.—ORIGIN AND HISTORY.

CHAPTER III.—DISTRIBUTION OF SIKHS, ETHNOLOGICAL AND ETHNOGRAPHIC GLOSSARY OF CASTES.

CHAPTER IV.—SALIENT FEATURES OF THE LIVES OF THE GURUS.

CHAPTER V.—THE SIKH RELIGION.

CHAPTER VI.—SIKH SECTS AND SUB-DIVISIONS OF JAT SIKHS.

CHAPTER VII.—CUSTOMS.

CHAPTER VIII.—CHARACTERISTICS AND MATTERS PERTAINING TO VILLAGE LIFE.

CHAPTER IX.—AGRICULTURAL.

CHAPTER X. –RECRUITING.